The Future
of the
Catholic Church
with
Pope Francis

GARRY WILLS

The Future
of the
Catholic Church
with
Pope Francis

VIKING

VIKING

Published by the Penguin Group

Penguin Group (USA) LLC

375 Hudson Street

New York, New York 10014

USA | Canada | UK | Ireland | Australia | New Zealand | India | South Africa | China

penguin.com

A Penguin Random House Company

First published by Viking Penguin, a member of Penguin Group (USA) LLC, 2015

Grateful acknowledgment is made for permission to reprint an excerpt from
Autumn Journal by Louis MacNeice (Faber and Faber). Used by permission
of David Higham Associates.

ISBN 978-0-525-42696-7

Printed in the United States of America

1 3 5 7 9 10 8 6 4 2

Set in Dante MT Std

Designed by Francesca Belanger

To Carolyn Carlson
for her guidance

Contents

IV: The Coming and Going of "Natural Law"

V: The Coming and Going of Confession

Key to Brief Citations

CD Augustine, *City of God* (*De Civitate Dei*), edited by Bernard Dombart and Alphonsus Kalb, fifth edition (Teubner, 1981), two volumes.

DF Edward Gibbon, *The Decline and Fall of the Roman Empire*, edited by J. B. Bury, seven volumes (Methuen & Co., 1909–12).

S 1 J. Stevenson and W. H. C. Frend, *A New Eusebius: Documents Illustrating the History of the Church to AD 337*, third edition (Baker Academic, 2013).

S 2 J. Stevenson and W. H. C. Frend, *Creeds, Councils and Controversies: Documents Illustrating the History of the Church, AD 337–461*, third edition (Baker Academic, 2012).

ST Thomas Aquinas, *Summa Theologiae*, four volumes (La Editorial Católica, 1958).

VC Eusebius, *Life of Constantine* (*Vita Constantini*), translated with introduction and commentary by Averil Cameron and Stuart G. Hall (Oxford University Press, 1999).

Introduction:
Reading History Forward

> In a higher world it is otherwise; but here below to live is to
> change, and to be perfect is to have changed often.
>
> —John Henry Newman[1]

> To be faithful, to be creative, we need to be able to change.
>
> —Pope Francis[2]

Pope Francis heartens some Catholics, but frightens others—both of them for the same reason, the prospect of change. The Catholic Church is the oldest institution in Western civilization. Surely the secret to its longevity is its ability to defy and outlast all the many breaks and discontinuities over the last twenty centuries. From that vantage point, a changing church is simply not the Catholic Church. Immutability must be built into its DNA.

It helps, in holding such a view, not to know much history. There was no need to know much. Since one begins from a certitude that the church was always what it has become, one simply has to extrapolate backward from what we have. We have priests, so we must always have had them— though they never show up in the Gospels. We have popes, so they must have been there too—they were just hiding for several centuries. We have transubstantiation, so we did not have to wait for the thirteenth century to tell us what that is. The beauty of the church is its marble permanence. Change would be its death warrant.

Early on, I was given a different view of the church from reading G. K. Chesterton's *The Everlasting Man*. It was published nine years before I was born, and it took me sixteen years after that to catch up with it—but I was intrigued, then, by a chapter called "The Five Deaths of the Faith." This offered a different story of the church's long life. For Chesterton, it was not a tale of certainty formed early and never altered. It was a story of hairbreadth escapes, as the church kept dying, of old age, or of inanition, or from external causes. There were many times when it could have died— when, by the laws of historical probability, it should have died—yet it was constantly reanimated from some supernatural deathlessness. Corruption should have killed it, or the Roman Empire should have, or the Renaissance, or Galileo, or Darwin, or Freud. "Christianity has died many times and risen again; for it had a God who knew the way out of the grave."[3]

This was not because it simply defied change. In fact, it often changed with the age—became Roman with the Roman Empire, shedding its Middle Eastern roots and adopting a Latin structure; became a supermonarchy in the age of monarchs; became super-ascetic in the age of Stoic contempt for the body; became misogynistic in the various patriarchies; became anti-Semitic when the world despised Jews. But when the age died of old age, the church somehow didn't. As Chesterton put it:

> It has not only died often but degenerated often and decayed often; it has survived its own weakness and even its own surrender . . . It was said truly enough that human Christianity in its recurrent weakness was sometimes too much wedded to the powers of the world; but if it was wedded it has very often been widowed. It is a strangely immortal sort of widow.[4]

Sometimes, of course, it clung too long to what it had worn as a new set of up-to-date garments. The recovery of Aristotle was a fresh and challenging thing when Albert the Great and Thomas Aquinas led it, but it became an unnecessary encumbrance when Rome thought it something too good to let go of. The Latin tongue looked, for a long time, like a universal language, spreading opportunities for communication, till it became an outmoded thing trammeled in its own particularities. The Irish practice of private confession introduced a deeper kind of spirituality for monastic specialists, till its broader use for everyone, including children, made it commonplace and subject to abuse.

The church outlasted things that seemed to undermine it—not because it was unaffected by these transitory things, but because it joined them, drew on other sources, and lived to adopt different new things. Instead of reading history backward, from its current form to a fictive immutability in the past, Chesterton led me to read history forward, from the early evidences and from the different guises the church had to adopt in order to survive. That is not only a more interesting story, but an exciting one—of narrow escapes and improbable swerves. It calls to mind Buster Keaton's *Seven Chances* (1925), in which Buster runs full speed down a sloping mountainside, pursued by a giant landslide of boulders, dodging some, leaping over others, maneuvering through repeated impasses, caught by a smaller rock that knocks him out of the path of a bigger one, ducking into cover that itself gives way. And then, toward the bottom of the mountain, an even greater menace forces him to run back up through the continuing rain of rocks.

Going back to read the church's story as it happened was called *ressourcement* (re-sourcing) in the 1940s and 1950s, when Pius XI and Pius XII silenced its practitioners. The only way to look back, for those popes, was to reaffirm what "always was" in the church, not to find anything new there. There can be no history at all for those who just retroject the present into the past. But Pope Francis champions *ressourcement,* as he told his fellow Jesuits at *America* magazine. Newman's concept of doctrinal development breathes through that interview:

> The joint effort of reflection [with the Orthodox Church], looking at how the church was governed in the early centuries, before the breakup between East and West, will bear fruit . . . St. Vincent of Lerins makes a comparison between the biological development of man and the transmission from one era to another of the deposit of faith, which grows and is strengthened with time. Here, human self-understanding changes with time and so also human consciousness deepens.[5]

The suppression of the "re-sourcers" is an old story with the church. Yesterday's heretic becomes today's authority—and vice versa. I want to trace, in this book, how change—far from being the enemy of Catholicism—is its means of respiration, its way of breathing in and breathing out. Even before Pope Francis, the Second Vatican Council had found in the church's sources that "the church" did not always mean what some of its defenders insist that it *must* mean. Their meaning is implicit in usages like "the church teaches," or "you must obey the church." For some, "the church" is the Vatican, the papacy, the *magisterium,* the church's teaching authority. But that apparatus was not there at the beginning. Another usage of "church" was older, broader, and better attested in the sources. Vatican II returned to that meaning when it proclaimed that the church is "the People of God."[6] This people includes all those who believe in, follow, and love Jesus.

This people first organized itself under the guidance of the Spirit imparted to it at Pentecost. It chose its own leaders, it tested authority, it rejected attempts to dictate to it from above. It had various leaders, playing them off against each other—James in Jerusalem, Peter in Antioch, Paul in Corinth. Its councils voted on doctrine through representatives (bishops) who were themselves elected by the people. In John Henry Newman's time, the *magisterium* was so far from this understanding of the church that he was silenced for claiming that the laity had *some* role in forming doctrine, and that the church could undergo *some* change (under the rubric of "development"). It was impossible for Newman to carry his thought further, developing its own implications. The very concept was quashed in its initial formulations. The need to hang on to set ways stifles creativity. Pope Francis describes the condition:

> Whenever we Christians are enclosed in our groups, our movements, our parishes, in our little worlds, we remain closed, and the same thing happens to us that happens to anything closed: when a room is closed, it begins to get dank. If a person is closed up in that room, he or she becomes ill![7]

We are now able to read history forward again, to test evidence and trace changes—changes that came, were changed themselves, and then fell away. We can see the People of God weathering all kinds of vicissitudes, while not losing belief, while still following Jesus, while still expressing love of him in the care for each other and for the needy. We can see the coming and going of the papacy as a worldly empire, the rise and final rejection of a "universal language," the rejection of the Jewish covenant and its renewed recognition, the fad for biblical fundamentalism returning to figurative readings, the condemnation of the body circling back to its recognition. I mean in this book to watch the phases of this process, the reaction of the church as a living body in real situations.

To say that change has often shaken the church does not mean that change is always an easy process. And we should not expect it to come from any one man, even though he is the pope. We sometimes think John XXIII changed much in the church. But he was not so much the initiator as the welcomer of changes long in preparation and not to be imposed, "top down," by fiat. Three of the changes I treat in this book—from the Latin liturgy, from rejection to acceptance of the Jewish covenant, and from the ideal of a state church to one of religious freedom—were made not by Pope John but by the Vatican Council he called together. He was in many ways a conservative in his tastes. He personally loved the Latin liturgy, and his own scholarship was pretty much restricted to editing writings of the quite autocratic Charles Borromeo.[8] But he did not try to mold the church in his own image. He knew that would be going against the true meaning of the church. He called in others to consider change. And the council fathers summoned or listened to prophetic scholars who had been silenced by autocratic popes—men named Daniélou, Congar, Chenu, Rahner, Murray.

The papacy is not a prophetic office. People may be lodging too much hope in the name Cardinal Bergoglio took for himself. No other pope has taken that name, probably for good reasons. Francis of Assisi was, notoriously, not a good administrator—prophets never are. The religious order he founded rushed off in all directions, splintered, and quarreled, while—in broader and lasting ways—the whole church was aerated and exalted by his example. It would have been more expectable for Bergoglio, a Jesuit, to have taken one of the Saint Francises from his own order—Saint Francis Xavier, for instance, or even Saint Francis Borgia. He made a riskier choice, but we would make the long shot even longer by expecting a prophet instead of a pope. Leonardo Boff, the leader of liberation theology, once avoided by Bergoglio, now embraced by Francis, thinks that, in this case, *nomen* truly is an *omen*. He says, "Francis is more than a name—it's a plan."[9] But Francis of Assisi was not good at plans, and the name can promise too much.

Though the pope has changed much in the style and presentation of the papacy, conservatives keep telling themselves that he has not changed dogma, and liberals say that even his stylistic changes have kept much they disapproved of in place. He has, for instance, canonized the authoritarian John Paul II, and retained Benedict XVI's favored disciplinary instrument, the Congregation for the Doctrine of the Faith. He has not only retained Benedict's choice as prefect of the CDF, Gerhard Müller, but promoted him to cardinal. And under Müller the harsh investigation of American nuns was allowed to continue.

The pope has said that to be truly Christian one must be a revolutionary, as Jesus was. "In this day and age, unless Christians are revolutionaries, they are not Christians."[10] But the man at the center cannot rebel against himself. The pope must, by his office, care for continuity and minimize disruption. It is true that some popes care more for continuity than for the life of the church—Paul VI and John Paul II were so urgent to keep continuity with the 1930 encyclical *Casti Connubii* that they wrote *Humanae Vitae* (1968) and *Familiaris Consortio* (1981), ignoring the voices of theologians, bishops, and the people. But that does not mean that a pope can just disregard any need for continuity. Though Francis can renounce the more ostentatious flourishes of his office, he cannot knock the props out from under the throne he sits on. Prophets levitate;

popes rarely do. Francis cannot simply draw up the ladder by which he climbed. That was as true of John XXIII as it is of Francis.

All popes show a proper deference to their predecessors; but no other pope had a predecessor still living, and living right next door. Some earlier popes had resigned or been forced from office, but they did not hang around to keep an eye on what their successor was doing. Francis is in the ticklish position of having to look over his shoulder, much of the time, at Benedict. The canonization of John Paul II, for instance, was an uncompleted project of Benedict. Francis completed it. The prefect of the CDF is another example of Francis's limited room for maneuver. Müller was not only a friend of Pope Benedict, he is the man he commissioned as the editor of his writings. Benedict also appointed him to the signature office he had held himself in a stormily contested tenure. No one could be more trusted to guard Benedict's legacy and reputation at the CDF. For Francis to reject him would be a direct insult to Benedict.

On the other hand, as the expert Jesuit Vaticanologist Thomas Reese has pointed out, Francis has done much to whittle down the centrality of the CDF, creating different centers of power in gradual shifts of emphasis and organization.[11] This is the kind of balancing act by which popes make change digestible, if not palatable. Francis, like John XXIII, calls on others to take steps moving the whole church, not just its ceremonial head. Liberals, for instance, have called for him to repeal the informal excommunication of sincere Catholics who have lapsed from some doctrinal demands. Francis has called on bishops to consider this question. But he has encouraged those who want to speak out to do so. He considers a hypothetical case in the confessional:

I also consider the situation of a woman with a failed marriage in her past and who also had an abortion. Then this woman remarries, and she is now happy and has five children. That abortion in her past weighs heavily on her conscience and she sincerely regrets it. She would like to move forward in her Christian life. What is the confessor to do?

He offers this simply as a matter for confessors to ponder, but he gives a hint where his own instincts lie when he says, "The confessional is not a torture chamber."[12]

Though church reform is a matter Francis cannot avoid, he says that the Gospel energy for that must look outward, at the other tasks the church has neglected, draining its power to carry out its commission from Jesus—to care for the sufferings of the poor, of immigrants, of sexual victims of all kinds. Reforms that seem hard can become almost incidental when energy is generated and expended on these missions. A constant emphasis of his talks as pope has been on going out to the periphery, the margins, the frontiers, to take God's love to them. And he wants Catholics to join with other Christian churches, East and West, in carrying Christ's message to those in need. It seems at first as if he is just taking on more tasks, more external missions along with internal reforms. But he says that getting priorities straight will help with all these efforts. That is why he criticized the endless and repetitive harping on things like abortion and contraception.[13]

It is a huge undertaking. If the pope is not a prophet, he does need to be something of an acrobat, like Buster Keaton dodging and scrambling down the mountain under the steady pursuit of boulders large and small. He has multiple tasks no one can perform alone, which is why he calls on others to pray for and support him. These are tasks the whole church must take up—tasks for us, for the People of God. He has made the church as the People of God a leitmotiv in his pronouncements, as in his major document, *Evangelii Gaudium:*

> [The church] exists concretely in history as a people of pilgrims and evangelizers, transcending any institutional expression, however necessary . . . The People of God is incarnate in the peoples of the earth . . . God furnishes the totality of the faithful with an instinct of faith—*sensus fidei*—which helps them to discern what is truly of God.

A pope who believes in *that* church will not try to change it all by himself—which is the best way to change it.

NOTES

1. J. H. Newman, *An Essay on the Development of Christian Doctrine* (Penguin, 1994), 100.
2. Pope Francis, *The Church of Mercy* (Loyola Press, 2014), 18.
3. G. K. Chesterton, *The Everlasting Man* (Ignatius Press, 1987), 250.
4. Ibid., 259–60.
5. Interview with Pope Francis, *America*, September 30, 2013. The interview was drawn from six hours of conversation over three days.
6. *Lumen Gentium* 13, *Gaudium et Spes* 11, in *Vatican Council II*, edited by Austin Flannery, sixth printing (Costello Publishing Company, 2007), 17, 174.
7. Pope Francis, *The Church of Mercy* (Loyola Press, 2014), 19.
8. As Peter Hebblethwaite wrote, "[Roncalli] had discovered his scholarly vocation, editing the 39 volumes of Saint Charles Borromeo . . . But it took a lifetime. The five volumes appeared in 1936, 1937, 1938, 1946 and 1957." But the books were so expensive few could buy them. *John XXIII: Pope of the Council* (Geoffrey Chapman, 1988), 54, 240.
9. Paul Vallely, *Pope Francis: Untying the Knots* (Bloomsbury, 2013), 198.
10. Pope Francis, *The Church of Mercy,* 13.
11. Thomas Reese, S.J., "Vatican's Doctrinal Congregation Isn't So Supreme Anymore," *National Catholic Reporter,* February 14, 2014.
12. Pope Francis, *America* interview.
13. Ibid.: "We cannot insist only on issues related to abortion, gay marriage and the use of contraceptive methods . . . We have to find a new balance; otherwise even the moral edifice of the church is likely to fall like a house of cards."

I

The Coming and Going
of Latin

ONE

Inclusion

When I was growing up I often heard that a strength of the Catholic Church was its universality. Go anywhere in the world, and you would find the same words and rites being used at Mass. This made people as different as Joseph de Maistre and Arnold Lunn say that a Catholic was at home anywhere. Latin knew no spatial or temporal limits. It was the perfect vehicle for conveying eternal truths, absolute everywhere. No wonder people fought so hard at the Second Vatican Council to keep this symbol and pledge of supra-temporal consistency. Latin was the eternal language for an eternal church.

The idea of a common language, one that can span cultural differences and bring people together, is perennially attractive. The most persistent effort at this is Esperanto, invented in 1878 by Ludwig Zamenhof. He came from the town of Bialystok, where people spoke Russian, German, Yiddish, and lesser-known tongues. After mastering these, Zamenhof dreamed of breaking down divisions in the community by creating a shared language all could own and be proud of. His broader hopes for creating peace through a unity of language were fostered by thousands of people around the world. He was nominated for the Nobel Peace Prize.

Other artificial languages have been contrived, along with attempts to unify the spelling, phonetics, and morphology of single languages—for instance, George Bernard Shaw's promotion of a new alphabet for English. At a less ambitious and therefore more common level, there have been attempts by national academies or prescriptive dictionaries to impose standard usage for any and all words. These have all been strangled in the thickets of particularity they were trying to erase.

Esperanto, precisely because it seeks a neutral common ground, loses the color, nuance, and historical resonance of native words spoken over time in specific cultural contexts. These words all have echoes of their former uses, in many layers. Different people are aware of different levels of that usage, but every native speaker recognizes some of them, and they lend richness to the words. The words when joined have rhythms and accents that vary according to the linkages, recognizing old partner-words, or perking up at striking collisions with surrounding words, accompanied with the arc of their phrasing, the tune of the language as sounded. Esperanto and its congeners will always seem sterile and empty next to words that buzz with such possibilities, as suggestive as they are elusive. That is why it is impossible to write real poetry in Esperanto. As a language with the lowest common denominator of meaning, it is all a wide, thin surface over nonexistent depths.

Latin, however, seemed for a long time to escape these common dangers of a common language. It did have a history, with historical resonance. For centuries it served as a lingua franca for those with differing first languages. It facilitated diplomatic and scholarly exchanges. It was the language not only of the Christian churches, but of the learned in many secular circles. Treaties were better drawn up in a language that extended to all parties. The civilization of a culture was judged by its degree of connection with the Latin language. That is why T. S. Eliot claimed that Dante is a more universal poet than Shakespeare, more accessible to those with the common heritage of Latin-derived Romance languages. (He hastened to say that this did not make Dante greater than Shakespeare, just a denizen of a wider culture.) As de Maistre wrote, "the European sign is Latin."[1] That was a problem. Latin was "universal" only for Europe. It was parochial so far as the rest of the world was concerned. Those who championed Latin as the best expression of the faith also thought, in Hilaire Belloc's familiar maxim, that "Europe is the faith." We no longer think that "universal" means European.

Even in the New World colonies of America, which were only partly non-European, there was a sense that one should find one's own ways of thinking and speaking, outside the matrix of Latinity. Dr. Benjamin Rush, the Revolutionary leader in Pennsylvania, said that people in a young country should develop their own new ways of learning. Though classically trained himself, he said that starting out with Latin and Greek would cramp the minds of American children:

> While the business of education in Europe consists in lectures upon the ruins of Palmyra and the antiquities of Herculaneum, or in disputes about Hebrew points, Greek particles, or the accent and quantity of the Roman language, the youth of America will be employed in acquiring those branches of knowledge which increase the conveniences of life, lessen human misery, improve our country, promote population, exalt the human understanding, and establish domestic, social, and political happiness.[2]

As a physician, Rush was especially upset at the long domination of medical theory by classical authors like Galen and Hippocrates. But other founding-era leaders, men like Thomas Paine and Noah Webster, also felt that training in the classical languages would inhibit freshness and creativity on American soil.[3]

When Benjamin Franklin established the Philadelphia Academy, which developed into the University of Pennsylvania, he ruled against a Latin language requirement. Later, when the school board reversed this policy, he tried to establish a separate school based on English.[4] He knew that Greek and Latin would be necessary for some graduate programs, especially those in divinity, but he did not want children to suffer the drudgery of learning Latin forms that they would never use in later life. He knew from experience that French had replaced Latin as the vehicle for international diplomacy.[5]

Nor were Americans the only ones trying to break away from the static Latin schooling of the past. The scientific revolution of the seventeenth

century led to the so-called "battle of the Ancients and the Moderns" celebrated by Swift and Pope in *The Battle of the Books* and *The Dunciad*. John
Locke had championed vernacular education in 1692:

> [The gentleman] ought to study grammar . . . but it must be the gram-
> mar of his own tongue, of the language he uses, that he may understand
> his own country speech nicely, and speak it properly . . . And to this pur-
> pose grammar is necessary; but it is the grammar *only of their own proper
> tongues* [emphasis added].[6]

The attempt to teach modern science in Latin led to the invention of stilted
and approximate terms based on Latin roots. That is why some early scientific work was carried on by academies and patrons' organizations apart
from the university systems. Franklin, the supreme autodidact, was in
communication with such scientific academies in other countries.

It took a long and dogged fight to break the hold of Latin as the basic
tool of education at the primary and secondary levels. Françoise Waquet
tells the story of that struggle, primarily from the history of her own
country, France, but with important looks around at the rest of Europe.[7]
Latin had not been taught to schoolboys as a way to appreciate important
works of poetry or philosophy. It was imposed precisely as "a discipline,"
the more severe the better, since it was supposed to be forming character
as well as rigor of thinking. (If clarity of thought was the goal, why not
just teach logic?) Locke and Franklin had early on exploded the concept
that learning Latin grammar was the way to learn other languages. Even
the claim that Latin gave a special entry into the Romance languages derived from it was disproved by Franklin. He had shown that it worked
better the other way around—knowledge of French and/or Italian made
it easier to pick up what Latin one might want for actual use.[8]

When one got beyond reading and composing by the rules, and actually read real poetry in the schools, it was still being learned as a chore, so
that few continued the reading after they left school. Benjamin Rush said
in the eighteenth century what was true of succeeding ones—that if boys

labored through a book or two of the *Aeneid* in a classroom, they did not go on to read the whole poem later.[9] Does one really know Vergil better for having read one book in the original than from reading the entire *Aeneid* in translation? Michel de Montaigne could say, even earlier, that "having learned" Latin was not the same as "knowing" it in later life.[10] The language was just a painful barrier to be crossed, making the first part of one's schooling the most arid. Even the well educated in France and England actually used what Latin they retained mainly in familiar tags and mottos. The British poet Louis MacNeice, who not only studied but taught Latin at the university level, had no illusions about the usual result of that teaching. It bestowed

The privilege of learning a language
That is incontrovertibly dead
And of carting a toy-box of hall-marked marmoreal phrases
Around in his head.[11]

What Rush called such "smatterings" have nothing to do with real scholarship.[12] Those who genuinely want to know and enjoy the classics can do that without imposing on others the labor of first indoctrination without any of the later enrichment. Of course, to get translations you must have a supply of learned people who know and can convey the meaning of the originals. And, ideally, teachers using such translations should be able to enrich them from their own knowledge; but it would impoverish general education to insist that only Greek scholars could teach Homer in the schools.

I have been talking so far about Latin in the broad world. Whatever happened there, one could always claim that Catholics, at least, had kept Latin alive as the language of the church. While it is true that Latin was used in the sacraments and documents of the church, its claim as a living medium of exchange had quickly grown thin. This was true at many levels. To start low down in the formation of the ministry, I recur to my days as a Jesuit novice in the 1950s. We were required to speak only Latin during the day, reserving the use of English to our recreation period after dinner. I had had four years of Latin at a good high school, and my *carissimi* (as we were instructed to call each other) had comparable backgrounds. But we used only "kitchen Latin" vocabulary and repeated locutions during the day, saving anything we wanted to say with richer meaning for our English exchanges. We took oral Latin tests in the same way, usefully restraining our answers to planned formulas as the safest in terms of matter and manner.

One might hope that as novices continued their studies, and became more practiced in Latin, its use would become more flexible and informative. But later, in my seminary philosophy classes, we actually used more English than Latin in studying Thomas Aquinas, and no one seemed to be reading the originals beyond assigned excerpts. I saw few priests in later life actually reading Latin works outside the formulas of their breviary. In the 1960s, after leaving the Jesuits, and getting a doctorate in the classical languages, I wrote a book on papal encyclicals. A few of these documents, the most famous ones, were available in English, but most of them were still in ecclesiastical Latin. To read them I had to go, in Baltimore, to Saint Mary's, the oldest seminary in America. There, text by text, I read them by slitting their uncut pages. If they were not being read there, where were they read?

The myth that Latin was a real means of living communication in the church took heavy blows at both of the ecumenical councils of the modern era. At the First Vatican Council (1869–70), conducted in Latin, bishops were less ready to use it and understand it than they pretended— which gave members of the Roman Curia an advantage for steering and limiting what went on. When bishops did speak up, they were not only halting in their attempts at spontaneous Latin, but they spoke in the different pronunciations of their own countries. Latin used by a bishop from Cyprus sounded like Greek to the Italian bishop of Lucca. In order to record the proceedings, a Roman secretariat arranged for twenty-three seminarians from different countries to try to puzzle out what their countrymen were saying, and their joint product had what were called "mediocre results." One of the scribes, according to Françoise Waquet, remembered that "during the first few days one often saw a smile breaking through the gravity of the Italian bishops and cardinals, when they heard the language of Cicero being spoken with inflections strange to their ears." Some bishops petitioned the pope to let them hold ancillary meetings in the different language groups to figure out what was going on. Waquet concludes her account of the event this way:

> Different accents had resounded in the very place where unity was supposed to reign, detracting considerably from the claimed universality of the Latin language.[13]

That was in the nineteenth century, when Latin was still the basis of instruction in most European schools, for laymen as well as clerics. A century later, at the Second Vatican Council (1962–65), when bishops and priests themselves were far less used to Latin outside church formularies, Archbishop Richard Cushing of Boston faced the language problem squarely by trying to pay for UN-style simultaneous translations the bishops could listen to through earphones. That was at the first session of the council. He was told that the Curia was exploring this proposal and would follow up on his request; but by the end of the second session nothing had been done, and Cushing left the council for good.[14] Maximos IV Sayegh, the Catholic Melkite patriarch, endorsed the request for simultaneous translation, to no effect.[15] He made his own addresses to the council in French.

It did not serve the Roman officials of the Curia to make communication easier. This lent a note of absurdity to the time when Cardinal Spellman of New York presided over one debate on retaining Latin in the liturgy and had to have his own speech read by another, since no one could understand his Latin. The Redemptorist priest F. X. Murphy, writing from Rome as Xavier Rynne, concluded, "Latin as a medium of communication at the Council proved to be less than a success."[16] Andrea Riccardi agrees: "The choice of Latin and the exclusion of simultaneous translation not only affected the ability of the fathers to understand what was happening; it also signified the choice of a mentality."[17] Latin is the language of dogma.

One can reply that the value of Latin comes not from the proficiency of its daily users, but from the stability of its rites and documents. The rites I will consider later; but the documents are not as firmly universal as they seem. The problem of sneaking subtle new meaning into creaky old formulas is harder to avoid than people think. Take, for instance, a famous dispute that arose from John XXIII's encyclical letter *Mater et Magistra* (1960). Paragraph 59 of that document referred to the modern world's increasing complexity of social interrelationships (*socialium rationum incrementa*). The first English translation authorized by the Vatican called this an increasing "socialization"—a valid translation, understandable by sociologists in a range of meanings; but the word suggested "socialism" to American readers and politicians, and for them socialism was synonymous with Soviet communism.[18] Oceans of ink were wasted on this contretemps.[19]

The problem, one may object, was not with the Latin, but with inadequate translators. But such a modern concept was going to be translated "in the head" by all people having different associations with the phenomenon being referred to. The misconception is that all such differences can be extruded from one controlling language. No language is univocal. To think so was to hope for Latin as a higher Esperanto, escaping nuance through a medium that reduces all meaning to a lowest common denominator. At the councils, even if no simultaneous translators put things in the bishops' native languages, they were mentally translating what they understood of the Latin into the specific cultural environment each man carried within. Those different worlds could not be ground into a single cultural mishmash called "timeless" Latin.

There is no universal language that can level and stunt the busyness of mind needed to put thinking into words. To succeed at that, one would have to anesthetize minds, to make thinking cease. And that, we may find, was the real hope offered by ecclesiastical Latin. It was not there to facilitate thought but to preserve it by freezing it. Some think it succeeded in that odd (they would consider it that "supernatural") effort. To prove that Latin is not "universal" does not break its real hold on those who cling to it. They never wanted it to be a leveler. For them, Latin's function was not to lower barriers but to raise them. It was never an inclusive Esperanto. More like a secret code of the elect.

NOTES

1. Joseph de Maistre, *Du Pape* (Charpentier, 1841), 134.
2. Carl J. Richard, *The Founders and the Classics: Greece, Rome, and the American Enlightenment* (Harvard University Press, 1994), 198.
3. Ibid., 192, 202, 215, 224. Also Meyer Reinhold, *Classica Americana: The Greek and Roman Heritage in the United States* (Wayne State University Press, 1984), 123–26.
4. Richard, op. cit., 221–22.
5. *The Autobiography,* in *Benjamin Franklin: Writings,* edited by J. A. Leo Lemay (Library of America, 1987), 1401.
6. John Locke, *Some Thoughts Concerning Education,* Section 168.
7. Françoise Waquet, *Latin, or the Empire of a Sign: From the Sixteenth to the Twentieth Centuries,* translated by John Howe (Verso, 2001).
8. Franklin, op. cit., 1401.
9. Richard, op. cit., 223.
10. Michel de Montaigne, "Du Pedantisme," in *Essais,* edited by Pierre Michel (Gallimard, 1965), vol. 1, 211–13.
11. Louis MacNeice, *Autumn Journal* XIII.
12. Richard, op. cit., 223.
13. Waquet, op. cit., 17–71.
14. "Xavier Rynne," *Vatican Council II* (Orbis Books, 1999), 206.
15. Mathus Lamberigts, "The Liturgy Debate," in Giuseppe Alberigo, *History of Vatican II,* English edition by Joseph A. Komonchak (Orbis/Peeters, 1997), vol. 2, 123–24.
16. "Xavier Rynne," *Letters from Vatican City* (Farrar, Straus & Company, 1963), vol. 1, 99–102.
17. Andrea Riccardi, "The Tumultuous Opening Days of the Council," in Alberigo, op. cit., 47.

18. The Vatican later changed the translation to an "increase in social relation-ships."
19. William F. Buckley Jr. was famously caught in this cross fire, though he did not think the pope was referring to communism. He called the encyclical "a venture in triviality." He did not think the pope socialist, just irrelevant—as his friend Russell Kirk said that Eisenhower was not a communist, just a golfer.

TWO

Exclusion

One of the heartiest defenses of church Latin came from the great Renaissance essayist Michel de Montaigne:

> We should not see the Holy Book, with the sacred secrets of our belief, bandied about in hallways and kitchens. Things once sacrosanct have become toys to play with. A subject so deep and revered should not be studied in a random or hurried way. It should be an act of quietness and recollection, to be begun with the *Sursum Corda* we say before prayer; and we should fit our very body to the expression of a different alertness and devotion. This is not a study open for anyone to indulge in. It is for those separately summoned by God's call—not for the evil or foolish, whom exposure to it will just make worse. It is not simply a story to be recited, but one to be plumbed with trembling and devotion. It is folly to think it can be spread to ordinary folk by being put in their own languages. They think mere difference of language keeps them from understanding what is written. I make bold to say that bringing it down to them just removes it farther from them. Simple ignorance, if reliant on others, is more useful and wise than knowing words that breed a reckless self-confidence. I hold that freely scattering out this holy teaching in all the vernaculars is more dangerous than useful.[1]

This is clearly different from the defenses of Latin considered in the preceding chapter. Those argued for a universal language, including as many people as possible, a language maximally understood. By that logic, Latin would fail only to the extent that it could not reach a wide audience. But Montaigne champions Latin because it keeps people out. It maintains the sacred by warding off the unworthy. There is no point in admitting people incapable or unwilling to be initiated into the secrets. In the ancient priests' cry, *Procul, Profani!*

Joseph de Maistre said, two hundred years later, exactly what Montaigne was saying in the sixteenth century: "If the people do not understand the [Latin] words, so much the better. Respect gains, and intelligence loses nothing. He who understands nothing understands more than he who understands badly."[2] It is not unusual for the keepers of a religious tradition to withhold its secrets from outsiders. The early Christian church observed such a *disciplina arcani* (guarding of the secrets) that people were forbidden to say the creed before unbelievers, and even beginning adherents to the faith were excluded from the communion part of the Mass.

In fact, this instinct is even wider than its religious uses. Some secular literature too has been cherished because it is confined to adepts. Certain kinds of knowledge, it is felt, should not be universally accessible. Even Benjamin Franklin, who favored easy instruction in the vernacular, said that truly special knowledge should be difficult to acquire. If, as many claimed, ancient philosophy, politics, and literature were so elevated above ordinary varieties of knowledge, then it is understandable that climbing up to them should be restricted to those willing to invest in more than ordinary effort:

> When youth are told that the great men whose lives and actions they read in history spoke two of the best languages that ever were [Greek and Latin], the most expressive, copious, beautiful; and that the finest writings, the most correct compositions, the most perfect productions of human wit and wisdom, are in those languages, which have endured ages and will endure while there are men; that no translation can do them justice, or give the pleasure found in reading the originals; that those languages contain all science; that one of them is become almost universal, being the language of learned men in all countries; that to understand them is a distinguishing ornament, etc.—they may be thereby made desirous of learning those languages, and their industry sharpened in the acquisition of them.[3]

But this draining off of great energy should take place only for those "that have an ardent desire," and only so long as "other studies absolutely necessary" are not neglected. For most people, Franklin maintained, such recondite knowledge is more ornamental than useful.

But, of course, some people feel that ornaments *are* useful. They are ardently sought precisely because they are rare, as gems or fine art can be rare and difficult to acquire. This fits with a more general feeling that the finest things need disciplined taste to be appreciated. From this it follows that really good art must be "difficult," with a matching hunch that anything instantly popular must be inferior. Anything ordinary people admired, including Shakespeare's plays and Verdi's operas, must have some taint. (The Elizabethan poet Ben Jonson felt that about Shakespeare, and Richard Wagner about Verdi.) The sacredness of religious language is merely an intensification of this instinct to keep the costly above ready purchase.

This is not—well, not always—mere snobbishness. It is true that knowing recondite things is not easy; but those who merely pretend to know them claim a superiority that is unearned. They affect a familiarity with other languages, or with "modern art," or with Einsteinian physics, striking a pose rather than studying the things themselves. Still, we should not let the poseurs deflect us from recognition that some tastes are not instantly acquired, that exacting standards should keep important knowledge precise, and that some secrets are worth keeping.

Of course, once an elite is formed in terms of a linguistic monopoly, privileges will accrue to mark out that elite, and some abuses are inevitable. Since knowing Latin was the mark of the cleric, one way to claim that status was simply to show evidence that one read Latin. This led to the oddity of English law called *privilegium clericale* (benefit of clergy), whereby one could appeal from a civil court (where beheading was the penalty for certain crimes) to an ecclesiastical court (where penalties were generally less severe) by showing a knowledge of Latin. The standard test for reading Latin became a verse of Psalm 51, beginning

Miserere mei, Deus—called the "neck verse," since it was used to escape hanging. Ben Jonson used that verse in 1598 to escape the gallows for manslaughter, getting off with a mere brand on his right hand.[4] This is just one of many ways Latin was used to mark out a privileged caste. But to those in authority, the advantages of exclusion outweighed any exploitations of it.

Mystery

For some, the great advantage of limiting knowledge of the truth by limiting the language in which it is transacted increased the value of that truth, even for those being kept in the dark. It was a blessing for them to be kept outside. It made them more reverent, and their reverence more meritorious. In the words of Felix Messerschmid, the twentieth-century German liturgist, the laity could sense the power of the Mass "independent of any comprehension in the natural sense of the word."[5] Mystery is enhanced by inaccessibility. Early in the nineteenth century, François-René de Chateaubriand wrote:

> Orisons in Latin seem to redouble the religious feeling of the crowd. Might this not be a natural effect of our penchant for secrecy? In the tumult of his thoughts and the miseries that beset his life, man believes that, by pronouncing words that are unfamiliar or unknown, he is asking for things that he needs but of which he is unaware. The charm of the prayer lies in its vagueness; for his troubled soul, which hardly knows what it desires, loves to form wishes as mysterious as its needs.[6]

This was not just the mystification of a Romantic. As early as the eleventh century, obscurantism was made holy by the pope. Gregory VII abolished a liturgy in Slavonic, restoring the Latin rite precisely because people could not understand it: "Had it been clear to all, it might perhaps have been less respected, or more easily ignored."[7] Dom Prosper Guéranger, often praised as the founder of the modern liturgical move-

ment, wanted wide participation in liturgical acts, but wanted it celebrated in a single rite for all, stabilized by a single language, Latin:

> While it is important for the language of the liturgical books to be fixed
> and inviolable, and not to be purely national, it is also in its nature to be
> mysterious; so it ought not to be vulgar.

For this it was not only "absolutely necessary" that the liturgy be in Latin;
it was also desirable that it be murmured by the priest in low tones, so
that the laity would not be distracted from its awe.[8]

The compulsion of mystery was explained by that reader of the human heart, Alessandro Manzoni, in his tale of a humble lay brother puz-
zled when a Capuchin priest admitted women to the monastery. The
priest threw off a formula, *Omnia munda mundis* (all things are pure to the
pure), forgetting that the brother knew no Latin. But he did not regret
that failure to communicate, since it was only an apparent failure:

> It was this very oversight that gave the words the right effect. If Fra Cris-
> toforo had begun to argue and produce reasons, Fra Fazio would have
> been at no loss to find other reasons to oppose against his; and heaven
> knows how and when it would have ended. But at the sound of the words
> so pregnant with mysterious meaning, and uttered with such an air of
> decision, he felt that they must contain the solution to all his doubts. He
> calmed down, and said: "Ah well! You know better than I do."[9]

The mystery should be wrapped in layers of further mystery. Only
that would be worthy of the sacred act, of the Mass, conducted by the
priest, as Guéranger writes, "in those fearful moments when he is placed
between heaven and earth," partly sealed off from the people to get close
to God.[10] This was theatrically underscored by the conduct of the Mass in
the Middle Ages and Renaissance. Not only was the priest turned away
from the congregation, engaged in his sacred action where they could not
see it; the whole sanctuary was sealed off by a "rood screen"—later modified to the communion rail declaring the territory not accessible to the

layman (or to any woman). Why expect anything other than an esoteric language in any rite so detached from connection with the community? Latin was just the natural expression of this separated sacredness.

Authority

But Latin was not only an expression of mystery. It stood for authority. For a long time that was true even of secular authority. Documents were in official Latin. Certificates and diplomas, school and other mottos, building inscriptions, emblems of societies were dignified by being in the formal tongue. There was actually an "inscription war" in seventeenth- and eighteenth-century France, when some institutions and monuments were beginning to be inscribed in languages other than Latin. This was called a disloyal abandonment of proud tradition. The French Revolution made this conflict flare up again, after it had subsided, with memories of the Roman republic in conflict with the modernism of the Encyclopedists.[11] Even today, some in America regret it if their college degree is not in Latin, as if it had been issued in a debased currency.

In the "Roman" church this tendency to see Latin as the natural language of authority had been deeply inculcated. *Roma locuta est,* "Rome has spoken," is the characteristic note of the papacy, and it is not accidental that one part of the Christian faith is called *"Roman* Catholicism." (Because "catholic" means, etymologically, "universal," John Milton said that it was contradictory to call something the Partial Whole.) The church prolonged the memory of the Roman Empire. The fact that the Christian church was born in part of the Roman Empire has led some people to think that Latin was the language of the early church. It was not. Greek, not Latin, was the common language of the Roman Empire, since the empire inherited lands acquired by the Greek conqueror Alexander and his ruling descendants.

Still, it was natural to think of the church as a sacred successor to temporal Roman rule. It was long a preacher's device to say that God had chosen to be incarnated at a time when there was a common culture for all of Europe, which at the time was equated with all the world. The ringing assertion of power in the Latin language was celebrated by Chateaubriand: "Is it not natural for us to speak to God in the finest idiom on earth, the one used by groveling nations to address their prayers to the Caesars?"[12] Latin, many felt, is more dignified, less subject to the degradations that modern languages suffer from daily use and lowly contacts. They agreed with Evelyn Waugh's criticism of John XXIII's concept of *aggiornamento* (updating), since "updating" the Latin liturgy would be like throwing it into the gutter, or the sewer, of modern usage.[13] We would no longer be hearing "Rome speak." Men like Waugh and Malcolm Muggeridge had come to the Catholic Church seeking authority, and they could not recognize it in any language but Latin.

If Latin was not, strictly speaking, *necessary* for enunciating religious truth, it seemed, in the eyes of many, to be the *natural* language of truth. It was what the deposit of faith had been formulated in; so it was best defended in those terms. This feeling that "things were not quite right" away from the Latin made Vatican officials queasy with the translation of *consubstantialis* in the creed recited at English vernacular masses as "one in substance." So they reinserted "consubstantial" into the approved English Mass. The meaning was the same, but somehow the Latinate form had more heft than "one in substance." It felt more securely locked down in place. And that, after all, was the desideratum. When Gregory VII forbade the use of Slavonic liturgies, he not only said that Latin would be more respected the less it was understood. He also said that if the people understood what the Latin is saying, they might interpret it for themselves, apart from meanings being given them by their priests. He meant to prevent it from being "badly interpreted by people of mediocre culture."[14] In this he anticipated the Reformation debates over "private interpretation."

The Logic of Exclusion

By the sixteenth century, control of doctrine could no longer be maintained simply by refusing to have it dealt with in any language but Latin. The Renaissance humanists had discovered the charms of Greek, which Erasmus praised as superior to Latin—as well as being the language in which the New Testament is written.[15] Erasmus was just one of those trying to establish the real meaning of the Gospels from study of their original. The leaders of the Reformation began to preach from and promulgate the Bible and catechisms in the English of Wycliffe, the German of Luther, the French of Lefèvre d'Étaples. Aided by the invention of the printing press, such works swept down in a torrent on the closed Latin citadel of Rome. It was not enough, in that situation, to keep the laity from straying by keeping all theology in Latin. One must now keep them from reading Bibles and church instructions in other languages (including even the original one, Greek).

In a panicky attempt to cope with so many different works and arguments coming at the church in a babble of different tongues, the papacy decided on a draconian measure. It would forbid the printing, possessing, or reading of any work on faith or morals that it considered wrong or misleading or dangerous—and it would name all such works. Paul IV published the first Roman list of forbidden books (*Index Librorum Prohibitorum*). It was a sweeping ban. Hundreds of authors' works were condemned in toto; a smaller but still large number of authors had particular works of theirs condemned. Anonymous works (common in that era) were condemned by title. Specific Bible editions and their translations were banned—thirty whole Bibles, and twelve New Testaments. The entire output of certain publishing houses (fifty-eight of them) was put off-limits because the companies had printed heretical works.[16]

That first Index was issued during the Council of Trent. But the council saw that it was not practical and set out to revise it. At first, some claimed that authors being scrutinized should be summoned to Trent to defend their work.[17] This had been an earlier practice when Rome was dealing with theologians accused of heresy. But why would Reformers heed such a summons—especially when they remembered what happened to John Hus at the Council of Constance? Invited there in 1415 to defend his teachings, Hus was promised safe conduct to represent himself—and then was burnt at the stake for heresy. At Trent, 150 years later, the bishops could not agree on how to revise the Index. For one thing, Trent was a small town with no significant library. Almost the only books available were those brought by the bishops' experts (*periti*). So the council charged the pope, back in Rome, to oversee revision of the Index—which Pius IV did in 1564.[18]

This Index relaxed somewhat the wholesale condemnation of authors' works. It kept that ban only for "heresiarchs" (leaders of significant heresies), naming Luther, Zwingli, Calvin, Balthasar Friedberg, and Schwenckfeld. Other presumed heretics were to be judged work by work. They could prove their innocence by submitting their works for review to the local bishop (the beginnings of the *nihil obstat* that all Catholics would later be required to get before publishing a book on theological matters). The principles for drawing up the Index were spelled out in an introduction, comprising ten rules. The rules implicitly banned any use of a translation other than the Vulgate Latin, and even editions of that had to be approved, to make sure notes and commentary did not stray. These rules were so encompassing on the principles of exclusion that all the actual books listed were already subsumed within them.

Nonetheless, the Index went on to create a long list of specific condemnations, whose production, possession, or reading would subject a Catholic to excommunication. What is more, a Congregation of the Index was set up to keep adding titles as they appeared. Eventually, the Index would include works of the leading scientists, philosophers, and historians of the modern era. It is a wonder that a Catholic college could exist into the twentieth century while unable to read some works of Locke, Milton, Hume, Gibbon, Voltaire, Rousseau, among the thousands of others banned in ever-renewed attempts to exclude unauthorized thought. The real wonder is that the church did not exclude itself out of existence.

But the church upped the ante in the nineteenth and twentieth centuries, adding to the Index of books two "Syllabi" of *ideas* to be banned—the first a Syllabus of Errors on church-state thought (issued by Pius IX in 1864), the second a Syllabus of the Errors of Modernism (issued by Pius X in 1907). To make assurance double sure that these concepts would be quashed, any priest being ordained from 1910 on had to take an "Oath Against Modernism" in which he vowed to observe all the bans in the Syllabus of Modernism (*Lamentabili Sane*), including observation of the Index of Forbidden Books. It was a futile effort, which soon became an embarrassment to priests, who either stultified themselves by submission to it or tacitly ignored it, more or less consciously deceiving their superiors, or their flocks, or themselves (until it was rescinded in 1967).

But the one thing that could not, for centuries, be ignored went back to the first barrier of exclusion that had been raised—the reservation of the Bible and biblical studies to Latin. In 1938, with much clanking of the church's ecclesiastical hierarchy, Catholic bishops in England commissioned a new translation of the Bible to replace the Reformation-era Catholic translation from the college of Douay. An eccentrically learned priest, Ronald Knox, given this charge, buried himself in the long effort. Naturally, since the bishops were sponsoring a translation for official use, it had to be made from the church's official Bible, the Vulgate Latin. By 1942, Knox had completed the New Testament, though it would not get final approval from the bishops till 1945. Then he was halfway through his translation of the Old Testament, whose final approval and publication came in 1955.[19] By that time, all the bishops' worry and hesitation about even attempting to change the old Catholic translation had been made obsolete.

In 1943, Pius XII finally approved translation and scholarship from the Bible's original languages (Hebrew and Greek). His encyclical *Divino*

Afflante Spiritu encouraged textual criticism of the originals and formal criticism of their content, scholarly tools long suppressed or denigrated in the church. The Vulgate quickly lost all popular authority. New translations by Catholics—or, more important, nonconfessional translation by scholars across denominational barriers—became the accepted currency. The tyranny of Latin was broken. The long, hard, hopeless endeavor to lock up the word of God in a language it was not written in was ending. There was still the battle to keep the liturgy in Latin, an effort that would not end for another twenty years (at Vatican II). There are still faint shots fired from that war—in the Society of St. Pius X liturgies, in Benedict XVI's encouragements of the Latin Mass, in the returned Latinisms of the revised English-language Mass, and such exercises of nostalgia. But the war is over. Like Japanese fighters holding out in their bunkers after V-J Day, only a few do not realize this.

NOTES

1. Michel de Montaigne, "Des Prières," in *Essais,* edited by Pierre Michel (Gallimard, 1965), vol. 1, 442.
2. Joseph de Maistre, *Du Pape* (Charpentier, 1841), 139.
3. Benjamin Franklin, "Proposals Relating to the Education of Youth in Pennsylvania" (1749), in *Writings,* edited by J. A. Leo Lemay (Library of America, 1987), 338–39.
4. Ian Donaldson, *Ben Jonson: A Life* (Oxford University Press, 2011), 135–37. Jonson later played with his close call in his comedy *Bartholomew Fair* (1614), where a proud illiterate refuses to use the *privilegium* to escape death: "I am no clerk. I scorn to be saved by my book. I'faith, I'll hang first" (1.4.4–6).
5. Felix Messerschmid, cited in Françoise Waquet, *Latin, or the Empire of a Sign: From the Sixteenth to the Twentieth Centuries,* translated by John Howe (Verso, 2001), 71.
6. François-René de Chateaubriand, *Défense du Génie du christianisme* (Garnier, 1926), 95.
7. Ibid., 42–43.
8. Prosper Guéranger, *Institutions Liturgiques* (Julien et Cie, 1819), vol. 3, 52–159.
9. Alessandro Manzoni, *The Betrothed,* translated by Archibald Colquhoun (Everyman's Library, 1951), 127.
10. Guéranger, op. cit., 159.
11. Waquet, op. cit., 238–41.

12. Chateaubriand, op. cit., 96.

13. Evelyn Waugh, *The Tablet*, August 21, 1965.

14. Waquet, op. cit., 43.

15. Leon-E. Halkin, *Erasmus: A Critical Biography,* translated by John Tonkin (Blackwell, 1993), 49–51.

16. *Index Librorum Prohibitorum,* 1559 (Houghton Library copy online).

17. John W. O'Malley, *Trent: What Happened at the Council* (Harvard University Press, 2013), 177–78.

18. Ibid., 206.

19. Evelyn Waugh, *Monsignor Ronald Knox* (Little, Brown & Company, 1959), 284–302.

THREE

God's Word Under Guard

The Word Guarded by Latin: Trent

Though the Vulgate has become a historical curiosity, it is important in this study of changes in the church to see how it came for centuries to be *the* Bible for Catholics, since the Vulgate came into being as itself a change, and one stoutly resisted. Only later would it enter that sacred realm of things that have been around for so long that people suppose they were always there, preserved because they are eternal. The New Testament was a Greek document, not a Latin one. The early creeds were also debated and formulated by Greek speakers in the East. Even in Rome, the language of the liturgy and preaching was Greek for the first two centuries. Neither Peter nor Paul would have known Latin; they spoke the koine Greek of all the Jewish Diaspora. To quote the great church historian Henry Chadwick:

> In 200 Tertullian in North Africa was pioneering the writing of Latin theology, but was simultaneously publishing in Greek. By the middle of the third century Latin became the predominant speech of western Christians, but there long remained Greek colonies at Rome, Carthage, the Rhône valley, and even Spain. Some in South Italy and Sicily remained Greek-speaking for a millennium; refugees from Persian and Arab attacks greatly increased the Greek-speaking population in the west in the sixth and seventh centuries.[1]

As Latin became the ordinary language of Christians in the West, the New Testament had to be translated out of its Greek original into various Latin versions. There was no single or official translation. Versions were made or copied as the need for them spread. What traces of these texts remain are now given the collective designation of the *Vetus Latina* (Old Latin) version, as if it were one shared Bible. That was never the case. When in the fourth century Damasus the bishop of Rome asked Jerome, a learned ascetic then in Rome, to improve and standardize the Latin of the Gospels and the Psalms, Jerome faced a bewildering collection of codices—with almost as many different versions, he said, as there were codices. Augustine too said that the Latin versions of the Bible available to him "differ so from codex to codex as barely to be borne."[2] Jerome therefore chose what he thought the best text from the mix, and he standardized their Latin style—without looking at the original Greek of the Gospels or Hebrew of the Psalms.

But over the next two decades he corrected more of the Latin texts, going beyond the Gospels and Psalms, and then began to translate them again, this time from the original Greek of the New Testament, and from the Greek translations of the Old Testament. Then, as he learned Hebrew, he began translating the Old Testament from its original language. In a life full of controversy, management of his Palestinian convent and study center, and prolific other writings, his Bible work was always hurried. It improved in his later translations, and in the parts of the Bible he gave new translations to when writing his extensive comments on the prophets. Thus he left his own bewildering pile of layered texts of "Jerome's Bible."

It was left to unnamed editors over the next two centuries to reduce the layers of his various campaigns, and what books remained in Old Latin, to one standard (*vulgata*) edition of "St. Jerome's Bible." The process of selection for this edition is lost in history, and its results are variable. For instance, Jerome wrote three Psalters—one the revised Latin, the other taken from the Septuagint, and only the third one taken from the original Hebrew. The Vulgate omits the Latin revision (and it is therefore mainly lost), includes the one from the Septuagint (which became the "Jerome" psalms), and left out the one from Hebrew—even though the later myth was that all the Vulgate Old Testament was from the Hebrew.[3]

Jerome's attempts to go back to the sources were resisted at the time. The Latin Bible that people had used was already sanctified by time. No less a figure than Augustine protested that Jerome would just confuse people by telling them that the gourd with which the Lord overshadowed Jonah in the Old Latin was now become a castor-oil vine.[4] Augustine, who knew little Greek and no Hebrew, said Jerome should stop his translations at the Greek, and not introduce confusion from the Hebrew, whose texts were obscure to begin with. Better stick to the time-tested.[5] There were hardly any trustworthy Hebrew manuscripts in the West for Augustine to consult, even if he had been able to read them.[6] Ironically, most of the arguments Augustine made against Jerome's Vulgate would later be used to defend the Vulgate against rival translations—that the traditions of the church should not be upset, that new ones would just confuse people, that God would not have let the church get along with a translation that was inferior. It was a recurrent view in history—that esoteric learning is just a nuisance to the ordinary believer.

But in the Middle Ages, the cult of Jerome and of "his" Bible grew steadily and piously. Men felt that it was a matter of divine providence that Jerome was given such fabulous linguistic skills, that his Vulgate was adopted by most churches of the West, and that it had proved so accurate and unquestionable. He must have been inspired in the same way that the prophets and evangelists had been—a fact underlined by his iconography, which showed him being dictated to by an angel, as the inspired authors were.[7] There was a specially close resemblance between pictures of Saint Mark writing his Gospel and Jerome translating it, since they were thought to have a certain affinity—accounting for their supposed burial in the same Roman church (Santa Maria Maggiore). The cult of one glowed over into the other. Jerome's Bible acquired a myth like the one he had mocked—that the Septuagint translation of the Hebrew Bible into Greek was so inspired by God that all seventy men doing it came up independently with the same translation for every word. Revered translations soon acquire the reverence accorded their source—just as, for some in America, the King James Version became the very word of God.

But the myth of Jerome ran into serious obstacles early in the sixteenth century, when Renaissance humanists, reading old texts with scholarly eyes, found all the contradictions and errors in the various layers of his translations and commentaries. Men like Erasmus and Lorenzo Valla found no basis for the idea that Jerome had rendered one true source in one true version.[8] By the time of the Council of Trent, defenders of the Vulgate no longer claimed that it was free of error because of direct inspiration. They retreated to more cautious ground, arguing that the church's long reliance on the Jerome Bible would not have been permitted by God if the Book was not the best guide for the faithful. Providence had become manifest by long sanction. Tradition was now the guarantor of Jerome. Rather than the Bible authorizing the church, the church now authorized the Bible (well, one form of it).

Yet the council did not (as many think) prohibit any translations but Jerome's. It just denied that any but his was authoritative. On April 8, 1546, it decreed that

> this ancient standard translation (*vulgata editio*), which is recommended by the long use of so many centuries in the Church, [should] be regarded as authoritative in public lectures, disputations, sermons, and expository discourses, and that no one may make bold to reject it on any pretext.

Nonetheless, as John O'Malley notes, the champions of the Counter-Reformation went beyond the actual words of the council and enforced a monopoly of the Vulgate. They did this in various ways, including the use of the revised *Index Librorum Prohibitorum*, in effect quashing all competition. A papal bull on the Latin Rite, along with decisions by the Congregation of Rites, gave no room for use of any but the Vulgate. Thus, on vernacular translation, "the myth took hold that the Council forbade it."[9] Many false "Tridentine" attitudes were imposed in the name of Trent.

The Word Guarded by Tradition: Vatican I

In saying that Jerome's Bible was sanctioned by tradition, the Vatican was opposing Luther's claim that faith should be based only on the Bible (*sola Scriptura*). By that test, Reformers had rejected things like Purgatory, indulgences, infant baptism, or auricular confession. Catholics could reply that the Bible cannot be entirely separated from tradition. After all, the canon of the Bible was only formed by the body of believers, sifting competing texts, and taking over a century to do it. Lived experience of the implications of the Bible were relied on to debate, over three centuries, the status of Father, Son, and Spirit, or the relationship of Jesus's divinity to his humanity. Even many Reformers accepted the doctrines of the Incarnation and the Trinity, which were not based directly on the Bible, but on inferences from it. Thus the bishops at Trent defended two channels (not "sources") of revelation. Formally, neither was given superiority over the other, since both were "from the Apostles." What the apostles had not written down, they passed on orally. In the words of the council:

> The Apostles are the source of the whole truth of salvation and rule of conduct. The Council clearly perceives that this truth and rule are contained in written books and in unwritten traditions that were received by the Apostles from the mouth of Christ himself or else have come down to us, handed on as it were from the Apostles themselves . . . preserved in unbroken sequence in the Catholic Church.[10]

O'Malley notes the trouble that was lurking in that claim to "unbroken sequence":

> Trent's insistence on continuity contributed to the Catholic historiographical tradition emerging at this time, in which continuity sometimes was so emphasized as to leave precious little room for change. The emphasis persists as a recognizable Catholic trait even to the present.[11]

This was a paradoxical appeal to time (longevity) in order to escape time (change). And, like the search for a timeless language (Latin), the search for a timeless tradition was dangerous. It denied the reality of history.

But by the time of the First Vatican Council, the idea of tradition as something wholly separate from the Bible had become the authority of the church's teaching (*magisterium,* basically the pope) to declare doctrine without reference to the Bible. Pius IX had asserted this dramatically in 1854 by declaring that the Immaculate Conception of Mary was a doctrine to be universally believed. This not only had no scriptural warrant; it had long been opposed by many Catholic theologians, including Bernard of Clairvaux, Albertus Magnus, and Thomas Aquinas (they thought this exempted Mary from the need to be saved by Christ). But Pius was reaching an inflated conception of his power, voiced at the council he called to declare the doctrine of papal infallibility. At that council, he told a cardinal who urged him to wait for a consensus in the church, "I am the Church." Thus, over opposition, he steered the council toward a definition of his infallibility in the most provocative terms:

> We teach and define as divinely revealed dogma that, when the Roman Pontiff speaks *ex cathedra,* that is, when in the exercise of his office as shepherd and teacher of all Christians, by virtue of his supreme apostolic authority, *he defines* a doctrine concerning faith or morals to be held by the whole church, he possesses, by the divine assistance promised to him in blessed Peter, that infallibility which the divine Redeemer willed *his Church* to enjoy in defining doctrine concerning faith and morals. Therefore, such definitions of the Roman Pontiff are of themselves, *and not by the consent of the Church,* irreformable.[12]

First, you notice, Christ gives the church infallible power, then the pope says that he has it apart from the church. Now both church and tradition could be disregarded, at the behest of the pope. The word of God, first locked up in the Latin language, then locked up by tradition sanctioning that language, was now triply locked up in the will of the pope. It would be a waste of time to study the language, genres, or formation of the Bible. It could only say what the pope says it said.

The Word of God as Christ: Vatican II

Yet the Catholic Church continued to esteem the Bible (how could any Christian not do so?). This esteem was increasingly hard to credit if free inquiry on the Bible was stultified by papal directives. So, as we have seen, Pius XII in 1943 gave warrant to scholars to use the tools of modern scholarship. Catholic scholars burst into a great surge of suppressed activity, studying the whole tradition related to the Bible in what was called, in French, a return to the sources (ressourcement). These scholars were soon equal to their Protestant colleagues in diligent research and fruitful inquiry. Pius panicked at what he had done, and issued his 1950 encyclical Humani Generis, deploring use of the new tools he had authorized, calling theologians back to the old Thomistic training:

> The Church demands that future priests be instructed in philosophy according to the method, doctrine, and principles of the Angelic Doctor, since—as we know from the experience of centuries—the method of Aquinas is singularly preeminent both for teaching students and for bringing truth to light . . . How deplorable is it, then, that this philosophy, received and honored by the Church, is scorned by some who shamelessly call it outmoded in form and what they call rationalistic in its method.

Given this cue, the Holy Office of the Vatican (formerly the Roman Inquisition) pressured the superiors of ressourcement priests to rein them in, with various results—taking away teaching positions, recalling books, forbidding further publication. This suppression affected most of the stars of the new Catholic theology—Karl Rahner, Henri de Lubac, Jean Daniélou, Yves Congar, Marie-Dominique Chenu, and John Courtney Murray, among others.[13] The silencings intensified when Cardinal Alfredo Ottaviani became pro-secretary of the Holy Office (the pope himself was secretary). Pius XII's respected biographer, Robert Ventresca, says that only the pope's death in 1958 prevented the censuring of the famous lay philosopher Jacques Maritain.[14]

It was rumored that Cardinal Angelo Roncalli, in Venice, was unhappy with *Humani Generis*. It is not surprising, then, that Ottaviani and others at the Curia were worried when Roncalli, right after being elected Pope John XXIII, announced that he was calling a council to open windows in the church and effect an updating (*aggiornamento*) of its approach. But the officials in place in Rome were confident that they could control the preparations, scheduling, and conduct of the Latin debates. They prepared initial schemata for the debates. When Ottaviani presented the schema on revelation at the initial session of the council, he claimed that it was the only document that could be debated. It could be amended, but no substitutes for it could be presented without a two-thirds vote. It was contrived to settle finally that tradition was a source of revelation like the Bible. Its very title was *De Fontibus* (*On the Sources*).

But he had, by the rules, circulated this draft to the bishops before they set out for Rome—to give them time to consider it. Some bishops asked theologians like Karl Rahner and Edward Schillebeeckx to write their considerations (*animadversiones*) on it. These were quickly circulated among the more liberal bishops, and made available in Rome to *periti* and journalists.[15] The liberal bishops were thus ready for the attempt to steamroll them. A majority present voted to reject the document, but it did not reach the two-thirds barrier. At that point, quiet appeals to John XXIII made him intervene and make an exception to the two-thirds rule, allowing the preparation of a whole new schema. It was the turning point that reversed the anticipated victory of the Curial conservatives. O'Malley calls it "the decisive moment for the direction [the council] would take."[16]

From this point, there was a vast undergrowth of informal debate and briefings from the *ressourcement* theologians, who filtered into Rome, invited by different bishops as *periti* or friends. Weekly night sessions were held in the different language groups, and Dom Helder Camara, the archbishop of

Recife, Brazil, held international sessions.[17] This infuriated Ottaviani, who asked the pope to tell the Jesuits that Rahner should be sent away from Rome. When Pope John asked who had invited him, Ottaviani had to answer that "Council Fathers" (bishops) had, and the pope said he should stay.[18]

The document on revelation, *Dei Verbum,* reflected the views of the *ressourcement,* that there is one source of revelation manifested in the Word Incarnate. Christ lives in his body the church, which is vivified by both scripture and tradition: "Holy Tradition and Holy Scripture are organically (*arcte*) interrelated and informative. For both, flowing from the same well-spring (*scaturigo*), have a way (*quoddamodo*) of intermingling in their motion to the same end" (*Dei Verbum* 9). The single spring (*isdem scaturigo*) could not be a more pointed rejection of the *duo fontes* that had taken over Catholic theology after Vatican I. And by uniting tradition and the Bible, this article denies that the pope can declare what tradition is without the consent of the church. Thus Vatican II expressly denied what Vatican I had declared. There were huge theological earthquakes shaking the council.

Other parts of the same document support the idea that church doctrine advances (*proficit,* 8), ending the long resistance to John Henry Newman's *Essay on Development.* Sections declaring the equal inspiration of both the Old and New Testaments (7, 11) proved important in the document on relations with the Jews (*Nostra Aetate*). Some Catholics noticed only one surface manifestation of the turmoil—the end of the Latin Mass. That is symbolically not inappropriate. The whole structure that had tried to maintain a uniform Latin culture was being undermined. It was like a new Pentecost, again speaking in many freed tongues.

NOTES

1. Henry Chadwick, *East and West; The Making of a Rift in the Church* (Oxford University Press, 2003), 8.
2. Augustine, *Letters* 71.6.
3. J. N. D. Kelly, *Jerome: His Life, Writings, and Controversies* (Harper & Row, 1975), 156; and Eugene F. Rice Jr., *Saint Jerome in the Renaissance* (Johns Hopkins University Press, 1985), 185.

4. Augustine, *Letters* 71.5.

5. Ibid., 71.4, 6.

6. Even Jerome did not really come to grips with the Hebrew until he acquired his own copy of Origen's *Hexapla,* which put in six columns the Hebrew text and five Greek translations of it. The work filled about twenty volumes of eight hundred pages, all copied by hand, and was "phenomenally expensive"—typical of the vast library and research team Jerome maintained, in his Bethlehem "hermitage," by drawing on the fortunes of his female patrons. No wonder Augustine thought the Hebrew was something beyond most Christian preachers' orbit. See Megan Hale Williams, *The Monk and the Book: Jerome and the Making of Christian Scholarship* (University of Chicago Press, 2006), 149–53.

7. Rice (op. cit., 173–74, 189–93) lists eight artists who showed an angel dictating his translation to Jerome, and notes a special resemblance to earlier works that showed an angel dictating his Gospel to Saint Mark.

8. The incisive work of Erasmus and Valla was joined by that of Johann Reuchlin, Lefèvre d'Étaples, and others. See Rice, op. cit., 175–79.

9. John W. O'Malley, *Trent: What Happened at the Council* (Harvard University Press, 2013), 93–99, 266–70. The Vatican Council, though it sanctioned the Vulgate, inhibited the study even of that Bible. The council, recognizing that the ignorance of priests needed some remedy, tried to make more intense study of scripture part of its reforms, but the humanists in Trent were thwarted by conservatives who preferred the study of Canon Law and Scholastic method, the means of their own advancement and control. See Louis B. Pascoe, S.J., "The Council of Trent and Bible Study: Humanism and Scripture Authors," *Catholic Historical Review,* vol. 52 (1966), 18–38.

10. Council decree of April 8, 1546.

11. O'Malley, *Trent,* 98.

12. Council document, *Pastor Aeternus,* July 8, 1870.

13. John O'Malley, *What Happened at Vatican II* (Harvard University Press, 2008), 87.

14. Robert A. Ventresca, *Soldier of Christ: The Life of Pope Pius XII* (Harvard University Press, 2013), 274.

15. Giuseppe Ruggieri, "The First Doctrinal Clash," in Giuseppe Alberigo, *History of Vatican II,* English edition by Joseph A. Komonchak (Orbis/Peeters, 1997), vol. 2, 236.

16. O'Malley, *What Happened at Vatican II,* 141.

17. Ruggieri, op. cit., 234–36, 247–49.

18. "Xavier Rynne," *Letters from Vatican City* (Farrar, Straus & Company, 1963), vol. 1, 168.

FOUR

Pentecosts

I t is almost inconceivable that for centuries the account of Pentecost (Acts 2.1–3.26) could have been read, in Western Catholic churches, only in Latin. What did clerics in those times think Pentecost meant? It was about breaking down linguistic and other barriers between people. It told of the Gospel being spoken or heard in various languages, none of which would have been Latin.

The First Pentecost

At Acts 2.1–11, the followers of Jesus, having huddled in a room for fifty days, experience a descent of the Spirit over them in tongues of flame— after which they break out onto the street and spread the news of Jesus to people who hear the message in their own languages. This is not a story to be read with fundamentalist literalism. Luke, the author of the Acts of the Apostles, is a theologian, who reads into the current situation of his church its deep spiritual meaning. In a fundamentalist reading, why would the Spirit wait fifty days, almost two months, after the risen Jesus promised to send the Spirit to his people?

The answer is in the very name "Pentecost." It is Greek for the fiftieth day (*pentēkostē hēmēra*). The Jewish festival of the Fiftieth Day marked the seven weeks the Israelites wandered from Egypt to reach Mount Sinai and the giving of the Law. The Jewish calendar therefore counted fifty days from Passover to recall that founding event.[1] At Sinai, Moses had as- sembled the people before the mount, before he went up to receive the tablets: "They took their stand at the foot of the mountain. Mount Sinai was all smoking because the Lord had come down upon it in the fire" (Ex 19.17–18).

Since the Kingdom of Jesus builds upon Jewish Law, Luke counts fifty days from the Resurrection to mark the loosing of new energies for "the apostles' deeds." The united people under Moses were gathered at the foot of Mount Sinai as the fire came down on it. In the same way, the people of Jerusalem are gathered at the meeting place of the apostles as the fire comes down on them. As Peter explains in the program-matic address he gives to the astonished crowd, the new inspiration will not abolish the old covenant; in fact, he explains the miracle of this preaching through many passages in the Jewish scripture—through Joel (Acts 2.17–21), Psalm 16 (2.25–28), Psalm 132 (2.30), and Psalm 110 (2.34–35).

As frequently happens with biblical symbols, there are many layers to this event. The Jewish Pentecost was also a harvest feast. The annual crop was a matter of vital importance in the rocky and irregularly fertile Palestine. The beginning of harvest was a time for the offering of prized "first fruits" in sacrifice. Its end—fifty days after the beginning—was marked by thanksgiving for the gathering of the crops. The harvest re-called, annually, the promise of the Lord to gather in his people from all the scattered Twelve Tribes.[2] The promise was frequently expressed—as by Isaiah (11.12):

> He will . . . gather together those driven out of Israel;
>> He will assemble Judah's scattered (*diesparmenous*) people
>> from the four corners of the earth.

Or by Jeremiah (29.14):

> I will collect them from all over the earth,
>> where I have scattered (*diespeira*) them.
>> And I will bring them back to this place.

Or by Ezekiel (11.17):

> I will gather them from among the nations,
>   and assemble them from the countries
>   over which I have scattered (*diespeira*) them.
>   And I will give them the soil of Israel.

Or by Zechariah (2.6):

> From the four winds of heaven
>   I shall gather you, says the Lord.

The account of Pentecost in Acts 2 is another preenactment of this ingathering of the Twelve Tribes. All those gathered to hear Peter are Jews, in town for the Pentecost feast (Acts 2.5). There are fifteen "nations" (*ethnoi*) named. But the eminent Jesuit scholar Joseph A. Fitzmyer notices that the first twelve are listed with bare names in a roughly geographical order, while three are added outside the catalog formula—Rome with its own modifiers, and "Cretans and Arabs" after the apparent conclusion of the list (2.10–11). He argues plausibly that the original catalog Luke used had twelve regions as types of the Twelve Tribes.

Then these gathered tribes are addressed by the twelve disciples—Luke prepared for this scene by explaining how the number twelve was restored after the defection of Judas (Acts 1.15–26). Jesus had, after all, chosen the twelve precisely to be the judges of the Twelve Tribes (Mt 19.28, Lk 22.30). This proves that the redemption of Israel was the first task and symbol of the Kingdom that Jesus brought with him. It is true that Peter, in the foundational announcement of the new impulse, says that Jewish leaders prompted others—the Roman occupiers—to crucify Jesus. "You used men outside the Law to destroy him by a hanging on the cross" (Acts 2.23). This has been taken as the expression of Christian anti-Semitism. But Jews themselves have often said that Temple bureaucrats killed the prophets. Elijah said, "The people of Israel . . . put thy prophets to death" (1 Kgs 19.10). Jeremiah denounced "their murderous plots against me" (Jer 18.23).

Peter is saying that Jesus is another in the line of prophets rejected by their own people. But he is reassuring the people that Jesus is their Messiah. The speech reaches its climactic conclusion in verse 2.36: "Let the entire house of Israel know beyond all doubt that God has made him your lord, the Messiah, the one you crucified."

Some later Christian preachers have made Pentecost the symbol of the church going out to all peoples, speaking their various languages. But Peter is speaking only to Jews, gathered together for their own festival. That is made clear in one of the groups clumsily added to the catalog of *ethnoi* at Acts 2.10–11, indicating that Jews from as far away as Rome can be included. It specifies that these are "travelers from Rome, not only Jews but converts (*prosēlytoi*)."[3] At this temporary ingathering of Jewish peoples, Jesus is preached by his own to his own, as the distinctively Jewish Messiah. A subsequent "mission to the Gentiles" will need a second Pentecost in this same Book of Acts (10.1–11.18), with a second miracle of languages heard and spoken across barriers.

The languages heard here should not be confused with the "speaking in tongues" (*glossolalia*), which Paul recognized, only to limit it, at 1 Corinthians 14.4–19. That is a mysterious effusion of the Spirit that is not clear without interpretation, and Paul therefore calls it worth far less than revelation, prophecy, or teaching (14.6). The miracle at the Pentecost of Acts 2 is that no interpreters are needed for everyone to hear in his own language the same message. Since all those present are Jews, either Palestinians or from the Diaspora, what differences of language would there have been? Peter is imagined as speaking the language of Jesus and his followers, Aramaic, which would be familiar in the Diaspora either in itself or in one of its Semitic cognates. There would be differences in dialects. Besides, some would more often be using the lingua franca of the empire, Greek, in which the New Testament is written. Others, more learned, probably knew the language of the original revelation, Hebrew. All these differences were transcended by the spirit of unity expressing the homecoming of all God's people promised for the End Time, of which this Pentecost is a harbinger.

The point is not the range of linguistic differences, but the unity felt as of a family speaking within its own circle—a Jewish message to Jesus's fellow Jews. There is an immediate understanding of what is being said. The message has been delivered. Some will reject it, but not because there was any fault in communicating it. This was not a case of *glossolalia* (ecstatic sound-making) but of *xenologia* (speaking others' language), a triumph of communication, not an obstacle to it. The same phenomenon will be noted and explicitly compared to this first Pentecost when Luke tells the story of a second one.

The Second Pentecost

The second time language barriers are not only crossed but eliminated is at Acts 10.44–46, and those involved are specifically non-Jews, unlike the audience in Acts 2. Yet the same miracle of understanding occurs, signaling that non-Jews are now for the first time receiving a Jewish Messiah:

> Even as Peter spoke these words, the Holy Spirit fell upon all those who were hearing him speak. This astonished the circumcised observants who had traveled there with Peter, because the favor of the Holy Spirit had been lavished on these Gentiles. For they heard them praising God in their own languages (Acts 10.44–46).

The audience hearing Peter at this point is the whole household of the centurion Cornelius, the Roman prefect at Caesarea. This would include the adult family members and their children, along with the slaves and military personnel attached to this headquarters. At the first Pentecost, the wonder is that Peter's audience hears him in its own languages. Here, the wonder is that the household, of various backgrounds, *responds* in language understandable to Peter's companions. They are the ones who must be convinced that Peter was right to eat with these Gentiles and to baptize them into the Jewish Messiah. The miracle is worked to make these circumcised Jews accede to the innovation.

We find this point reemphasized when Peter and his followers return to Jerusalem and have to explain their dealings with Cornelius. "When Peter came back to Jerusalem, he was criticized by the circumcised for entering the home of those who had not been circumcised and eaten with them" (Acts 11.2–3). Peter then tells them the whole story of his dealings with the foreign centurion. Cornelius was a devout man, God-revering (*phoboumenos ton Theon*), who had made many generous donations to the Jews and prayed with them (Acts 10.2)—the action of the many God-reverers known from the excavations at the synagogue of Aphrodisias. Close dealings with such uncircumcised sympathizers of Israel were common, and needed no justification. But Peter had eaten with Cornelius in an "unclean" house serving foods outside the prescriptions of the Law. To justify this, he needed a miracle to equal that which had made the Jews speak with a unified mind at the first Pentecost.

And the miracle occurred. The Spirit accepted the Cornelian household before Peter could, making it praise God in a shared communication. As Peter tells his fellow Christian Jews in Jerusalem:

> "As I began to speak, the Holy Spirit fell upon them, just as it had upon us at the former occasion. And I was put in mind of the Lord's word, 'John baptized with water, but you will baptize in the Holy Spirit.' So if God gave to them the same gift as he had given us when we came to believe in lord Jesus as the Messiah, who was I to withhold God from them?" On hearing this, they were calmed, and they gave God honor, saying, "O it is true that God has granted a life-giving change of heart even to Gentiles" (Acts 11.15–18).

Luke is presenting here the resolution of an issue that had been engaged over thirty years before he wrote, in Paul's account of the clash with

Peter in Antioch (Gal 2.11–14). There, Paul rebuked Peter for refusing to eat unclean food with the uncircumcised. By the time of Acts, late in the first century, this split has been healed and the position of Paul is not only honored but actually attributed to Peter, leaving no room for disagreement anymore.

That Luke is addressing the extension of salvation out from the Jews to other peoples is clear from a very rare adjective he makes Peter use in his speech to Cornelius—*prosōpolēmptēs* (Acts 10.34), from *prosōpon* (separate character) and *lambanō* (choose). Peter says that God is not "particular-people-choosing," in contradiction to the concept that he has only one chosen people. This does not mean that God did not in fact choose the people of Abraham, since Paul says that God cannot go back on his word (Rom 11.2), and all salvation comes from the Jews (11.26). All that Paul and Luke are saying is that choosing one people does not exclude others. Peter continues, "In every people, one who reveres God and acts in accord with right is welcomed by him" (Acts 10.35).

The vision meant to convey this to Peter is a glorious affirmation of the entire creation as coming from God and belonging to him:

> A vision came to him—he sees the sky open and an apparatus descending, as in a great sheet lowered to earth by its four corners. In it were contained all manner of four-legged animals, and things that crawl on the ground or fly in the sky. And a cry came to him, "Rise, Peter and slay these animals for eating." But Peter said, "Never, Lord! For I have never eaten the profane and unclean." But the cry came again to him, "Do not profane what God makes pure." Three times this occurred, and then the apparatus was suddenly swept up into heaven (Acts 10.10–16).

This vision of a generous inclusiveness reclaims creation. It stands over against other first-century visions, largely Gnostic, that saw creation as divided, illusory, in the grip of evil. It is the theme of praise songs like Psalm 148, which raises a chorus of all created things—including the "unclean" animals not considered "profane" at Acts 10.12:

Praise the Lord on earth,
you water-spouts and ocean depths . . .
all mountains and hills,
all fruit-trees and all cedars;
wild beasts and cattle,
creeping things and winged birds (Ps 148.7, 9–10).

The meal to which the vision invites Peter, and which he will soon share with Cornelius, recalls the eschatological meal so often invoked in Jewish literature—and by the Christian Eucharist. In fact, the earliest records we have of the Eucharist—in four places in the second-century *Didache* and in Justin Martyr—are just such celebrations of the Lord's creative mercy.[4] There is no "consecration formula" in the four, and the only scripture quotations are from Jewish scripture—there was no other Bible to be cited in the early days of the church. Indeed, Luke's description of the dinner at Emmaus is a "theologizing" of the Eucharistic meal as Luke's contemporaries experienced it—a sifting of Messianic prophecies from "all the Law and prophets," followed by the acknowledgment of Jesus as the Messiah promised to the Jews. They experience Jesus as close to them in "the sharing of the bread" (literally, the "breaking," *klasis*). But after this moment of closeness, he disappears.

The disciples, on the way to Emmaus, had been disheartened by the death of Jesus and the end of their concept of a Messianic kingdom—they are rebuked by their travel companion as "unperceptive (*anoētoi*) and sluggish of heart" (Lk 24.25) for not seeing that the Messiah must be a suffering savior:

Then, starting from Moses and going through all the prophets, he gave the deep meaning (*diermēneusen*) of them all as referring to him . . . He vanished, and they said to each other, "Were our hearts not set on fire, as he spoke to us along the way, as he opened (*diēnoigen*) the meaning of scripture?" (Lk 24.27, 32).

This is Luke's exposition of what happens at the Eucharistic meal of his day. We should consider its vast distance from the Mass as it was celebrated for centuries in a language foreign to most of the attendants at the meal. The disciples are given to understand the words of their (Jewish) scripture, expounded carefully in terms they could understand and respond to—not with sluggish hearts, but with hearts on fire. It is those words, and the shared experience, that bring them close to Jesus.

Most people find the foundation of the Eucharist meal not in Luke's tale of Emmaus but in his account of the Last Supper (Lk 22.17–20). But that is even less a model for later practice. For it to be that, we should have Luke telling us that at the moment of consecrating the bread and wine, Jesus got up, turned away from the disciples at table, and muttered in a language they did not understand. Even that is not a true parallel to the Mass as practiced. For that, Jesus would not only have turned away from them and stopped talking to them—they would have to have been roused up and placed at a distance from the person they had sat down at table with, behind some hastily thrown-up rood screen or communion rail. What a mockery that made of the two Pentecosts, in which the Jews first and then the Gentiles were addressed in the words they knew best and could handle most intimately, quickening the mind and rousing the heart. As substitutes for that, we used to be given "mystery," distance, esoteric rites and terms, things more to be revered the less they could be understood. The reign of Latin was a massive betrayal of all that Pentecost means.

Vatican II, by bringing the word of God and the shared experience of discipleship back to believers, was a proof that the church could change in the right direction after so many centuries of harmful change. By changing, the church was reanimated. Pentecost is the feast of that favorite New Testament word, *parrhēsia,* "all-speaking." It proclaims outwardly all that we believe inwardly. As Pope Francis says about the apostles who went out from Pentecost, "If we go out to bring his Gospel with love, with a true apostolic spirit, with *parrhēsia,* he walks with us, he goes ahead of us, and he gets there first."[5]

The lesson of past Pentecosts is that the word of God should be embodied in many languages and cultures, crossing barriers, uniting not by an imposed uniformity, but by a mutually heartening diversity. That is what Pope Francis urges on us in *Evangelii Gaudium:*

> We would not do justice to the logic of the incarnation if we thought of Christianity as monocultural and monotonous. While it is true that some cultures have been closely associated with the preaching of the Gospel and the development of Christian thought, the revealed message is not identified with any of them; its content is transcultural. Hence in the evangelization of new cultures, or cultures which have not received the Christian message, it is not essential to impose a specific cultural form, no matter how beautiful or ancient it may be, together with the Gospel. The message that we proclaim always has a certain cultural dress, but we in the Church can sometimes fall into a needless hallowing of our own culture, and thus show more fanaticism than the true evangelical zeal.[6]

In line with this sense of Pentecostalism, the pope warned against the "ideologization and exploitation" of the Latin Mass.[7] By contrast, he praised precisely those Jesuit experiments in acculturation of the Gospel that were condemned by the Vatican in the past—"the Chinese rites, the Malabar [South Indian] rites, and the Reductions in Paraguay."[8] Jesuit adaptations of the Gospel to different cultures were still under hostile investigation during Benedict's reign. So slowly does change make its way in the church.

NOTES

1. Joseph A. Fitzmyer, *The Acts of the Apostles* (Doubleday, 1998), 233.
2. Ibid., 233–35.
3. Proselytes ("newcomers") were non–ethnic Jews who had accepted circumcision and become full observers of the Law, as opposed to *theosebeis* (the "God-

revering"), who were sympathetic to the Jews but had not been circumcised. Fitzmyer, op. cit., 449–50.

4. There are two versions of the same ceremony at *Didache* 9.1–4 and 10.1–7. The other oldest reports are in Justin Martyr—*The First Apology* 65.3 and *Dialogue with Trypho* (Philippe Bobichon text, Fribourg, 2003), vol. 1, 496.

5. Pope Francis, *The Church of Mercy* (Loyola Press, 2014), 19.

6. Pope Francis, *Evangelii Gaudium* (United States Conference of Catholic Bishops, 2013), 59–60 (par. 117).

7. Interview with Pope Francis, *America,* September 30, 2013.

8. Ibid.

II

The Coming and Going
of Monarchy

FIVE

Church Without State

MARTYRS AND PASSIVITY

U ntil the ratification of the First Amendment to the Constitution of the United States, it was unheard of for a state to be without an official religion. Other beliefs could be tolerated, if they did not challenge the state's own authorized cults; but they were inevitably slighted, or treated with less respect. They could be indulged, that is, so long as they kept a comparatively low profile. Outsiders had to remain discreet, verging on invisibility, making themselves politically irrelevant. Should they rise to a level of salience that questioned or undermined the predominant cultural values, they were normally silenced by either ridicule, intimidation, threat, banning, or execution. The modes of killing heretics down through the ages have been inventive and extensive—stoning, suffocating, starving, hanging, burning, and dismembering by axe or saw or animals.

Persecuted Christians

It was a boast of early Christianity that, as a religion not recognized by the pagan Roman Empire, it had experienced the whole range of repressive violences reserved for dissent. Late in the first century of the Common Era, the Letter to Hebrews took a kind of grisly relish in the repertoire of sufferings that had been or would be visited on believers. The Letter to Hebrews called the roll of horrors:

> Some were torn apart, not accepting release in order to get a higher resurrection. Still others underwent trial by insult and the lash, even by chains and imprisonment. They were stoned, sawn asunder, slain by a

knife's blow. They lived homeless in sheepskins and goatskins, deprived, afflicted, ill-treated, these people better than the world deserved; driven into deserts, and mountains, and caves, and earthen tunnels (Heb 11.35–38).

Since martyrs became Christianity's early rock stars, some yearned for as many of these torments as they could get, and famous martyrs were executed in many different ways before one of the expedients "took." Polycarp, thrown into a fire, was not consumed by it, so he had to be stabbed to death.[1] Catherine of Alexandria broke the wheel that was supposed to break her, so she had to be decapitated. A Carthaginian martyr, Saturus, told that the Christians would be killed in the arena by a leopard, or a bear, or a boar, hoped to be devoured by all three. He was exposed to each in turn, but had to have his throat slashed in order to die.[2] Faced with a novice killer (*tirunculus gladiator*), Perpetua had to guide his wavering (*errans dextera*) knife into her throat.[3] The second-century bishop of Antioch, Ignatius, wanted to die every kind of death:

> Burning, crucifixion, grappling with lions, stabbings, amputations, wrenching of bones, rending of limbs, crushing of the entire body, the worst tortures of the devil—bring them all to me![4]

The desire for martyrdom became the mark of the "true" Christian. After all, Jesus had said, according to all three Synoptic Gospels, that his followers must "take up your cross," imitating him in his death (Mk 8.34, Mt 10.38, Lk 9.23). Only those who died for Jesus could be his perfect imitators.[5] Even the twelve apostles had their devotional fame, not because Jesus chose them to be the judges of the Twelve Tribes, but because, according to legend, they all died as martyrs. (Candida Moss marshals the historical evidence to prove that "we simply don't know how any of the apostles died, much less whether they were martyred.")[6]

The early martyrologies are full of people who succeed in reaching their desired goal of death. The church historian Eusebius told of six young men who went to the governor of Caesarea and demanded to be thrown to the beasts.[7] A Sicilian martyr, Euplus, shouted in front of a closed courtroom, "I wish to die, since I am a Christian"—and he was allowed in, to his death.[8] The church father Tertullian said that all the Christians in one Asian town asked a proconsul there to grant them the privilege of martyrdom. He killed a few of them, then said, "If you are so eager to die crazily, do it yourself with a rope or off a cliff."[9] Ignatius of Antioch, quoted above, pleaded with his fellow Christians in Rome not to save him from the arena's animals, showing what Geoffrey de Ste. Croix calls his "pathological yearning for martyrdom":[10]

> I beg you, do me no unwelcome favor. Let the beasts eat me . . . Entice them instead, to become my tomb . . . I will be favored by their eagerness for me, and I pray to find them with sharp appetites. I will entice them to eat me hungrily, unlike those they were too hesitant to touch. Even if they shy from me, I shall make them do it.[11]

It was said that a certain Germanicus did just that—pulled a slow animal on top of himself and forced it to eat him, astonishing the crowd with his hardihood.[12] A woman in Pergamum, Agathonike, saw some martyrs being burnt alive in a fire and asked to join them, crying out, "This meal was made to be mine. I must eat such glorious fare."[13]

Since Tertullian said "the blood of Christians is seed" from which the church grew, it was considered important to have ample seed.[14] Eventually, altars all around the world would have relics of martyrs in them. The supply was maintained by legends like that of the eleven thousand virgins martyred in Cologne alongside Saint Ursula (a tale followed in detail by Carpaccio in his ten paintings for the Scuola di Sant'Orsola in Venice). The ossuary from a Roman necropolis, discovered in 1104 at Cologne, supplied many relics from its trove.[15] Any bone found in a catacomb was considered a martyr relic. By the fourth century, the church calendar was filled with days commemorating martyrs.[16]

The veneration of martyrs reached such a pitch by the fourth century that Augustine of Hippo nervously tried to dial back the fervor, insisting

that martyrs should not be worshiped. Exaggerated tales of their immunity from fear and pain had presented them as superhuman, surpass-
ing even Jesus—who, after all, confessed to fear in his agony in the
Garden of Olives.[17] Tale after tale presented martyrs as practically laugh-
ing their way through their own death. Their smiles baffled their executioners.[18] The Carthaginian martyrs spoke of "offering as a challenge our
joy in suffering" and mocked the "eagerness of crowds to see it."[19] This
imperviousness to death amounted to what Candida Moss calls the deify-
ing (*theōsis*) of martyrs.[20] The editor of the *Passion of Perpetua* argues that
her guiding the knife into her own throat shows that "so great a woman
could not be killed if she did not will it herself."[21]

Eusebius was typical in his celebration of the joys of martyrdom. Of
one scene, which he claimed to have witnessed himself, he wrote:

> As some were given the death sentence, others—group after group—
> rushed up to the judge's bench professing their Christianity, heedless of
> menace and ready for any kind of torture, rapturously speaking of their
> reverence for the Lord of the universe, and receiving their sentence with
> joy and laughter, so that they sang and prayed cheerfully to the Lord of
> the universe with the very last breath they drew.[22]

Augustine argued against seeking martyrdom. For him, such a quest
amounted to the sin of suicide. He read the Golden Rule backward, as it
were, saying that to love another as oneself implies loving oneself as one
does others. One may not seek one's own death any more than one should
seek another person's.[23]

But the cult of martyrs was too deeply involved in Christian identity
for Augustine to make much of a dent in it. He had first opposed the Donatists' relish for martyrs as their way of condemning those Christians
who had proved weak in the persecution under Decius. But his need to
compete with the Donatists made him capitalize on his own diocese's
possession of a relic of the "first martyr," Saint Stephen.[24] Eusebius had
earlier said that the bones of the martyr Polycarp were more precious

than gems, and deserved a worthy shrine.[25] Augustine had only some dust purporting to be Stephen's, but he too built an impressive basilica for it and other martyr relics.[26]

In fact, Augustine could not resist a favorite argument for the truth of the Christian faith—that so many had been willing to die for it. As Candida Moss writes, "Suffering is the process by which moral and doctrinal superiority can be established. The claim that martyrdom authenticates mission is an established rhetorical move."[27] Only a supernatural religion could produce such unnatural results. But those using this rhetoric will not accept the truth of other religions for which people are ready to suffer (like modern jihadists). Also, to complete this picture of religion being punished by its enemies, the persecutors are presented as malicious, even diabolical, adding a further proof that only God's enemies could perpetrate such horrors. Persecuting Rome became the Babylon of Revelation, and more generally the Antichrist.

Persecuting Romans

But there is something odd about this picture of Romans as fiends in a frenzy against God. The Romans were in fact fairly lackadaisical persecutors. The empire was exigent and hard-edged in crucial areas, in tax collection and in technological know-how (for things like roads, bridges, aqueducts, arches, and domes). But it was surprisingly loose and soft around the edges when it came to the cults and religious traditions of its member states. By strategic fuzziness, Rome largely avoided giving offense to local pieties. Rome had formed a bring-your-own-god pantheon by welcoming Greek deities in Latin disguise, and many other "strange gods" benefited from this open-house approach.

The Romans' record for religious conformism was lax, despite brief suppression of cults like the Druids or the Bacchants. And these, like the Christians, were not normally condemned for their beliefs but for alleged crimes (*flagitia*). The authorities showed little or no interest in private beliefs. The executions of Christians were sporadic, intense but irregular, usually local and/or brief. In the first century CE, there was just one brutal spasm in one city—Nero's punishment for what he claimed was the crime of arson in 64 CE. There was a long hiatus between this isolated event in the first century and the middle of the third century, when Decius and Valerian instituted the first general policy against Christians. Geoffrey de Ste. Croix, in an influential essay, wrote:

> We know of no persecution by the Roman government until 64, and there was no general persecution until that of Decius. Between 64 and 250 there were only isolated, local persecutions; and even if the total number of victims was quite considerable (as I think it probably was), most individual outbreaks must usually have been quite brief. Even the general persecution of Decius lasted little more than a year, and the second general persecution, that of Valerian in 257–9, less than three years. The third and last general persecution, by Diocletian and his colleagues from 303 onwards (the so-called "Great Persecution"), continued for only about two years in the West, although it went on a good deal longer in the East. In the intervals between these general persecutions the situation, in my opinion, remained very much what it had been earlier, except that on the whole the position of the Church was distinctly better: there were several local persecutions, but there were also quite long periods during which the Christians enjoyed something like complete peace over most of the empire.[28]

In other words, there were only twelve or so years of persecution over the course of three hundred years.[29] Though martyrologies told of executions of thousands, W. H. C. Frend reasons that named martyrs of the Decian persecution figure in the dozens, though hundreds, unnamed, may have suffered—surely not the thousands that are claimed.[30] Even Origen, whose father was a martyr and who longed to be one himself, had to admit that early martyrs were few (*oligoi*) and "easily countable" (*euarithmētoi*).[31] Gibbon and others have noted that far more Christians would be killed by other Christians than were ever killed by pagan Romans.[32]

Peaceful Coexistence

Thus, in most of the years throughout the first three centuries, "Christians not only lived peacefully among the Romans, they flourished and rose to positions of prominence and power."[33] Even the tales of persecutors seizing church property show that wealth had been accumulated. For the years of the long peace, David Potter says that "martyrdom had seemed more a theoretical than a real possibility," since "most people managed to get along most of the time."[34] The historian Ramsay MacMullen writes that "from around AD 100 to 312, Christians as such avoided attention . . . In sum, the church before Constantine seems to have kept itself to itself."[35] Indeed, one of the reasons for the late and feckless attempt to expunge Christianity was its exponential growth throughout the last half of the third century—a development that combined with a crisis of authority in the Roman Empire itself.

In periods of relative calm, religious dissidents in most cultures try to live inconspicuously, not in open defiance of the majority's belief. Though Eusebius and other early church historians looked back at the first centuries through the filter of the last and most destructive persecution, the church looked very different when viewed from its beginnings. It was expressly and insistently nonconfrontational. Paul and the Gospels inculcated a get-along spirit with Rome. As Paul wrote:

Let everyone submit in mind (*psyche*) to the authorities over them. There can be no power but from God, and those exercising it are put there by God. Those who refuse to submit are opposing God's own disposition, and this opposition brings a judgment on itself. Rulers are not a menace to the orderly but to the disorderly. Would you avoid the fear of power? Be orderly, and you will win its approval, since it is God's instrument for good order. If you are fearful, it is because you are disorderly. The sword is given to be used. It is an instrument to give the disorderly hard discipline. It must be accepted, not only as discipline but as duty. That is why you must pay taxes. The collectors are doing God's work, for which they are appointed. So meet all your obligations, tax by tax, exaction by exaction, submission by submission, respect by respect (Rom 13.1–7).

Those are odd words from a man who was probably killed by the Roman authorities. But Nero did not execute Paul for being a Christian. It was for a specifically alleged crime, arson. And Paul was not an outlier in counseling submission to the Roman authorities. The Peter of his supposed First Epistle says the same thing: "Be submissive in the Lord to whatever social structure there is—to the king who supervises, as well as to officials who carry out his ordinances, for the punishment of criminals or for support of the law-abiding" (1 Pet 2.13–14).

These apostolic admonitions were in perfect accord with the teaching of Jesus in the Gospels, as one can see from his familiar dealing with tax collectors and Roman soldiers. When provocateurs tried to tempt him into defying the Roman taxation, he said, "Give (*apodote*) Caesar his due" (Mk 12.17, Mt 22.21, Lk 20.25). That verb, *apodote*, is the same Paul used for paying the Roman taxes (Rom 13.7).[36] Jesus was compliant enough with Romans giving orders that he told his followers, "Whoever might command (*aggareusei*) you to go one mile, accompany him for two miles" (Mt 5.41). Hardly the advice of a revolutionary.

The attitude of Christians in the second century was still one of cooperation with the empire, not confrontation, as we see from the *Letter to Diognetus*. It presents Christians as different from their surrounding culture, yet not as a threat to it:

> Christians are not set apart from others by homeland or language or customs. They do not live in cities reserved for them, with their own special idiom or unusual mode of life. They do not have a special mindset or contrivances of human cleverness, they are not part of some human sect (as others are). Wherever they happen to be, in Greek or other territories, they conform to local custom, clothing, diet and the rest, yet in another part of their lives they show an amazing agreement on their unique (*paradoxam*) self-government. They are in many countries, but as transients

(*paroikoi*),[37] sharing all things as natives, yet undergoing all things as strangers. Everywhere they are at home, yet without a homeland . . . They pass the time on earth, but their homeland is heaven.[38]

Given Roman laxness and Christian cooperation, why did any persecution at all take place? How, as Gibbon put it, did Christians sometimes "exasperate the mild indifference of antiquity"?[39] This was not usually the result of Roman determination to ferret out dissent and quash it. When Christians began to look troublesome, it was often because of friction in the interacting spheres of Jews, Jewish sympathizers (*sebomenoi ton Theon*) who were being peeled off by Christians, and Christians who were themselves divided on how close to or far from their Jewish roots they must steer their conduct. The first Roman discussion of the Christians we know of did not take place until 111 CE, when Pliny the Younger, a governor in Pontus, wrote Emperor Trajan asking how to handle these odd people (*Letters* 10.96–97). Someone had anonymously sent Pliny a list of Christians to be suppressed. He did not know what offense they had committed, and could not find any except that they met secretly as a group—which Trajan had forbidden in his effort to reduce the threat arising from guilds in Rome. Trajan answered that Pliny should not go looking for Christians, and should pay no attention to anonymous accusations.

A similar story is told by Tacitus of Nero's purge in 64 CE, when Jews or Christians or both had turned in some of their fellows as guilty of the crime of burning Rome (*Annals* XV 44.15).[40] There seem to have been efforts by outsider groups to keep their own precarious Roman concessions by playing off one group against another—which, after all, was how the Crucifixion came about.

The initiative for persecution did not come from any central Roman source until 250, when Decius proposed a kind of loyalty test for the empire—certificates (*libelli*) were issued to those who made a pro forma offering of grain or incense to the gods. This was imposed, Candida Moss argues, "from a desire to unify the Roman empire rather than from a decision to root out Christians."[41] Even then, this could be evaded in the countryside, since enforcement was usually confined to the cities.[42] In the Decian persecution, Cyprian avoided martyrdom in Africa by going to a country retreat. In the Diocletian one, Bishop Peter of Alexandria did the same—though both men were killed in a later stage of the suppression. But as Christian numbers crested and Roman rule became more vulnerable at the beginning of the fourth century, there was a last spasm of conflict before Constantine got out ahead of the changes in society.

Honoring "Normal Gods"

What was the most basic Roman objection to the Christians? A. N. Sherwin-White said it was their obduracy (*contumacia*), while Geoffrey de Ste. Croix said it was their "atheism."[43] Romans were astounded that the customary gods should be ignored or denied—since the gods demanded so little in the way of intellectual commitment. The cults were more patriotic symbols than theological tests. Christians did not join in the social cohesion demanded at a time of social stress. This was equivalent to spitting on the flag during wartime in America. The Roman gods were a vehicle of social solidarity. Their rites had little creedal force—which made the refusal of them seem all the more perverse. Contrary to a common view, Christians were not asked to sacrifice to the emperor:

> No emperor being officially numbered among the gods of the Roman state until he was dead . . . emperor-worship is a factor of almost no independent importance in the persecution of the Christians.[44]

The gods were culturally important to ordinary people because they had a tutelary aspect. Individual gods were invoked for particular needs, and the aggregate of recognized gods was a symbol of society's values. These were the "normal" (*kata physin*) gods referred to by a judge as he condemned a Christian: "Who stops you from worshiping your god along with the normal ones? You are just asked to honor the gods everyone recognizes as such."[45]

Augustine would mock the way pagans called on gods to help them do even ordinary things—they could hardly get across a doorstep without honoring specific gods of hinge and threshold and lintel. He called these a "mob of vulgar deities" (*turba quasi plebeiorum deorum*).[46] He made this sound sinister, though Chesterton found something "homey" in the cluster of gods around daily Roman life:

> What strike us in the Italian cults is their local and especially their domestic character. We gain the impression of divinities swarming about the house like flies; of deities clustering and clinging like bats about the pillars or building like birds under the eaves. We have a vision of a god of roofs and a god of gate-posts, of a god of doors and even a god of drains. It has been suggested that all mythology was a sort of fairy-tale; but this was a particular sort of fairy-tale which may truly be called a fireside tale, or a nursery tale; because it was a tale of the interior of the home.[47]

That is an almost exact description, in rosier tints, of Augustine's savage attack on the god of doors (Forculus), the god of hinges (Cardea), and the god of thresholds (Limentinus).[48]

We find later instances of this desire for tutelary help in Christianity itself. Guardian angels and patron saints have for centuries been made to favor countries, cities, guilds, professions, and tasks. Stunning altars and chapels were built for Saint Ananius, the patron of shoemakers. Candles have been lit for Saint Thomas More, the patron of lawyers. These intercessors have rather faded now—Saint Christopher, the protector of travelers, has traveled off—but the great historian of magic practices, Keith Thomas, argued that Catholic cultures were less prone to witchcraft and witch hunts than Protestant ones, because they had guardian angels, holy water, the sign of the cross, and the rosary to protect them from demons. "It was only the Reformation which disturbed the situation by drastically reducing the degree of immunity from witchcraft which could be conveyed by religious faith alone."[49] That was the Roman attitude toward their own patron deities.

By the fourth century, when the convulsion of the last persecution was over and the task of clearing away all pagan temples and traces of the gods was beginning, Augustine and others could present all the pagan gods as devils in disguise, as deep enemies of the one true God.[50] But we can assume that Christians did not go around in the early centuries saying that the gods were devils. Remember how Paul called the Roman institutions divinely ordained. Christianity was not, at its origin, a suicide mission.

The Church of Martyrs

But once Constantine had made Christianity the favored religion, his biographer Eusebius began energetically building an image of the early church as locked from the outset in a death struggle with the pre-Christian state, in one long series of horrendous conflicts and bloody martyrdoms:

> It was Eusebius who made martyrdom a nearly continuous presence in the life of the church. Christians had described themselves as suffering for Christ long before Eusebius, but the process of redefining the *church* as a persecuted church was really initiated in his *Church History.*[51]

What had begun as a religion without state became, retrospectively, a religion against the pre-Constantinian state and a religion wholly supportive of the Constantinian state.

Those who followed the Eusebian program kept collecting and savoring tales of gory martyrdom—what Keith Hopkins and Mary Beard call a "sacred pornography of cruelty."[52] There was a literature that exhausted every variety of assault that can be made on every part of the human body.[53] Later iconography required that Saint Agatha display on a salver her severed breasts, and Saint Lucy her extruded eyes. Despite all this ingenuity of torture and defiance of pain, one form of death became canonical—the throwing of Christians to the lions. And there was a favorite locale for this archetypal death—the Roman Colosseum.

Though Ignatius of Antioch called for many modes of death, he made one especially vivid, describing himself as "God's wheat, to be ground by the teeth of wild beasts (*theria*), vindicated as Christ's pure bread."[54] He is often described as being killed by lions, but he never specifies what beast might be loosed against him—with good reason. There were many possibilities. The Carthaginian men killed with Perpetua had been mauled to death by a leopard, a bear, and a boar—not lions. Perpetua herself was knocked about by a wild cow (*ferocissima vacca*), as a way to ridicule her gender.[55] Though she was injured in this way, she could not guide the animal to the best way of killing her, as she later guided the executioner's knife to her throat.

That tale gives us an important clue to the Roman form of execution, *damnatio ad bestias* ("death sentence by animals"). Perpetua and her servant Felicity were not given the dignity of attack by male beasts. One aim of the sentence was to humiliate. As Brent Shaw says, "The choice of the animal was unusual, but was a deliberate one on the part of the authorities: they wished to mock the sex of the condemned women by using one of their own, a wild cow, to destroy them."[56] And humiliating Christian men was as important as humiliating women. Though they would be "thrown to the beasts" anyway, why waste a majestic beast on them? Better an ugly boar, sneaky leopard, or blundering bull. The highlight of the show was made more glamorous by saving majestic lions to pit against muscular gladiators (not pacific Christians).

The Roman motive for not choosing the lion to kill Christians was the Christians' reason for preferring that match. It was more spectacular. No wonder people have given Ignatius a death by a lion's teeth grinding him, though he nowhere says anything but *theria* (Greek for *bestiae*) will kill him even if he has to prod them into doing it. And just as we do not know what method was used for his martyrdom, we do not know where he died. It is usually assumed that it was in the Colosseum, since that has become famous mainly not for gladiators fighting with each other, or for wild animal hunts—the usual fare—but for the death of Christians.[57] Some people are surprised to learn that historians throw cold water on this myth: "The fact is that there are no genuine records of any Christians being put to death in the Colosseum."[58] There probably were some Christians slain there, but not of sufficient fame or numbers to leave any contemporary notice of the fact. Even medieval myths about the Colosseum did not include any memory of martyrs:

> Although it seems to us inconceivable that this tradition should have been completely forgotten through the Middle Ages, the standard medieval view of the building certainly did not link the Colosseum with the fate of the saints. Although other shrines associated with martyrs were keenly venerated, there is no sign of any religious appropriation here. Significantly, the pilgrim guide to the Wonders of Rome picks out, for example, the Circus Flaminius (another Roman spectacle arena) as a place of martyrdom, while the Colosseum appears as a "Temple of the Sun."[59]

Although other martyr myths took shape later, the great push in defining Christianity as the church of martyrs occurred just when persecution ceased. Eusebius was busy making this the case in the East, but the Western church was not far behind. The bishopric of Rome, with its partly legendary history, had been a comparative backwater in the first three centuries, when the great theological battles were taking place in the Greek-speaking East—at Alexandria, Antioch, Caesarea, Nicomedia, Chalcedon, and other places of learning and controversy. Rome based its importance on the unhistorical claim that Peter had been bishop there, the first "pope." This local see created a legendary history based less on scholarly achievement than on an unbroken line of bishops who were martyrs.

What could be a greater authentication of true Christianity? It was claimed that twenty-six of the first twenty-seven bishops of Rome were martyrs, even the ones who served through long periods when there was no persecution. J. N. D. Kelly could find evidence for only two real martyrdoms in that lineage (not counting Peter, though he is presumed to have died—as an outsider—in Rome).[60] All these supposed early bishops of Rome went into the church's calendar of saints, on the grounds that martyrs are ex officio saints. The Roman church would finally claim to be the one true church, since "real Christianity" is a church of martyrs. It was an argument that had worked when all twelve apostles were declared martyrs.

NOTES

1. *The Martyrdom of Saint Polycarp* 16, in Herbert Musurillo, *The Acts of the Christian Martyrs* (Oxford University Press, 1972), 15.
2. *The Martyrdom of Saints Perpetua and Felicitas* 19.21, in ibid., 126–31.
3. Ibid., 21 (130). Stephanie Cobb notes that "the throat is a particularly feminine part of the body, and tends to be locus of death for women in tragedy." L. Stephanie Cobb, *Dying to Be Men: Gender and Language in Early Christian Martyr Texts* (Columbia University Press, 2008), 178.
4. Ignatius of Antioch, *Letter to the Romans* 5.3.
5. Candida Moss, *The Other Christs: Imitating Jesus in Ancient Christian Ideologies of Martyrdom* (Oxford University Press, 2010), 45–74.
6. Candida Moss, *The Myth of Persecution* (HarperOne, 2013), 136.
7. Eusebius, *The Martyrs of Palestine* 3.2–4.
8. *The Acts of Euplus* 1, in Musurillo, op. cit., 310.
9. Tertullian, *To Scapula* 5.1.
10. Geoffrey de Ste. Croix, "Why Were Early Christians Persecuted?" in M. I. Finley, *Studies in Ancient Society* (Routledge and Kegan Paul, 1974), 237.
11. Ignatius of Antioch, *Letter to the Romans* 5.2.
12. *The Martyrdom of Saint Polycarp* 3, in Musurillo, op. cit., 4.
13. *The Martyrdom of Saints Carpus, Papyls, and Agathonike*, in Musurillo, op. cit., 26.
14. Tertullian, *Apology* 50.13.
15. Giovanna Nepi Scire, *Carpaccio: Storie di Sant-Orsola* (Electa, 2000), 114–15.
16. R. A. Markus, *The End of Ancient Christianity* (Cambridge University Press, 1990), 98–99.
17. Carole Straw, "Martyrdom," in Allan D. Fitzgerald et al., *Augustine Through the Ages* (Eerdmans, 1999), 538–42.
18. Glenn Bowersock, *Martyrdom and Rome* (Cambridge University Press, 1998), 60–61. Cobb, op. cit., 118.
19. *The Martyrdom of Perpetua* 17, in Musurillo, op. cit., 124.
20. Moss, *The Myth of Persecution*, 163–64.

21. *The Martyrdom of Perpetua* 21, in Musurillo, op. cit., 130). Brent Shaw argues that the extraordinary prominence given Perpetua had to do with her high social standing. Shaw, "The Passion of Perpetua," in Robin Osborne, ed., *Studies in Ancient Greek and Roman Society* (Cambridge University Press, 2004), 286–325.

22. Eusebius, *Ecclesiastical History,* edited by Kirsopp Lake (Harvard University Press, 1926), 8.9.5. Moss demonstrates the leading role Eusebius played in showing the whole early history of the church as a history of martyrdoms (*The Myth of Persecution,* 217–34).

23. CD 1.19–21. Augustine criticized any Christian use of a pagan model like Lucretia for killing oneself to prove one's virtue. For his opposition to the Donatist view that only martyrs are perfect Christians, see S 2.289.

24. Nine of Augustine's Stephen homilies are collected as *Sermons* 314–20, 323, 324, and his relics are given lengthy praise at CD 22.8. His three sermons on the favorite African saint Perpetua are Numbers 280–82, discussed at Shaw, op. cit., 315–19. Peter Brown argues that bishops had to incorporate the fervent devotion to martyrs into the institutional church. Brown, *The Cult of the Saints* (University of Chicago Press, 1981), 9–11, 27–29.

25. Eusebius, op. cit., 4.15.43.

26. Augustine, *Sermons* 156.10 and 313G.3.

27. Candida Moss, *Ancient Christian Martyrdom: Diverse Practices, Theologies, and Traditions* (Yale University Press, 2012), 163.

28. Ste. Croix, "Why Were Early Christians Persecuted?," 211–12. Bowersock also notes that persecution was normally limited to cities, not the countryside (op. cit., 41–56).

29. Moss, *The Myth of Persecution,* 159.

30. W. H. C. Frend, *Martyrdom and Persecution in the Early Church* (Basil Blackwell, 1965), 413. He argues that even the Great Persecution could not account for the thousands of victims claimed for it: "As in the Decian persecution, prudence generally guaranteed safety" (ibid., 536).

31. Origen, *Against Celsus* 3.8.

32. Gibbon referred mainly to the slaughter of Huguenots, others to the crusade against Albigensians. But Ramsay MacMullen points out that the Christians killed thousands in their first years after Constantine, in the factious wars of Donatists, Arians, Nestorians et al. and their foes. MacMullen, *Voting About God in Early Church Councils* (Yale University Press, 2006), 56–66. Gibbon realized that the Christians lost no time in "imitating the conduct of their pagan adversaries" (DF XVI, 77). But Geoffrey de Ste. Croix points out that the Romans punished cult nonobservance while Christianity killed others for deep mental crimes ("heresy"): "Heresy, Schism, and Persecution in the Later Roman Empire," in *Christian Persecution, Martyrdom, and Orthodoxy* (Oxford University Press, 2006), 201–29.

33. Moss, *The Myth of Persecution,* 152.

34. David Potter, *Constantine the Emperor* (Oxford University Press, 2013), 227, 237.

35. Ramsay MacMullen, *Christianizing the Roman Empire, A.D. 100–400* (Yale University Press, 1984), 35.

36. Reza Aslan tries to extract a "historical" Jesus-as-revolutionary from the Gospels. He reads the "give (*apodote*) to Caesar what is Caesar's" to mean "renounce Caesar and reclaim God's land of Israel": "That is the zealot argument in its simplest, most concise form"—*Zealot: The Life and Times of Jesus* (Random House, 2013), 78. By that logic, Paul's "pay (*apodote*) your taxes" would mean "renounce your obligation." He bases Jesus's claim that the land belongs to the Jews on Jewish Law, though Jesus more often contravened Sabbath and kosher rules than any Roman edicts.

37. The First Epistle of Peter uses the same word when urging Christians to be "transients" (*paroikoi*, 13.11) who are beyond reproach.

38. *Letter to Diognetus* 5.

39. DF XVI, 2.76.

40. For Christians to ingratiate themselves with authorities by turning on each other has occurred in the recent as well as the remote past. Michael Budde shows that priests and bishops turned in their fellow believers to modern totalitarian states: Budde, "Martyrs and Antimartyrs: Reflections on Treason, Fidelity and the Gospel," in Budde and Karen Scott, *Witness of the Body: The Past, Present, and Future of Christian Martyrdom* (Eerdmans, 2011), 156–62.

41. Moss, *Ancient Christian Martyrdom*, 12.

42. Bowersock, op. cit., 41–54.

43. A. N. Sherwin-White, "The Early Persecutions and Roman Law Again," *Journal of Theological Studies* n.s. 3 (1952), 199–213. Ste. Croix, "Why Were Early Christians Persecuted?," 216. Ramsay MacMullen adds some citations on Christian "atheism," though he finds Sherwin-White and Ste. Croix mainly in agreement (op. cit., 128).

44. Ste. Croix, "Why Were Early Christians Persecuted?," 216.

45. Eusebius, *Ecclesiastical History* 7.11.9.

46. CD 4.11.

47. G. K. Chesterton, *The Everlasting Man* (Ignatius Press, 1987), 142.

48. CD 4.8.

49. Keith Thomas, *Religion and the Decline of Magic: Studies in Popular Beliefs in Sixteenth- and Seventeenth-Century England* (Penguin, 1973), 588–89.

50. CD 9.18–23.

51. Moss, *The Myth of Persecution*, 216.

52. Keith Hopkins and Mary Beard, *The Colosseum* (Harvard Univesity Press, 2005), 105.

53. Gibbon gives the repertory of deaths described: "racks and scourges, with iron hooks, and red-hot beds, and with all the variety of tortures which fire and steel, savage beasts and more savage executioners, could inflict on the human body." DF XVI, 2.144.

54. Ignatius of Antioch, *Letter to the Romans* 4.1.

55. *The Martyrdom of Perpetua* 20, in Musurillo, op. cit., 128.

56. Shaw, op. cit., 289.

57. Though popular imagery now fills the arena with lions, whole menageries were pitted against each other. Elizabethan Englishmen had a grisly taste for bear baitings, using attack dogs. But the Romans had a much more extensive range of animal-on-animal and animal-on-man killings, featuring such large beasts as elephants, rhinoceroses, hippopotamuses, bears, bulls, boars, ostriches, ibexes, and other curiosities to be killed or to kill each other. Hopkins and Beard, op. cit., 44–49, 94–103.

58. Ibid., 103.

59. Ibid., 167.

60. J. N. D. Kelly, *The Oxford Dictionary of Popes* (Oxford University Press, 1986), 5–24. The two actual martyrs are Fabian (236–50) under Decius, and Sixtus II (257–58) under Valerian. No "popes" were slain during the Great Persecution—partly, perhaps, because the see was vacant for three and a half years during it (ibid., 25).

SIX

Church with State
ASCETICS AND RESISTANCE

I n the fourth century, the whole character of Christianity changed drastically. It took on a new relationship with the world around it, which required a revision of its internal order and ideals. It went from a socially suspect religion to a socially favored one, from a loose arrangement of local communities to an empire-wide set of beliefs, practices, and discipline. These changes meshed with a secular reorganizing of the empire by the energetic Constantine. What had been a tetrarchy, with Eastern and Western empires, each under two rulers (an Augustus and a Caesar), was now forged as a single empire, with Constantine as monarch.

An important element in this new entity was the Christian church, whose cohesiveness Constantine promoted for his own purposes. Christians had been a solvent force in the pagan scheme of things, a minor but persistent irritant. But Constantine's father, the Western emperor Constantius Chlorus, had fostered good relations with Christians in his part of the Tetrarchy; and Constantine, who meant to unite all the empire under his rule, saw that Christianity might be a connective (rather than disruptive) force in his friable domain. What had been scattered enclaves of devotion had developed a network of communication and exchange between communities, with efforts at a common teaching and ritual. It had "overseers" (bishops) able to negotiate terms with him, a capacity he meant to reinforce and expand.

As the emperors had shifted their power centers out of Rome to guard the borders, the role of the Senate evaporated. Legions promoted their generals for empire in the musical-chair successions/usurpations of the third century. This demoted the senators from the role they had played when Augustus created the empire—as a legitimating gesture toward

Rome's republican past. H. A. Drake makes the plausible claim that Constantine used Christian bishops to convey moral legitimacy on his rule, much as Augustus had used the Senate.[1] If he became the bishops' patron, they could become his protectors. In order to effect this Constantine had to mute the differences among Christians—the heresy hunting typified by Irenaeus's second-century book *Against the Heretics*—and promote concord. He did this by financing frequent meetings of the bishops to resolve their differences.

As Diarmaid MacCulloch puts it, Constantine became the bishops' generous "travel agent," using subsidized travel by royal post on the empire's excellent roads, and supplying the free lodging and food for bishops and their trains at the places where they met.[2] In the time of Constantine's son Constantius, according to Ammianus Marcellinus, "By the traffic of bishops back and forth in the imperial post service, to attend what they call their 'synods,' the emperor damaged the nerves of travel in an effort to make this religious activity fit his own purpose."[3]

Constantine also undertook an immense building program to create Christian basilicas, finding a replacement for the stability that had been symbolized in pagan temples. Promoting legitimate celebrators of the Christian mysteries in these grand new structures was another way to give his reign a solid base. This was a direct contribution to the Christian communities, which he also subsidized with immunities from taxation. He gave donations to the poor, to be distributed by bishops, making their role both more desirable and more manipulable.

Some Christians were made uneasy by partnership with a worldly power that had hitherto been an active or possible foe. A sign of Christianity's spiritual nature had been its potential or actual defiance of worldly power. How could it now become the beneficiary of that power? In Gibbon's later words, this could suggest that "the prerogatives of the King of Heaven were settled, or changed, or modified, in the cabinet of an earthly monarch" (DF XXI). A church without martyrs was still a disorienting prospect. Martyrs, as the "true Christians," had been guarantors of the true church. Worship had taken place at the martyria. What could replace them? The church was suffering from a martyr gap. What could fill it?

Asceticism

If Rome would not kill Christians, competitive self-punishment could make them all but kill themselves with fasting, scourging, loneliness, and inventive deprivations. As R. A. Markus notes, there was an unslaked need for martyrdom, if only virtual martyrdom—of the kind supplied by virginity, as a way to cut off life's continuation in offspring. The virgin anticipated the End Time, careless of a worldly future. As Averil Cameron notices, there was a "repeated association of virginity with martyrdom."[4] Jerome and Ambrose praised virginity as superior to marriage. The same virtual martyrdom could be accomplished by isolation from the world in hermit cells like that of Antony or monastic communities like that of Pachomius. "With the ending of the age of persecution, monasticism came to absorb the ideal of the martyr."[5] Peter Brown has described the great shudder away from the body that swept through late antiquity in the age of the Desert Fathers and consecrated virgins. The Egyptian desert became a kind of outer space with heroic astronauts venturing into its devil-haunted remotenesses. In this "counter-world," the monk became as impervious to the fear of pain or starvation as the martyrs had been fearless before death.[6]

Christian life had a new ideal, described perceptively by W. H. C. Frend:

The monk, like the martyr, was the athlete and soldier of Christ. Each fought the demons in his own way, the martyr as witness to Christ, the ascetic in his struggle to maintain his spiritual ascent to Christ. This was the challenge of the desert where the demons had their abode. The extremes of mortification and self-torture to which the monk subjected himself might be compared to the pangs endured by the martyr, and the punishment even of being eaten by wild beasts was simulated by some of the more venturesome spirits . . . With the ending of persecution, the substitution of ascetic for martyr as the height of the Christians' goals became complete.[7]

This set up a new division within the church, between the "true" Christians and a second-best cadre that relied on the prayers of their betters to help them toward heaven. Eusebius described the situation in his *Proof of the Gospel:*

> Two ways of life were thus given by the law of Christ to his Church. The one is above nature, and beyond common human living; it admits not marriage, child-bearing, property, nor the possession of wealth . . . Like some celestial beings, they gaze down upon human life, performing the duty of a priesthood to Almighty God for the whole race.[8]

It should be noticed that Eusebius gives the ascetics a priestly role. They are the intercessors most powerful in praying for the church.

This was an entirely charismatic view of the church, going back to the priestless New Testament, where the gifts of the Spirit were bestowed on those favored with spiritual insight or leadership. David Brakke argues that the inspiring role of the ideal monk, the Antony or the Pachomius or the Simeon, made him a guru for others, implicitly undermining the bureaucratic view of the church encouraged by Constantine. Rather than submit to an authorized hierarchy, many people revered "the informality and fluidity of the prevailing guru sytem in eremitical and semi-eremitical monasticism."[9] The guru out-holyed the merely appointed leaders. John Chrysostom wrote that a monk surpasses in dignity even the most philosophical and benevolent king.[10] The ascetic would even more obviously outrank a humanly elected bishop. Euchites drew the conclusion that authorized bodies, even in the church, should not interfere with the lonely quest for sanctity.[11]

Thus, despite the effort of Athanasius and others to recruit star holy men into the priesthood or into bishops' chairs, famous monks refused ordination, which they considered a step down from their holy heights. Some monks, ordained against their will, refused to celebrate the Eucharist.[12] In order to avoid forcible ordination, the famous Pachomius moved from one hiding place to another.[13] The monk Ammonius went further, cutting off an ear to show he could not perform the duties of a priest. When the archbishop Timothy of Alexandria still pressed him to accept ordination, he threatened to cut out his tongue as well—and was finally left to his saintliness.[14] The first canon issued by the Nicene Council was a condemnation of those ascetics (like Origen) who castrated themselves (S 1.383–84).

It is hard to appreciate today the drive to remain otherworldly just when worldly acceptance was being bestowed on the church by Constantine. Even those who did not remain monks had tried out that vocation for a while—Jerome, for instance, and John Chrysostom, and Basil—and continued to uphold it as an ideal even after they left off their own endeavor. Admirers of Athanasius claimed that he had spent some time as a monk—for the same reason that admirers of the apostles claimed that they must have been martyrs. They were assumed to live the perfect life, even without any evidence for that. Athanasius did not claim he had ever been a monk, but wrote that being exiled gave him the status of a virtual martyr.[15] When Melitius was exiled from Egypt to the mines in Palestine, he organized what he called a "church of the martyrs."[16]

The cult of the martyrs deepened just when martyrs were no longer being made. The calendar was crowded with their feast days, so that "a Christian who attended a church service would be liturgically thrust back into the age of the martyrs."[17] Shrines like that of the martyred Saint Felix, raised by Paulinus of Nola, became a congested goal of pilgrimage.[18] People communed with the luridly described trials of the martyrs by chaining and beating themselves. Some ate only grasses.[19] There was a competition in self-denial, in doing without sex or sleep or food or clothes. The holy man or woman became a naked, starving, shivering person in a sleepless trance—the type of holiness later presented in the gaunt figures of the Magdalen and the Baptist as sculptured by Donatello. "Christian asceticism of the third and fourth centuries tended to move from salutary self-discipline to extremes of self-torment which only increased preoccupation with the body."[20] Such excesses upset the less adventurous. Anticipating Augustine's plea that one should not seek martyrdom, Athanasius warned monks against starving themselves to death by fasting or driving themselves crazy with sleeplessness.[21] We are back to Nicaea's legislation against self-castration.

Perfectionism

Ascetical feats may seem the acts of eccentric individuals, but the reverence widely given them shows they expressed some urgency of the church. A similar resistance to worldliness and yearning back for a tie with the martyrs took the very practical turn of fights over control of sacred spaces and sacraments after the persecutions. Christians who had resisted persecution said that only they had the right to honor those who died from it. These "confessors" denied that people who surrendered to the persecutors, or who fled their posts, could hold or resume bishops' chairs or administer sacraments. These were called deserters (*lapsi*) or traitors (*traditores*)—as later people would be called "quislings." People baptized by a *lapsus,* or by a priest ordained by a *lapsus,* had not received a valid sacrament. They needed to be rebaptized, or newly ordained, by keepers of the true tradition.

In Africa, Donatists took this stand, denying that a *lapsi*-elected bishop, Caecilian, could hold the see of Carthage. In Italy, the Novationists disputed who should return to the empty chair of the bishop of Rome. In Egypt, the Melitians embroiled Alexandria in contested successions. These heirs of the martyrs were not all ascetics—but they were perfectionists, who tried to keep the church pure by denying leadership to the impure, the compromised, the contaminated. Constantine took it as his first task, in dealing with Christians, to heal this division between the *confessores* and the *lapsi*. It was a task not sought out but imposed upon him. It was thrust on his attention by the Donatists during the first phase of his rule—when he had taken control of the Western empire by defeating Maxentius in 312 and was negotiating terms for the Eastern empire with Licinius. (Only after he defeated and killed Licinius, in 324, would he address the problems of the whole church, with an inclusive meeting at Nicaea.)

Donatist bishops in Africa, who saw Constantine's rise to power from his Christian-friendly father's part of the empire in Gaul, asked for a hearing before Gallic bishops to oust Caecilian from Africa's main see at Carthage (S 1.341–42). Constantine, in his newly won Italian territory, summoned Gallic bishops from the north to Rome, to meet with African bishops from the south, reinforcing the assembly with fifteen Italian bishops. He told the Donatists to bring the charges against Caecilian, who was allowed to have seven of his own advocates with him (S 1.343). Constantine made every effort to ensure fairness, and made unity his aim. "The respect which I pay to the lawful Catholic Church is so great that it is my wish that you should leave no schism whatsoever or division in any place."[22]

The meeting's decision, reached in 313, confirmed Caecilian in his seat—which just made the Donatists appeal the sentence. Constantine, who was nothing if not patient in his toil for union, called a second council, to be held in the Gallic forum the Donatists had asked for originally. Though he expressed his impatience that the matter was being protracted "with persistent obstinacy," he provided travel warrants, at the Donatists' request, for bishops representing more of Africa (from the provinces of Byzacena, Tripolitania, the Numidias, and Mauritania) "so that they may all arrive speedily" at Arles (S 1.344). But this council also went against the Donatists. They had condemned their fellow Christians who obeyed pagan Rome; they had not thought they might oppose a Christian emperor. But they would not turn over their beloved martyr shrines to people who had collaborated with the state that martyred them.

This cult of the martyrs was a point of fierce and patriotic pride for the Donatists. For them to give up their many shrines was a desecration of all that they held holy. Monnica, Augustine's mother, who had Donatist traits beyond her Berber name, tried to keep up her cult of the martyrs even when she had followed her son to Milan. Augustine was amazed that she would give up something so dear to her out of respect for Milan's bishop, Ambrose.[23] Constantine, when he took on the Donatists, was dealing with an unbudgeable part of his new reign in the West. The African purists were as dissociated from his universalist ideal as the Desert Fathers and consecrated virgins. Peter Brown says the Donatists had the tough cohesion of a new chosen people:

> It contained the secret of a success unparalleled in the history of the Early Church. For like Nonconformity in Wales, the Donatist Church had won over a provincial society, isolated, self-respecting, suspicious of the outside world, to its form of Christianity.[24]

After several more attempts to force the Donatists out of their enclaves, Constantine at last gave up, confessing his own failure and leaving the outcome to God:

> Until the Heavenly medicine shows itself, our designs must be moderated so far as to act with patience, and whatever in their insolence they attempt or carry out, in accordance with their habitual wantonness, all this we must endure (S 1.351).

When Constantine's son Constans tried again to suppress the Donatists in 347, Donatus replied, "What has the Emperor to do with the Church?" (S 2.29). It is an ironic comment, since the Donatists had first pushed the emperor to intervene in church affairs. But it shows that resistance to institutional authority took many forms, even after institutional authority seemed to have come to Christianity.

Catholicity

Constantine still thought he needed (and so must foster) religious unity among Christians. As soon as he had secured his supremacy over all the empire, he called the greatest meeting of bishops ever, at which he meant to play the peacemaker. Constantine's own claim was that over 300 bishops attended.[25] A symbolic number was later invented and accepted by church celebrants—318, the number of Abraham's servants at Genesis 14.14. Modern estimates put the number under 300, with only 5 bishops from the West (and 2 presbyters from Rome).[26] Nonetheless, "it was by far the greatest number of bishops ever gathered together up to then."[27] Eusebius, who was present, says that "the number of bishops exceeded 250" and "the number of presbyters and deacons and of the many other attendants who accompanied them was beyond calculation" (VC 3.8). Thus it is reasonable to call this the first Catholic (*kath-holou*, for "entire") and ecumenical (*oikoumenē*, for "populated world") council of the church.

Constantine said that he changed the venue of the council from inland and mountainous Ancyra to Nicaea for two reasons: a warmer climate and proximity to his capital at the time, Nicomedia (S 1.383). It is reasonable to suppose that he also had in mind the difficulty of lodging and provisioning such a large assembly for two whole months (from late May to late July). Nicaea was on the great Roman road that ran by the Lacanian Lake. He may well have hoped that his personal presence could produce more harmony than had prevailed at the councils (Arles and Antioch) where he was just represented by Ossius. This does not mean, as many have supposed, that he ran the Council of Nicaea. Only bishops could vote there, and he was not even a baptized Christian yet. (He could not attend Mass at what is called his own council.) He was trying to enhance the office of bishop and to build a corporate spirit among its holders. He would not do anything to diminish their voting power, as T. D. Barnes rightly points out.[28] His influence was real, but was probably exercised through the presiding bishop, Ossius.[29]

What were the bishops and their large support staffs doing through those two months? There is no record of the proceedings. The council is now famous (and contested) for the Trinitarian creed it agreed on. But it had many other items on its agenda. In his *Life of Constantine*, Eusebius makes it seem that the main goal was bringing East and West together on the date of Easter (VC 3.5, 14–20). That was, indeed, the focus of extensive texts issued just after the council, trying to give uniformity to the most important liturgical expression of the empire-wide church. Constantine himself devoted a long letter to the subject (anti-Semitic in divorcing the date of Easter from the Jewish Passover, VC 3.17–20), and Eusebius wrote an elaborate treatise *De Pascha*.[30] Like the other matters dealt with in the council, this one would remain unresolved for a long time. (The council, in Canon 3, also mandated an unmarried clergy, a rule long neglected.)

An especially pressing problem was that of determining the authority of individual bishops. Indeed, most of the twenty canons issued by the council deal with bishops' election, or installation, or orthodoxy (S 1.383–90). Bishops were elected, normally by presbyters. But the procedures for this were not uniform—some were not accepted or understood, some were erratic or irregularly followed. The status of even the most famous bishops had been challenged, both before and after the council. Athanasius was said to have been too young for the office, Ambrose to have been consecrated too soon (one week) after his baptism, Augustine to have been elevated when another was still in the chair. Nicaea tried to set firm standards—for election by presbyters, confirmation by neighboring bishops (a minimum of three, including the metropolitan of the province), only one man for each see, and none ever to be translated from one see to another. It is a sign of the noncompliance in this last requirement that Constantine's own bishop, Eusebius (of Nicomedia, not Caesarea), was transferred from Nicomedia to Constantinople when that imperial capital was completed—and this Eusebius, an Arian, is the man who baptized Constantine on his deathbed.[31]

Even aside from the election and confirmation procedures, there were many disputed episcopal chairs because of the perfectionists' refusal to readmit *lapsi*-tainted bishops. Nicaea dealt with the challenge Melitius had offered to Alexander as bishop of Alexandria. These disputes would merge with later attempts to disqualify bishops on grounds of orthodoxy— embroiling the *lapsi* quarrel with the Arian problem. The council tried to set standards for the readmission of Novationists and Paulinians, after a period of repentance, posing problems of coexistence between two quali- fied bishops for the same post. The problems persisted, and in some places increased.

The question of Arianism was not as prominent at the council as it would seem in retrospect. The issue had arisen in an earlier council, called at Antioch to settle a challenge to Eusebius in the chair of Caesarea. Euse- bius was deposed, as having "Arian" views on the divinity of Christ. At Nicaea, Eusebius presented his own case, reciting a creed he called tra- ditional to his church. In a letter he wrote to his church in Alexandria, he says that this was accepted by the council as orthodox (S 1.390–94). But when the council formed its own creed, the emperor (at Ossius's sugges- tion?) introduced a nonscriptural word for the Son, *homoousios* (same- beinged). Two bishops, supporters of Arius, did not sign this creed, and were deposed. (Arius could not be deposed, since he was not a bishop—he was exiled.) Eusebius, also a supporter of Arius, writes his letter to explain why he signed the creed—*homoousios* can have several meanings.[32]

Nicaea has the reputation of settling the meaning of the Trinity, and of doing it with the emperor's seal of approval. But Eusebius's claim that *homoousios* left much to interpretation was confirmed by the fact that Constantine restored the two bishops who had been holdouts, and did the same for Arius himself (S 1.401). Another resisting bishop was the Euse- bius (of Nicomedia) he made metropolitan of his new capital, and from whom he accepted baptism. He worked to reconcile all those condemned at Nicaea—not only Arius, Eusebius, and Theognis (the bishop of Ni- caea, where they met), but the Novationists, the Paulinians, and the Meli- tians. He had, remember, given up his attempt to force the Donatists back into the fold. His ideal seemed to be the one Ronald Knox would ridicule in his attack on ecumenism as "Reunion All Round."

Constantine followed this policy of maximum conciliation and omnidirectional inclusion after the council. When Athanasius was deposed at the later Council of Tyre (335 CE), Constantine exiled but did not depose him (letting no other bishop take his chair). John Henry Newman thought that Constantine fostered heresy by his temporizing preference for unity over doctrinal purity. He accuses Constantine of what was, for Newman, the great sin of "eclecticism," the antidogmatic principle that accepts the "Creed as a formula of peace, not of belief." He was willing "to endure or discountenance error" because he "subjected religious principle to expediency, and aimed at peace, as a supreme good."[33]

What Newman fought in his effort to reimpose dogma on the nineteenth-century Anglican church looks bigoted now. Constantine, in his effort to hold together a fissiparous religion, tried to break Christianity out of its purist enclaves (some fanatical) by having as many as possible bishops talk to each other as often as possible, and by reassuring all parties of the bishops' proper credentials. He championed cosmopolitanism over provincialism. The process he initiated was continually breaking down, and he worked continually to repair it. He compromised because he knew the kinds of resistance he would get if he did not temporize, trim, and negotiate toward fragile states of peace.

Constantine has the unearned reputation of introducing "caesaropapism" into the church, the union of the spiritual and the temporal power. T. D. Barnes says that this view was largely formed by German scholars in the time of Bismarck's "Reicheskirche," and has little to do with the actual Constantine, who was more the "eclectic" Newman condemned him for being.[34] Constantine even sounds like a pluralist of modern times when, in relaxed conversation with his guests, he said what Eusebius records:

On one occasion, when entertaining bishops to dinner, he let slip some such words as these in our hearing; "You are bishops of those within the

Church, but I am perhaps a bishop appointed by God over those outside."
In accord with this saying, he exercised a bishop's supervision over all his
subjects, and pressed them all, as far as lay in his power, to lead the godly
life (VC 4.24).

He mollified factions in the church and sought common ground even
with "outsiders." In a speech delivered before he had won the East away
from Licinius, he professed his belief in the Christian mysteries, but did
not confine his concern to those inside the church. He was also thinking
of the outsiders:

> We strive to the best of our ability to fill with good hope those who are
> uninitiated in such doctrines, summoning God as our helper in the
> undertaking.[35]

Even the emperor's last-minute interjection of the term *homoousios* into
the council was probably an effort at conciliation. The *homo-* element
("same") was soon contrasted with a *homoi-* element ("similar"), in the adjective *homoiousios*, making the Son like (but less than) the Father. Yet
homo- was often used for "agreeing-with," as in the adjectives *homonous,
homologos, homomathetes*. How *much* "like the Father" must the Son be to
equal him?

Constantine was probably taking the word *homoousios* as a compromise on all the slight disagreements on degree of divinity for the Son.
This is proved not only by his later actions in accommodating Arius but
by his words in summoning the council at Nicaea. He thought that distinctions were slight and could easily be solved by a spirit of agreement.
He advises the contending parties:

> Now, therefore, do ye both exhibit an equal degree of forbearance, and
> receive the advice which your fellow-servant righteously gives. What
> then is this advice? It was wrong in the first instance to propose such
> questions as these, or to reply to them when propounded. For those
> points of discussion which are enjoined by the authority of no law, but

rather suggested by the contentious spirit which is fostered by misused leisure, even though they may be intended merely as an intellectual exercise, ought certainly to be confined to our own thoughts, and not hastily produced in the popular assemblies, nor unadvisedly intrusted to the ears of the multitude . . . Let therefore both the unguarded question and the inconsiderate answer receive your mutual forgiveness . . . For as long as you continue to contend about *these small and very insignificant questions,* I believe it indeed to be not merely unbecoming, but positively evil, that so large a portion of God's people which belongs to your jurisdiction should be thus divided (S 1.377, emphasis added).

This is the voice of Newman's "eclectic" Constantine, not of Jacob Burckhardt's "caesaropapist" one. But Constantine found he could as little stop the Trinitarian quibbles of Alexandria, Caesarea, and Nicomedia as he could quash the martyr shrines of Donatists. Yet he labored at compromise until his death. It was only when the fight of his sons to inherit the empire was resolved in the triumph of Constantius over his brothers that the empire was enrolled on one side of the conflict—the Arian side. And when that happened, there were ringing defiances of the state by church leaders recalling the old martyr days. Hilary of Poitiers defied state blandishments as well as threats, saying Antichrist is still Antichrist, even if he "does not flog our back but tickles our belly" (*non dorsa caedit sed ventrem palpet*).[36] Ossius, the ally of Constantine, became the defier of his son:

Do not intrude into ecclesiastical matters, and do not give commands to us concerning them; but learn from us. God has put into your hands the kingdom; to us he has entrusted the affairs of the Church (S 2.42).

Athanasius would defy Constantius dramatically. He and others were just echoing what Donatus said in 347: "What has the Emperor to do with the Church?" (S 2.29).

If the church was no longer oppressed by the state after Constantine, it was hardly merged with it. Resistance to power existed on many levels, from private withdrawal and asceticism, from perfectionists opposed to state sponsorship of the *lapsi*, from opportunists taking state patronage to use for their own purposes against the state, and from homoousian theologians calling Constantius a heretic and the Antichrist. The church had gone from existing without a state to existing along with it. It was still not a church acting with and as a state. But that development was coming.

NOTES

1. H. A. Drake, *Constantine and the Bishops: The Politics of Intolerance* (Johns Hopkins University Press, 2000), 41–56, 467–82. Ramsay MacMullen argues that "the Roman senate was a model" for the bishops' synods: *Voting About God in Early Church Councils* (Yale University Press, 2006), 19.
2. Diarmaid MacCulloch, *Christianity: The First Three Thousand Years* (Viking, 2010), 214; VC.
3. Ammianus, *Roman History* 21.16.18.
4. Averil Cameron, *Christianity and the Rhetoric of Empire* (University of California Press, 1991), 70.
5. R. A. Markus, *The End of Ancient Christianity* (Cambridge University Press, 1990), 71.
6. Peter Brown, *The Body and Society* (Columbia University Press, 1988), 212–24.
7. W. H. C. Frend, *Martyrdom and Persecution in the Early Church* (Basil Blackwell, 1965), 47–48.
8. Eusebius, *The Proof of the Gospel* (*Demonstratio Evangelica*), translated by W. J. Ferrar (Macmillan, 1920), 48.
9. David Brakke, *Athanasius and the Politics of Asceticism* (Oxford University Press, 1995), 85.
10. John Chrysostom, *A Comparison Between a King and a Monk*, translated with an introduction by David G. Hunter (Edwin Mellen Press, 1988), 69–76.
11. Henry Chadwick, *The Early Church*, revised edition (Penguin, 1993), 179.
12. Brakke, op. cit., 83.
13. Ibid., 113–14.
14. Ibid., 109.
15. Athanasius, *Defense of His Flight* 11–17.
16. T. D. Barnes, *Athanasius and Constantius: Theology and Politics in the Constantinian Empire* (Harvard University Press, 1993), 14.
17. Markus, op. cit., 99.
18. Peter Brown, *Through the Eye of a Needle* (Princeton University Press, 2012), 227–30.
19. Chadwick, op. cit., 180.

20. Gillian Clark, *Iamblichus: On the Pythagorean Life* (Liverpool University Press, 1986), xiii.

21. Brakke, op. cit., 87–89, 186–87.

22. Eusebius, *Ecclesiastical History*, edited by Kirsopp Lake (Harvard University Press, 1926), 10.5.20.

23. Augustine, *Confessions* 6.2. Peter Brown notes other Donatist elements in Monnica: "In a society that valued sheer physical continuity in life and death (Monnica, after all, had once wished to 'rejoice in grandsons after the flesh,' and had hoped to be buried in her home soil), these [Donatist] bishops were thought of as the 'sons of the martyrs,' as surely as the despised Catholics were the 'sons of Caecilian.'" *Augustine of Hippo*, new edition (University of California Press, 2000), 215.

24. Brown, *Augustine of Hippo*, 215.

25. Eusebius, *Ecclesiastical History*, 1.9.21.

26. Ramsay MacMullen (op. cit., 41) makes a "low ball" guess of 200 bishops in attendance. R. P. C. Hanson compromises on the number of bishops as 250 to 300: *The Search for the Christian Doctrine of God: The Arian Controversy, 318–381* (Continuum, 1988), 156.

27. Hanson, op. cit., 152.

28. T. D. Barnes, "Constantine, Athanasius, and the Christian Church," in Samuel N. C. Lieu and Dominic Montserrat, *Constantine: History, Historiography, and Legend* (Routledge, 1998), 7–20, especially 10–11.

29. Hanson, op. cit., 154–57.

30. The *De Pascha* (PG 24.693–706) survives only as a long fragment, translated and analyzed by Mark DelCogliano, "The Promotion of the Constantinian Agenda in Eusebius of Caesarea's *On the Feast of Pascha*," in Sabrina Inowlocki and Claudio Zamagni, *Reconsidering Eusebius: Collected Papers on Literary, Historical, and Theological Issues* (Brill, 2011), 25–38.

31. The two Eusebii, of Caesarea (the more famous now) and of Nicomedia/Constantinople (the more powerful then), are sometimes confused because they were not merely coevals but Arianizing allies. But the tendency of Easterners to take the same classical names can confuse the record of the time. We get many an Athanasius ("immortal-like"), Arius ("warlike"), Alexander ("man guarder"), Eudoxius ("famous"), Eugenius ("noble"), Theodore ("godsend"), and Eusebius ("reverend").

32. The *ousia* (being) in *homoousios* was later distinguished from *hypostasis*, as "substance" and "person." But Hanson (op. cit., 181–202) rightly argues that each term was, taken singly, fuzzy, and that they were for a time either synonymous or reversible in meaning.

33. John Henry Newman, *The Arians of the Fourth Century*, third edition (E. Lumly, 1871), 273, 252.

34. Barnes, *Athanasius and Constantius*, 165–75. Barnes discusses the influential work of Eduard Schwartz, but the Bismarck era also produced Jacob Burck-

hardt's *The Age of Constantine the Great* (revised edition, 1880). Barnes deplores Burkhardt's impact on the study of Constantine in "The Constantinian Reformation," reprinted in his *From Eusebius to Augustine* (Variorum, 1994), V 41–42.

35. Constantine, "Speech to the Assembly of the Saints" 11.1. Barnes argues for the authenticity and sincerity of this speech: *Constantine and Eusebius* (Harvard University Press, 1981), 73–76.

36. Hilary of Poitiers, *Against Constantius* 5.

SEVEN

Church with State

WHO OWNS CONSTANTINE?

When the state suspended its opposition to the church, how were Christians supposed to respond? How could an otherworldly religion work out living relationships with the vast worldly power of the Roman Empire? According to the Gospel of John (18.36), Jesus told Pilate, "My reign is not of this worldly order (*kosmos*)." In fact "reign over this earthly order" (*kosmos*) is just what Satan had offered to Jesus, according to Matthew (4.9). And Luke (4.7) says why the offer was rejected—because of its condition: that Jesus "kneel down before me." Is that always the price of worldly power—subjection to the devil? It is true that Jesus said, "Pay Caesar what is Caesar's" (Mt 22.21)—but that made Caesar the Other. It was *contrasted with* paying to God what is God's. There were two obligations. But what if Caesar becomes an ally, a patron, a partner? When does paying Caesar become obeying Caesar, and when does obeying Caesar slide into being Caesar?

True, both Paul and the letter of supposed Peter said that Christians should accept the state's rule as from God—and that was when the state was not well disposed toward Christianity (sometimes persecuting it, always disapproving). How could Christians comply with a hostile state but refuse compliance to a favoring one? Should Constantine's offer to build basilicas at all the sacred places of Christianity be rebuffed? Individuals could do that—could go off into the desert, or stick with forms of Christianity not approved by the state (Donatist, Melitian, Novatian, or whatever). But could bishops as a body refuse to take the exemption from taxation offered by Constantine? Compliance was much easier than resistance, and ways to justify this were not long in coming.

The New Moses

One of the first and most ingenious of these justifications came from Constantine's celebrant, Eusebius. As we have seen, Eusebius's *Ecclesiastical History* helped create a mythical age of martyrs. But that just made Eusebius work more energetically to justify a postmartyr church for the age of Constantine. The issue he faced squarely was that Constantine was not even a baptized Christian (until his deathbed). The emperor could not attend Mass, where he would have been expelled at the end of the Mass of the catechumens. To avoid that humiliation, he probably never even became a catechumen (it would have been mentioned if he did). Not only was he not a priest in the new religion. He was in fact the highest priest of the old (the persecuting) religion, since he pointedly retained the pagan Roman title of Pontifex Maximus. How then could he be accepted as a patron and guide for a religion he was not part of?

To rationalize this situation, Eusebius did what all early Christians did—he looked to the Old Testament for guidance. For centuries, the only Bible the Christians had was the Old Testament, reflecting on which was at the core of the earliest liturgies. The first visual arts of the church were almost entirely devoted to Old Testament subjects, to Jonah, Noah, Daniel, David, and especially Moses—Moses at the burning bush, Moses striking the rock, Moses giving the tablets.[1] Eusebius was shrewd enough to notice that Moses, though a leader of God's people, was not a priest. He did not and could not offer sacrifice. That was reserved to his brother Aaron and Aaron's descendants. So Eusebius compared the unbaptized Constantine to the non-priestly Moses. Moses could bring the Law down from Sinai, but he could not offer the sacrifices commanded in the Law. In the same way, Constantine could preside over the council defining Christian worship, though he could not conduct (or even attend) that worship himself. Constantine, then, could be the leader of the Christian people as Moses was the leader of the Jewish people, though neither was a celebrant of the people's religious cult.

Modern students of Eusebius's *Life of Constantine* have analyzed how thoroughly it is patterned on the life of Moses.[2] The parallels are emphasized.

1. Constantine was brought up in an Eastern court, as Moses was in Pharaoh's palace. Constantine, as the son of a Western tetrarch, spent his youth as a security pledge at the court of the Eastern tetrarchs Diocletian and Galerius. Since these were the principal enforcers of the Great Persecution, Eusebius equates them with the Pharaohs in whose court Moses was raised (Ex 1.5–7). Both Moses and Constantine, in the words of Eusebius, were raised "in the heart of the palace and family circle of the tyrants," but both became "tyrant slayers" (VC 1.12). It was an early preachers' theme that Moses had acquired the wisdom and lore of Egypt before he broke his people free from that rich but oppressive world. T. D. Barnes argues that Constantine acquired classical learning at the sophisticated court of Diocletian, so he understood thoroughly the religious world he was leaving behind.[3]

2. Constantine's father, Constantius I, as the Western Augustus, was not an enthusiastic persecutor, which Eusebius takes to mean that he was in fact a quiet Christian (VC 1.15–17). In this he resembles the father-in-law of Moses, the Midianite Jethro, who favored Moses' mission to his people (Ex 3.18).

3. While tending Jethro's flocks, Moses had the vision of a burning bush, from which God called him back to Egypt, where he could save the Israelites (Ex 3.2–17). Before Constantine's battle for the West at the Milvian Bridge, he too had a burning vision, the shape of a cross in the sun, with a three-word text under it saying "Win with This"— *En toutōi nika* (VC 1.28–29).[4]

4. Constantine did not understand the message in the sun until Christ, appearing in a dream, told him to issue battle standards for his troops (like the eagle standards taken into battle by Roman legions). These were to resemble the shape he saw in the sun (VC 1.29). He was told what form the standard should take—the cross shape is the Greek letter chi, drawn over the stem of the Greek letter rho, the first elements in the Greek title of Jesus CHR(istos) (VC 1.31).[5] This battle standard, called the *labarum*, is like the wonder-working staff that God includes

in his instruction to Moses about the burning bush (Ex 4.2–3)—the one used, for instance, in striking water from a rock (Nm 20.6–11).

5. Moses used his miraculous staff to part the Red Sea, so that the Israelites could pass through it—while behind them it closed on the pursuing troops of Pharaoh, drowning them (Ex 14.16–28). Eusebius expressly compares this with the way Constantine pushed the army of Maxentius into the Tiber, where Maxentius drowned (VC 1.38).[6]

6. As Moses received on Mount Sinai the Law that would govern the People of God, so Constantine called the Great Council of Nicaea that would establish the creed by which Christians would live. This parallel is implicit in the run of comparisons with Moses, and T. D. Barnes persuasively argues that Eusebius would have made it explicit but for the fact that he died while finishing the book:

> Had Eusebius lived longer, he would doubtless have penetrated beneath these superficial resemblances to the deep similarity between the achievements of the two men [Moses and Constantine]: like "God's ancient prophet," Constantine was a law-giver who showed God's people how to live, prosper, and attain happiness, both in this world and hereafter.[7]

In this way, Eusebius both exalted and limited Constantine's role in God's providence. He is the savior of his people, but also their servant. This is the first in a long line of efforts to distinguish political power from church authority. It seems neat and convincing at a first glance. But how in practice does one keep the two apart if they are used in tandem?

One might say that Moses was the protector of his people in a physical sense. He baffled the Egyptian army. He took the people to their physical space (though he did not get all the way there himself). With God's help he provisioned them, providing water from the rock and manna from the sky. These are things Constantine and other rulers could do for the Christian people. But Moses' authority was not confined to military, logistical, and economic services. He defined what the people should believe. He destroyed the Golden Calf. He delivered the Law. He said who could be priests and what they should do (Ex 32.26–29). He enforced doctrine as well as discipline.

Thus, casting Constantine as Moses did not really limit his authority in the way that Eusebius might have hoped. Admittedly, Constantine let the bishops define belief, saying he was there simply to enforce it once they had made their decision. But he had discretion on the ways and degrees of enforcement. And when the bishops disagreed among themselves, he created orthodoxy by enforcing one set's views against the others'. (In practice, he tried to enforce a compromising mixture of views—but that too was a way of establishing an authoritative position.) When he tried to oust Donatists from their shrines, he failed; but he still had to adjudicate the ongoing squabbles over church property. That was more evident when he decided who were orthodox enough to provide the sacraments in basilicas he had built around the empire (six in Rome alone). Was building churches a secular, not a religious activity? In order to give bishops exemption from taxes, or money to distribute to the poor, he had to decide which contender for any bishop's chair should be accepted as legitimate.

I have already mentioned how this intervention of the emperor in doctrinal disputes tore people apart when Constantius took the Arianizing side of disputes on the Trinity and the Incarnation—disputes that Constantine had "settled" by fudging the issue. This and other quarrels would entangle the emperor in religious matters for most succeeding centuries. Those who told the emperor to stay out of the way one day were appealing for his intervention on the next. Donatist bishops in Africa were the first to call on Constantine for help, but their later African opponents, including Augustine, successfully asked the emperor Honorius to overrule the bishop of Rome, Zosimus, in order to condemn Pelagius.[8] When the presbyters of Milan, wanting to get rid of the Arian legacy of their former bishop, had chosen Ambrose as his successor, and Ambrose refused to serve, the presbyters asked Emperor Valentinian to make Ambrose take the office, and the emperor complied. Was the church ordering the state in this case, or the state ordering the church? How can we distinguish one from the other? Eusebius's assignment of roles, clever though it was, would not settle the disputes looming as Christians tried to justify compliance with state favor.

Saint Silvester

Eusebius's biography was typical in many ways. It shows that Christians felt they had to work out their collaboration with the state by pondering their personal ties with Constantine, who continued to be a mythogenic figure. That posed a special problem for Christians in the West, since Eusebius was defining the church in the East and for the East, where Constantine ruled in his new city of Constantinople. These councils, like the major early controversies of the church, were conducted in Greek. Some in the West had to wait for the Nicene canons to be translated into Latin before they could comply with them. It was not until the fifth century that Rufinus translated Eusebius's *Ecclesiastical History* from the Greek. Rome played a minor role, when it played any, in these world-shaking events. Constantine, after winning his first important victory (but not the most important one) in Rome, at the Milvian Bridge in 312, had slipped away to found a new Rome, which became the center of the empire. It is true that he built major basilicas in and around the original Rome; but he made it clear that the founding church of Christianity was at the Holy Sepulchre in Jerusalem. He dispatched all the bishops gathered at the Council of Tyre to the dedication of this basilica, sending costly gifts to it, where Eusebius and others gave grand orations (VC 4.43–46). Helena, of course, Constantine's mother, drew much attention to Jerusalem by her visit and heavy donations there (VC 3.41–43).

By the end of the fifth century, the church in Rome was particularly weak. It was ruled by the Ostrogoth lord of Italy, Theodoric, who made Ravenna the intellectual as well as political center of the West (with Boethius and Cassiodorus as his scholars-in-residence). In Rome, by contrast, there were two flawed claimants to the papacy, one (Lawrence) in the Lateran Palace that was the customary seat of the papacy, and the other (Symmachus) outside the city walls in the Basilica of Peter. To bolster the claims of Symmachus, biographies of former "popes" were created around contentious issues in the situation of Symmachus, giving him supposed precedents for all of his claims. This polemical use of imagined biographies helped begin the creation of the *Liber Pontificalis,* tracing an unbroken line of bishops from the fictive office of Peter.[9] This maneuver is called by George Demacopoulos "Papal biography as a narrative weapon."[10] In this blossoming of imagined lives, one of the most lastingly successful was a *Life of Silvester.*

"Silvester" gave Rome its needed link to Constantine. The point of history that was seized on was the undeniable fact that Constantine's first famous battle had been fought in 312 to "free" the Christians at Rome, and he had given imperial properties to the bishop of that city. But in manipulating the hazy records of the early bishops, inventors of the new "history" got the wrong pope.[11] Miltiades was Rome's bishop at the time of the battle at the Milvian Bridge, but he died two years later, and Silvester became bishop for a long reign. By a simple change in chronology, Silvester became the bishop who helped Constantine win his great battle under the slogan "Win with This." It was relatively easy to give Silvester a false biography, since the real one was so insubstantial. J. N. D. Kelly says of Silvester:

> Although pope for almost twenty-two years of the reign of Constantine the Great (306–37), an epoch of dramatic developments for the church, he seems to have played an insignificant part in the great events that were taking place, and only one or two glimpses of him, negative but instructive, survive.[12]

Once the false date was accepted, a number of problems in Rome could be solved by creative remembering. How did the first Christian emperor make it to his deathbed without becoming a Christian? How could he have been baptized by an Arian? How could he have treated Rome so negligently? The solution was simple: just deny that most of these things

happened. In this busy time of "papal" biographies, the *Actus Silvestri* became so popular that three hundred manuscripts of it survive.[13] The Silvester legend would grow and be amplified in the Middle Ages, and serve
later as the basis for the most famous and important of church forgeries
(the Donation of Constantine). The basic elements of it were popularized
in Jacobus de Voragine's wildly popular *Golden Legend* (c. 1260).[14]

The *Golden Legend* account of Silvester was theatrically told in church
fresco cycles—in Tivoli, in Rome's Santi Quattro Coronati, and in Giulio
Romano's Constantine Room of the Vatican.[15] But it is best seen in the
Silvester chapel of the Franciscans' Santa Croce church in Florence, brilliantly restored in the 1990s. This is Maso di Banco's masterpiece of the
1330s, filling the chapel with seven great frescoes. It gives the canonical
"history" of Pope Saint Silvester.

1. *The Leprosy.* After contracting leprosy, thought to be incurable, the
   desperate pagan Constantine turned to magicians for a cure. They
   said he must bathe in the blood of three thousand innocent babies.
   Maso's picture shows the anguished Constantine in a high carriage
   stopped by hysterical mothers shrieking in fear for their babies. The
   iconography is that of Herod on his throne commanding the slaughter
   of the Holy Innocents. But Constantine is a good pagan, and he re-
   lents out of mercy.
2. *The Dream.* Two figures appear to Constantine in a dream. He takes
   them to be gods, though they tell him to seek out Silvester, Rome's
   bishop, who is hiding from pagan persecutors on Mount Soracte. Silvester, they say, will put him in a bath more healing than any infant's
   blood.
3. *The Mountain.* Soldiers find Silvester on Mount Soracte and lead him
   down to meet Constantine. Little remains of this fresco but some
   rocky scenery and Silvester on his horse descending a mountain path.
4. *The Pictures.* When Constantine tells the bishop his story, Silvester
   shows him pictures of Peter and Paul, convincing him that he has
   seen a Christian vision.
5. *The Baptism.* After instructing Constantine in the faith, Silvester bap-
   tizes him in the sacred bath, and his leprosy is instantly cured.

6. *The Bull.* Constantine's mother, Helena, has acquired the Jewish faith in the Holy Land, and she brings twelve rabbis to convince her son that he was baptized into a false religion. The fresco shows Constantine enthroned, Helena and her rabbis on his left side, two pagan philosophers as judges on his right side, and Silvester standing before them. *The Golden Legend* gives a clever argument against Christianity to each of the first eleven rabbis, with Silvester's neat responses. The twelfth rabbi impatiently gives up the arguments and has a wild bull brought in. He then whispers a devil's name to the bull and it keels over. Maso shows Silvester resuscitating the bull with the name of Jesus.

7. *The Dragon.* This scene, one of the earliest pictures of Rome as a ruin, shows how the pagan city has declined. A dragon has slain citizens with its deadly breath. While Constantine (who will rebuild the city) looks on, Silvester descends into the pit where the dragon lurks and ties its muzzle shut. But before he can do that, two magicians, who came to see how he would cope with the monster, have come close enough to keel over from its stench. Silvester, coming back up from the pit, reanimates them. This is a complex story told with the clarity of Maso's master, Giotto. It shows Silvester before and after (going down and coming back) and the magicians before and after (dead and risen). Constantine holds the orb of rule that he is about to give over to Silvester—because, by the time of Maso, the life of Silvester has been used as the basis for a later myth, which would alter the political situation of Europe for centuries. The charming folktale had become a political weapon.

Saint Constantine

In the eighth century, a momentous addition was made to the fifth-century tale of Constantine's cure and baptism. According to the new forgery, the *Constitutum Constantini*, the emperor set up a subsidiary place in the East out of deference to the real capital of the empire, the "apostolic see" in Rome. Constantine gives ("donates") temporal rule over the West to the pope. In fact, he recognizes papal rule over all the bishops and patriarchs of the church, including "the four principal sees, Alexandria, Antioch, Jerusalem, and Constantinople."[16] He also concedes property rights "in Judea, Greece, Asia, Thrace, Africa, and Italy."[17] Constantine then takes the crown off his own head and gives it to the pope. When the pope refuses to substitute that for his sacred crown, Constantine gives him a tiara to wear when he acts as temporal ruler. Enacting his own subordination, Constantine takes the bridle of the pope's horse, performing the duty of a groom.[18] After the pope has accepted his temporal supremacy only in part, Constantine says he will withdraw to the East, because "where the supremacy of priests and the head of the Christian religion has been established by the heavenly emperor, it is not right that there an earthly emperor should have jurisdiction."[19]

The *Constitutum Constantini* was cited by pope after pope trying (often ineffectually) to exert his right to rule. As Samuel Lieu writes, "The earliest certain appeal to the *Constitutum* was made by Pope Leo XI in a letter to Michael Cerularius, the patriarch of Constantinople, in 1054; from then on it was frequently employed in papal claims to territorial possessions."[20] Even when it was ignored by rival rulers, they did not bother to question the authenticity of the document. It was too extravagant in its claims. It did not need to be challenged—yet men ignored it at their peril. Whenever it became possible for a pope to exercise his power, he had a supposed justification in the *Constitutum*. It was not a document that could stand scrutiny, as Nicholas of Cusa recognized. Even the future pope Pius II, a scholar, wrote an exposé of it before he became pope—but he never published the rebuttal. Then, in 1440, the Renaissance humanist Lorenzo Valla demolished the document in one of the most thoroughgoing acts of literary demolition ever undertaken.

The document was absurd. How could Constantine give what he did not have? How could he give the ruling of armies to a "vicar" of Jesus who renounced violence? How could he subordinate the patriarchate of Constantinople when Constantinople had not yet been founded? Valla mocks the pictures of Peter and Paul that Silvester showed Constantine—still on display in his time.[21] He has special fun with the tale of the dragon that devastated Rome until Silvester tamed it in Constantine's presence. The dragon demanded to be given virgins on the Kalends of each month. How did he know it was the Kalends (suggesting he had a calendar in his pit)? What did he do with the virgins? Eat them? "Was he content with such scant and occasional food?" Rape them? What would the offspring of a huge dragon and a tiny virgin look like? Valla gets so fed up with people peddling this nonsense that he addresses them directly: "Shut up, most imbecile of men—or should I call you most criminal?"[22]

Though Valla's work became a delight of scholars and further grounds for revolt by Luther, the official church continued to revere Constantine as a saintly son of the church. Valla destroyed the Donation myth in 1440—yet for the 1520s Raphael planned, under two popes' direction, to celebrate the myth in the largest of the papal apartments of the Vatican. Raphael died before he could complete the Constantine Room, but his leading pupil, Giulio Romano, covered the walls with the basics of the story—Constantine's vision of the cross, his victory at the Milvian battle, Silvester baptizing Constantine, and the Donation. In this last picture, Constantine kneels before Silvester in his towering throne and offers the image of Victory as a sign of rule. The religious problem of complying with earthly power is obviated if all earthly power can do is serve and support the church. Reversing Luke's tale of Jesus's temptation, the Silvester of myth says that he will comply with Roman authority if it will "kneel down before me." The myth makes Constantine nothing but a lackey of the pope (holding his horse's reins). Though the West did not formally make Constantine a saint, as the East did, it treated him as a saintly servitor of the pope.

Saint Helena

Constantine was also given a holiness by association, since his mother is a canonized saint who gave rich treasures to the church in Jerusalem and

Rome. Helena is celebrated along with her son on the feast of the Holy Rulers, May 21. In the West, her feast is celebrated on August 18, and her connections with Rome are made to boost Constantine's connections there. Her myth was elaborated in conjunction with his, as we saw in the Maso di Banco picture of her seated by Constantine to watch the debate between Silvester and twelve rabbis. The official story was that Constantius Chlorus, the father of Constantine, had first married Helena, and then divorced her to marry Theodora, daughter of the emperor Maximian. Scholars doubt that Constantius, a Caesar of the empire on the way to becoming an Augustus, could marry a lowborn woman—Helena, according to Ambrose, was a *stabularia,* what we would call something like a "waitress."[23] It was normal at the time for a man to have a *concubina* who was not of the station he held or aspired to—much as Augustine had for years a mistress who gave him his beloved son, Adeodatus.[24] No one knows what happened to Helena until Constantine came to power at his father's death, but presumably he had remained close to her, since he elevated her to the station of Augusta and made her the dispenser of many benefactions, especially in the Holy Land.

Eusebius tells of her journey to Jerusalem (VC 3.42–43). As the leading patriarch in Palestine, he probably conducted her on what Averil Cameron and Stuart Hall say was more an imperial progress than a pilgrimage.[25] He relates how she consecrated and beautified churches in Bethlehem and the Mount of Olives. But in this, the only firsthand account we have of her time in the Holy Land, he never mentions what later became her most famous act, the finding of the true cross. There is good reason for this. What purported to be the cross had already been honored in Jerusalem before she arrived there, and the myth of her "invention" (finding) did not start to spread until fifty years after her death.[26] The earliest famous account of it came seventy years after that death in the eulogy of Theodosius by Ambrose.[27]

Because of her trip to the Holy Land, she was connected with the spread and intense popularity of relics from the cross, a connection often marked in devotional sites—for instance, in Rome's suburban church of Santa Croce in Gerusalemme, near her mausoleum, where she was buried in the porphyry sarcophagus now in the Vatican Museum.[28] The Franciscans, because their founder bore its stigmata, were special devotees of the Holy Cross. Remember that it was in Santa Croce, their church in Florence, that Maso di Banco elaborated in bright frescoes the whole story of Silvester. The same church had a cognate fresco series telling of Helena's invention of the cross, painted by Agnolo Gaddi. This story was popular on the walls of churches, especially in Franciscan churches. Cenni di Francesco di ser Cenni painted it in Volterra, Masolino in Empoli, and Piero della Francesca (brilliantly) in Arezzo.[29]

The devotion to the cross led to two different feasts in the sacred calendar—the feast of the Invention of the Cross (May 3) and of the Exaltation of the Cross (September 14). Wherever the cross was honored, Helena was celebrated, and Constantine was remembered. Reclaiming Constantine was a campaign with many ancillary sorties. In the Helena myth, what Lieu calls "the fertile late antique imagination" shows what it could do "to bring Constantine and his family into greater prominence in the providential history of Christianity."[30] In the later competition of the church with Charlemagne, in the divisions of the Avignon exile, and in all clashes with the Eastern church, great advantage went to the side that could claim Constantine. As we saw in the last chapter, some tried to resist Constantine's state by ascetical or perfectionist withdrawal. But for many others in the church, owning Constantine (or pretending to) was seen as the key to power.

Older critics of Constantine as a "caesaropapist" saw him using power to take over or corrupt a poor victim church. In fact, the church grew stronger under Constantine by using *him,* getting him (at least sometimes) to side with "orthodoxy," punish "heretics," strengthen and centralize the network of bishops, build churches, and subsidize the services inside them. It used to be said that the ancient Greeks took their Roman captors captive.[31] In the same way, the church made Constantine an inadvertent captive. But the church also needed an independent source of authority. For that, it had to capture Peter.

NOTES

1. Angela Donati, *Pietro e Paolo: La storia, il culto, la memoria nei primi secoli* (Electa, 2000), 47, 125, 126, 127, 130.

2. See, for instance, the commentary on the *Life of Constantine* by its editors, Averil Cameron and Stuart Hall (VC 35–38, 73, 84, 192–93); Anna Wilson, "Biographical Models: The Constantinian Period and Beyond," in Samuel N. C. Lieu and Dominic Montserrat, *Constantine: History, Historiography, and Legend* (Routledge, 1998), 113–21; and T. D. Barnes, *Constantine and Eusebius* (Harvard University Press, 1981), 271.

3. Barnes, op. cit., 73–74. Barnes supposes that Constantine had met Lactantius, "the Christian Cicero," during his residence in the court of Diocletian—he later made Lactantius the tutor to his son Crispus.

4. The Western church adopted a Latin variant, *In hoc signo vinces,* "With this sign you will win."

5. The other source for this dream, Lactantius's *Deaths of the Persecutors* 44.5–6, does not mention the vision in the sun, and it gives a different shape to the *labarum*—what is called a *staurogram* (upright cross with a rho rounding at the top), not a Christogram (sideways cross athwart the rho). Cf. J. L. Creed, *De Mortibus Persecutorum* (Oxford University Press, 1984), 63, 119.

6. Eusebius had already used the parallel between the Red Sea and the battle at the Milvian Bridge in his *Ecclesiastical History* (9.9.4–6). This may have been the seed for all the later comparisons with Moses.

7. Barnes, op. cit., 271. Anna Wilson (op. cit., 119–21) agrees that Constantine is compared to Moses precisely as a lawgiver.

8. Peter Brown, *Augustine of Hippo,* new edition (University of California Press, 2000), 361–64.

9. George E. Demacopoulos, *The Invention of Peter: Apostolic Discourse and Papal Authority in Late Antiquity* (University of Pennsylvania Press, 2013), 108–14.

10. Ibid., 107.

11. Samuel Lieu, "From History to Legend and Legend to History: The Medieval and Byzantine Transformation of Constantine's Vita," in Lieu and Montserrat, op. cit., 144–45.

12. Ibid., 27.

13. Jan Willem Drijvers, *Helena Augusta* (E. J. Brill, 1992), 36–37.

14. Jacobus de Voragine, *The Golden Legend,* translated by William Granger Ryan (Princeton University Press, 1993), vol. 1, 62–78.

15. Cristina Acidini Luchinat and Enrica Neri Lusanna, *Maso di Banco: La cappella di San Silvestro* (Electa, 1998), 19–20.

16. Text and translation of the *Constitutum* in Christopher B. Coleman, *The Treatise of Lorenzo Valla on the Donation of Constantine* (Russell & Russell, 1950), 12–13.

17. Ibid.

18. Ibid., 14–17.

19. Ibid., 16–17.

20. Samuel N. Lieu, "Constantine in Legendary Literature," in Noel Lenski, *The Cambridge Companion to the Age of Constantine* (Cambridge University Press, 2006), 303.

21. Coleman, op. cit., 142–43.

22. Ibid., 146–47: *"Silete, imperitissimi homines, ne dicam sceleratissimos."*

23. Ambrose, *On the Death of Theodosius* 42.

24. Bill Leadbetter, "The Illegitimacy of Constantine," in Lieu and Montserrat, op. cit., 77–80.

25. Cameron and Hall, op. cit., 292.

26. Drijvers, op. cit., 81–82. Lieu, "Constantine in Legendary Literature," 304.

27. Ambrose, loc. cit., 43–51.

28. Mark J. Johnson, "Architecture of Empire," in Lenski, op. cit., 285.

29. Bruce Cole, *Piero della Francesca: Tradition and Innovation in Renaissance Art* (HarperCollins, 1991), 90. Ronald Lightbown, *Piero della Francesca* (Abbeville Press, 1992), 123.

30. Lieu, "Constantine in Legendary Literature," 305.

31. Horace, *Epistles* 2.1.156: *"Graecia capta ferum victorem cepit."* "Captive Greece captured its rough conqueror."

EIGHT

Church with State

The fake Donation of Constantine, written in the eighth century, re-members enough of the era it was misrepresenting to have Constan-tine give Rome's bishop supremacy over the patriarchates of "Alexandria, Antioch, Jerusalem, and Constantinople." By then it was customary to treat the polycentric church as a Pentarchy, the rule of five—those named in the Donation, plus Rome. The imbalance is obvious—all the centers of church power and influence were in the East. Rome was the outlier. For the first four centuries, that was not where the action was. The great coun-cils, the main creeds, the highest debates (on the Trinity, the Incarnation, on where decisions were being made and who would make them) took place in the part of the world where Jesus had been born, lived, and died—and where Constantine had decided to set up his hub of the empire.

What claim did Rome have for getting in on the action? Its main cre-dential was "apostolicity." Other cities claimed that they were where an apostle worked or died, but only Rome had a double apostolicity. *Both* Peter and Paul died there. So far as we know, that was all they did there. The city figures in early church history only because Paul wrote to the brothers and sisters that he was on his way to Rome. There was already a thriving community of believers in Rome—he greets twenty-five people by name before his first arrival there. Peter is not among them, nor will there be any other bishop by the end of the first century, for Ignatius of Antioch to appeal to, as he did to all the other cities he addressed.

This doubleness of apostolic deaths was offered as the city's creden-tial. Playing one card would not have worked. But two were trumps. All the earliest references to Rome's honor paired the two men acclaimed in what Victor Saxer calls an "inseparable singleness of cult."[1] Peter is not singled out or given primacy in the earliest references to the city's apostolicity—in the letter of Rome to Corinth (attributed to a certain Clement), in the letter of Ignatius to Rome, in Irenaeus's treatise on heresies.[2] In early inscriptions (for instance, in the catacomb under San Sebastiano), they are invoked as a team, often as Peter-and-Paul, but sometimes as Paul-and-Peter.[3] It is clearly not thought that prayers would be as powerful if one were separated from the other in these invocations. Even when Irenaeus accepted the idea of a succession of bishops in Rome, he said it was from both Peter and Paul (S 2.127). It was a tradition that could be remembered (faintly) into the ninth century, when Pope John VIII called himself the "vicar of Peter and Paul."[4] The two were not even separated by giving them separate feasts in the liturgical calendar. June 29 is the feast day of both Peter and Paul.

I was deeply impressed by the singleness of the initial cult in Rome when I visited the scholarly exhibit created, at the Palazzo della Cancelleria, for the Jubilee Year 2000.[5] That displayed all the earliest representations of Peter and Paul—in wall paintings, figurines, clay vessels, plaques, and prayer tokens. The two men are shown not only side by side but embracing—in a fresco, a stone relief, or an ivory panel.[6] When the two are not simply shown in conjunction or embracing, their different roles are represented in the *traditio legis* convention, in which a seated ruler hands a law document to an official meant to carry it out. In this case, the seated Christ is shown handing the Law (a scroll) to Peter. But Paul is not excluded. He stands on the favored right hand of Jesus.[7] The underlying message is made clear in an apse of the Mausoleum of Santa Constanza, which shows the two on either side of Jesus as shepherds, each with equal flocks of sheep. This reflects the traditional division of labor by which Peter ministers to the Jewish Christians and Paul to the Gentile Christians.

Remember that most artwork in the earliest days was of Old Testament subjects. Thus, when Peter began to be depicted separately, it was often as a new Moses, bringing the Law into the Christian era. He works the Mosaic miracle of striking water from a rock.[8] This explains the *tradi-*

tio legis bestowal of the scripture on Peter, while—on Christ's favored right side—Paul strikes the orator's pose, taking the Law to new lands and people. This is clear on a fourth-century reliquary, in which Jesus, while handing the scroll to Peter, turns away from him to his right (Paul's side), and Jesus himself strikes the orator's pose with raised hand—Paul looks up at the hand, not down toward the scroll.[9] Thus, when the two men are shown with separate tasks, it is because they are addressing separate audiences, not because of any difference of authority or closeness to Jesus (both are equidistant).

Thus Rome's claim to importance lay in the conjoined authority of Peter and Paul. Pope Damasus (366–84) in one of his poems referred to the presence of the two saints' relics at San Sebastiano as attesting "the powerful names of Peter *paired with* Paul" (*nomina . . . Petri pariter Paulique*).[10] The idea of a primacy for Peter was first tried by Pope Stephen (254–57), and he was mocked for it by Bishop Firmilion of the Cappadocian Caesarea, who writes that Stephen is "defaming the blessed apostles Peter and Paul" when he "proclaims that he occupies by succession the chair of Peter" (S 2.270–71). It was not only the Eastern church that repudiated a special claim by Rome. Bishop Cyprian of Carthage, who had written that Peter was made the head of the church, later said that Peter was just a symbol for any and all bishops—a point he spelled out in defying Stephen's ruling on the treatment of *lapsi*. At that point he called Pope Stephen's claim to sole Petrine power "arrogant or extraneous or self-contradictory, [a thing] which he wrote without due instruction and caution" (S 2.267).

The novelty of the claim to sole power in Peter seemed absurd on the face of it—that Jesus would rest the whole future of his disciples on one man, isolated from the other disciples. (Jesus, remember, had forbidden his followers to have any preeminence among them—Mk 9.33–37, Lk 14.7–11). Augustine and others wrote that a Petrine lordship would displace Jesus himself as the head of the mystical body, the rock on which the church is founded. That is why the early view of Matthew 16.18, "On this stone I will raise my gathering," was that Peter stood for the community—a reading confirmed by the fact that the ancillary promise "Whatever you ban on earth" is later in Matthew (18.18) said of the whole community: "Whatever you [plural] may ban on earth it will have been banned in heaven."

Vice Petri

Yet by the third century, bishops of Rome claimed to stand *vice Petri,* "in the place of" Peter, as the ruler over the whole church, East and West. *Vicis,* "stand-in," can mean successor or substitute. It is used of things changing about (as in *vicissitudo*) or of interchanging places (as in *vice versa*) or as agent (as in *vicegerens*). *Vicarius* comes from this word, and bishops of Rome claimed to be vicars of Peter, his "stand-ins." The ablative *vice* means "in the place of" (Peter, or whomever). But even if Jesus had done something so odd as to commit the destiny of the whole Christian church to one man, why would that power be continued without interruption in someone else pretending to have all the first man's supposed powers? Who would succeed Peter? Not some bishop of Rome, since there were no bishops in Rome.

Succession in the political world of monarchs was most often asserted by family descent—and, sure enough, Peter, like early bishops of Rome (which he was not), was married; and some even had sons who inherited. As late as the sixth century, Silverius (536–37) became pope after his father, Hormisdas (514–23), held that office. A more famous pope, Gregory the Great (590–604), was the great-great-grandson of Pope Felix III (483–92). But most of the time popes were elected, under shifting rules and with contested outcomes, some winning by bribes, some being muscled in by secular families or rulers. One Ostrogothic king put Silverius in office, and another deposed him.[11]

Originally, succession was not only uncertain in method but sketchily recorded. The Roman church, not having a bishop until the second century, could not have recorded a line of bishops before that, and was hazily sketched in after that. The list was confected in retrospect, as Eamon Duffy says, "based on scraps of half-remembered information, or simply invented."[12] The aim was not history but symbol:

> The earliest list to survive for Rome is the one supplied by Irenaeus, and in it this symbolic function is very clearly at work. Irenaeus underlines the parallels between Apostles and bishops by naming precisely twelve bishops of Rome between Peter and the current incumbent, Eleutherius. The sixth of these bishops is named Sixtus. It all seems suspiciously tidy.[13]

In short, where records were lacking, they were simply made up.

Even if we could suppose that Jesus meant to invest one bishopric with power over all others, why would he have chosen the distant Western outpost, away from all the theological energy and dense prose-lytizing of Eastern centers—Jerusalem, Caesarea, Antioch, Ephesus, Nicomedia, and other places? We know nothing of Peter's and Paul's activities in Rome (other than their dying), but we know how both men acted in Jerusalem and Antioch, and of their influence in the church at Corinth. If (*per impossibile*) we are to imagine Peter as a bishop anywhere, it would have to be in Antioch, where he quarreled with Paul and won by being more in accord with Jerusalem practice (Gal 2.11–14). Rome was hors de combat for over a century.

If Stephen was the first to claim a supremacy based on Matthew 16.18, he resembled later popes in a way traced by George Demacopoulos in *The Invention of Peter*. He notes that popes tend to make their most extreme claims not from positions of strength but from weakness.[14] They assert vast authority when they are least able to make the assertion stick. Having little to lose, they make a kind of compensatory gesture. In most cases, their assertion is not given much weight at the time, but each maximum claim is later remembered as part of an accumulating tradition of them, and can give grounds for selective later use. That is the story of the Silvester myth (confected in the sixth century) and the Donation of

Constantine (formulated in the eighth century), which were seriously invoked from the tenth century on. The Symmachan forgeries and False Decretals fit this pattern. Even as late as the nineteenth century, Pius IX at his weakest—stripped of his temporal holdings and challenged by Catholics like Lord Acton and John Henry Newman—made his most defiant declarations of papal preeminence and infallibility.

Demacopoulos notes that even popes with reputations as strong rulers calibrated their assertions of Petrine identity, omitting or tempering it when they had some basis for negotiation with rulers in the West or patriarchs in the East, resorting to it when they made statements for principle's sake, though no practical outcome was likely.[15] These prudent men had observed or experienced that claiming a monopoly of power in the church is an occasion for opponents to protect their own claims to be the churches of Peter. Remember that it was Stephen's assertion of sole power that made Cyprian agree with Eastern bishops, even though he had given Rome a special privilege before Stephen overstated his case.

The claim of a universal church of Peter, ruled from Rome, was the occasion for and the recurrent provoker of Eastern separatism from the West. When Pope Felix III said that he had a right to settle the Acacian schism over Monophysitism in the Eastern patriarchies, he was rejected. When Felix's adviser Gelasius succeeded him in the see of Rome, he wrote a famous letter (to the emperor Anastasius) justifying the earlier interference in the affairs of Constantinople. (This letter will come up again.) The flamboyant gesture of Gelasius was so futile, and came from so smart a pontiff, that Demacopoulos believes the pope knew it would not fly in the East, whither it was purportedly addressed. He thinks it was meant to shore up the pope's weaknesses in the West:

> It is difficult to believe that Gelasius ever expected this letter to heal the Acacian schism or to effect imperial subordination to the papacy. Instead, it is conceivable that Gelasius' Petrine posturing in the *Ad Anastasium* allowed the pontiff to assert for his domestic audience that foreign bishops and the emperor himself (Gelasius' "son") took their theological cues

from the chair of St. Peter. Whatever role the *Ad Anastasium* may have played in Gelasius' Eastern diplomacy, it allowed the pontiff to conjure an illusion of international respect that no other domestic authority (lay or ecclesiastic) could equal. This was possible in part because Gelasius' domestic audience could not possibly have understood how little attention foreign leaders (both lay and ecclesiastic) paid to Gelasius' Petrine bluster.[16]

Where popes had reason to hope for good relations with other bishops, they learned to scale back their pretensions. Thus Gregory I (590–604), who huffed and puffed when the bishop of Constantinople called himself "the ecumenical patriarch," kept the reins loose where he was showing greater successes—as in England. He had dispatched to that pagan land a monk from the monastery he had founded—Augustine, the future archbishop of Canterbury. When Augustine worried about keeping his outpost in line with Rome, Gregory told him to rely on his own discretion and the conditions of the country: "Gregory urged him to adopt whatever customs seemed likely to be helpful to the infant church in England, regardless of their source."[17] It comes as no surprise that the evangelization of England was one of the truly great achievements of Gregory. Even Gibbon paid this tribute:

> The conquest of Britain reflects less glory on the name of Caesar than on that of Gregory the First. Instead of six legions, forty monks were embarked for that distant island, and the pontiff lamented the austere duties which forbade him to partake the perils of their spiritual warfare. In less than two years he could announce to the archbishop of Alexandria that they had baptized the king of Kent with ten thousand of his Anglo-Saxons, and that the Roman missionaries, like those of the primitive church, were armed only with spiritual and supernatural powers (DF XLV, 5.38).

Later popes were not as wise as Gregory—they quashed the successful efforts of Jesuits to spread the Gospel in Asian and South American cultures by framing their message in terms understandable in a foreign culture. This resembles the determination to keep all ministry of the sacraments in Latin. In fact, the supremacy claims of the pope resembled in many ways the church's self-limiting adherence to Latin. Both were advanced under a claim that they united when in fact they divided. When other bishops argued that Peter was a symbol of the whole church, not of one man's office, they were declared heretical or excommunicate. This drove off Eastern churches, as it would later drive off Protestant ones. Owning Peter meant, for Rome, losing much of the world.

Rome of the popes did not understand the Gospel passage where the disciples of Jesus, sent out for their own first missionary effort, came back bragging of their exclusive power. One of them made a claim for them all: "John said, 'Leader [*epistata*], we found a man casting out devils in your name, and we stopped him, since he was not with us.' Jesus said, 'Why did you stop him? You see, whoever is not against us is with us'" (Lk 9.49–50). Gregory, at least part of the time, understood that saying: "He told his friend Leander of Seville, who had enquired about the correct method of baptizing, that 'Where there is one faith, a diversity of usage does no harm to the church.'"[18]

Vice Christi

The title Vicar of Peter was meant to establish primacy over other bishops around the world. The decisive break from being just one of the two apostles who died in Rome was a long time in formation, but placement of him above all other bishops of the West and patriarchs of the East came when the papacy was set apart with its own term. The pope, like many bishops, had been called "papa." But his special form of fatherhood did not come until it was named, in the eleventh century:

> The new status of the apostolic see was reflected in the emergence of a new term, apparently first used by Clement II in 1047: papacy, *papatus*. Constructed on the analogy of bishopric, *episcopatus*, it expressed the idea that there existed a rank or order higher than that of bishop.[19]

Colin Morris argues that, for all the early claims of the bishop of Rome, the concept of the pope as a universal ruler—with a *plenitudo potestatis,* a full panoply of powers—was "a special feature of the centuries after 1050."[20]

Slumbering claims like the Donation of Constantine and the False Decretals were revived and put in systematic order:

> Leo IX [1049–54] drew at length on the Donation of Constantine when he expounded the nature of Roman authority to Michael Cerularius, patriarch of Constantinople; and Hildebrand asked Peter Damian before 1059 to compile a collection of texts on the prerogatives of the apostolic see. The irony was that most of the material which was being used, although of this they had no conception, was the product of ninth-century forgery, and they were thus reconstructing, not the apostolic age, but a church order designed for polemical purposes by the imagination of a Carolingian author.[21]

This was the time when popes launched crusades in the Holy Land and Spain, backed inquisitions, empowered mendicant orders, anointed kings, put whole countries under interdict, and assumed many initiatives never thought of before. But institutional power did not satisfy the popes who wanted a more intimate access to the consciences of all believers, prescribing all belief and behavior. Christ's own access to the believer was more important than Peter's sway over bishops. So the pope took on a new title: he was *vice Christi,* the Vicar of Christ:

> The statement that the pope acts in place of Christ (*vice Christi*) appears in Peter Damian and in a few writers of the early twelfth century, but the first application to the pope of the precise title "Vicar of Christ" seems to be early in the twelfth century in Honorius's *Jewel of the Soul* (*De Gemma Animae*), which makes its special character quite clear: "The pope is the Vicar of Christ and all the bishops are vicars of the apostles." Its appearance about 1150 in the *De Consideratione* of Bernard of Clairvaux was particularly significant because of the huge influence of the work. The first pope to use the title was Eugenius III in 1153, and thereafter its acceptance was widespread.[22]

Most of us modern Catholics have grown up taking for granted the title Vicar of Christ for all popes. It is enough to make us forget the stand-ins Jesus described as being his real representatives. Describing the final judgment of men, Jesus said:

> The Ruler will tell those on his right hand, "Approach, you blessed of my Father, take possession of the reign prepared for you from the cosmic beginnings. For I hungered and you gave me food. I thirsted and you gave me drink. I was an alien and you welcomed me, I was naked and you clothed me, I was ill and you tended me, I was in prison and you came to me." Then the vindicated will respond to him, "Lord, when did we see you hungry and we fed you, or thirsty and we gave you drink? When did we see you as an alien, and we welcomed you, or naked, and we clothed you? When did we see you ailing and we tended you, or in prison and we went to you?" And the Ruler will reply, saying: "In truth I tell you, whenever you did these things to the lowliest of my brothers, you were doing it to me" (Mt 25.34–40).

No powerful person is *vice Christi*. But all the poor are *vicibus Christi*, "in the places of Christ."

NOTES

1. Victor Saxer, "Il culto degli apostolico Pietro e Paolo," in Angela Donati, *Pietro e Paolo: La storia, il culto, la memoria nei primi secoli* (Electa, 2000), 73: "*il loro culto era stato considerate un tutt'uno indivisibile.*"
2. 1 Clement 5.4–7; Ignatius of Antioch, *Letter to the Romans* 4.3; Irenaeus, *Against the Heresies* 3.2 (S 2.127).
3. For examples of both orders, see Donati, op. cit., 67.
4. John W. O'Malley, S.J., *A History of the Popes: From Peter to the Present* (Sheed & Ward, 2009), xv.
5. The lavishly illustrated catalog of the exhibit, with scholarly essays, is Donati, op. cit.
6. Ibid., 52, 53, 134. This iconography was remembered as late as the twelfth century in a mosaic of their embrace at Monreale, Sicily.
7. Ibid., 50, 51, 52, 132, 148, 149, 155.
8. Ibid., 47, 125, 126, 127, 130.
9. Ibid., 155.

10. Ibid., 78.

11. J. N. D. Kelly, *The Oxford Dictionary of Popes* (Oxford University Press, 1986), 59–60.

12. Eamon Duffy, *Saints and Sinners: A History of the Popes,* third edition (Yale University Press, 2006), 26.

13. Ibid., 14.

14. George E. Demacopoulos, *The Invention of Peter: Apostolic Discourse and Papal Authority in Late Antiquity* (University of Pennsylvania Press, 2013).

15. Ibid., chapter 2 ("The Many Faces of Leo's Power") and chapter 5 ("Restraint and Desperation in Gregory the Great's Petrine Appeal").

16. Ibid., 101.

17. Duffy, op. cit., 70.

18. Ibid.

19. Colin Morris, *The Papal Monarchy: The Western Church from 1050 to 1250* (Oxford University Press, 1989), 107.

20. Ibid., 1–6, 205–10.

21. Ibid., 107–8.

22. Ibid., 206. There was an earlier reference to the pope as the Vicar of Christ at a Roman synod of 495, but the pope of the time, Gelasius I, did not use the title himself. See Kelly, op. cit., 48.

NINE

Church as State

WHO OWNS THE SWORD?

If the church is not resisting the state, or truckling to it, or dominating it, how should a right relationship with it be described? Should the norm be cooperation? If the state is doing something immoral, doesn't cooperation become a complicity in sin? Even to cooperate, you need two distinct operatives. How to keep the two within their own spheres? Is the distinction that of the material to the spiritual, of the temporal to the eternal, of the secular to the sacred? Pope Gelasius tried to make such a distinction in 494, in the letter to the Eastern emperor mentioned in the last chapter. This missive, as I noted, had no real effect at the time; but it was put to many uses later. It seemed to make a neat separation between what the pope calls *auctoritas* (of the church) and *potestas* (of the state). "There are, of course, two things (*duo quippe sunt*) that mainly rule the world: sacred authority of the priest, and power of the prince."

This distinction (sacred/secular), like cognate ones (spiritual/material, eternal/temporal), has an implicit hierarchy in it. One of the components is higher than the other, and so should trump it in any conflict. The state must render earthly justice, but it must do so morally; and the church is the arbiter of morality. That is made clear at other points in the letter. Gelasius tells Anastasius that the pope can determine the fate of the emperor's soul:

I ask that you listen to me pleading in this life rather than (may it never happen) hear me accusing you at the last judgment (par. 4).

If the emperor does not follow the pope's direction on excommunicating Acacians, he returns to the evil days when the state created martyrs to the truth:

So, you can see, Emperor, that I desire peace for the church, and I will hold to that peace even if my blood must be shed in order to secure it (par. 6).

The distinction in the pope's letter is hierarchical, of one sphere existing above the other. The power to rule in the lower sphere is only valid so long as it accepts direction from above.

John Courtney Murray, in the twentieth century, would try to make "the Gelasian doctrine" a defense of American-style religious pluralism; but Gelasius had nothing like that in mind. He was not defending a plurality of churches; just the opposite. He was trying to get the emperor to quash one form of religion, Monophysitism, in favor of the superior (and solely legitimate) orthodoxy. In fact, all the talk of two spheres, sacred and secular, led to one of the more weird distortions of scripture, the claim that church-state relations were properly thought of as the "two swords" of Luke 22.36–38, where Jesus mysteriously tells his followers they should sell their cloak to buy a sword, since troubles are coming. But when they say, "See, here are two swords," he cuts them off with, "Enough of that!" (*Hikanon*).

Jesus was clearly not advocating violence. When Peter uses one of the swords to cut off an ear of the high priest's servant, Jesus restores the ear, showing he had come to heal wounds, not inflict them. He tells Peter (Mt 26.52), "Put the sword back in its holder. Don't you know (*gar*) those taking to the sword are killed at the sword (*en makhairei*)?" The sword he told them to buy is clearly a symbol—but of what? There have been many interpretations of this, some highly fanciful. Ambrose in the fourth century said the two swords of a Christian are his two intellectual defenses—the Old Testament and the New Testament. This and all other interpretations make Jesus himself talk of two swords. Actually, he just mentioned one (to say, later, it must be forsworn). The disciples alone mention two, and they are acting foolishly (as usual).

But as the papacy grew in power during the twelfth century, the two

swords of Luke's Gospel became the embodiment of Gelasius's two powers. Jesus had told Peter to give up the use of the sword, by which men
just perish. But now his words, "Put the sword back in its holder (literally
its place, *topos*)," became an exhortation to keep it in its scabbard (*vagina*)
for use whenever "Peter" needs it. Bernard of Clairvaux, whose *De Consideratione* (*Pondering the Papacy*) had promoted the pope as the Vicar of
Christ, with a *plenitudo potestatis,* also used the Luke passage on two
swords to show the pope's right to use both swords, one directly, the other
indirectly:

> Both swords therefore belong to the church, the spiritual and the material
> sword—the one is to be used *for* the church, the other *by* the church. This
> latter sword is in the priest's hand, the former in a military hand, but only
> when directed by the priest who guides the emperors' hand.[1]

Bernard of Clairvaux gave this influential advice in a book-length letter to Pope Eugene III. He had feared that the pope—a monk from his
own monastery of Clairvaux—would not be hard enough for the demanding office. The *De Consideratione* is a powerful example of the "mir-
ror of princes" instruction, describing the high responsibilities of a ruler.
Bernard told his pope-pupil to be ruthless in purging his Curia of corrupt
and incompetent climbers; to assert his rights as "the controller of events
without an equal" (3.13). Bernard was a backer of the Second Crusade, not
only to reclaim the East but to impose order on the forces of the West.

Bernard preached the crusade with torrential eloquence—and sent it
off to disaster. His protégé increased the power of his office by giving indulgences to all those who took the sword (and perished by it). The
papacy took flight with Bernard's wind under its wings. Innocent III
would realize all the hopes Bernard had for a world ruler—his Fourth
Crusade would be even more calamitous than Eugene's, veering off to
conquer a Christian capital (Constantinople) and making the separation
of East and West even more unhealable. It visited similar ravages on the

West with his indulgence-fueled crusade against Albigensians in France. During all this time, the two-swords reading of Luke would become more entrenched, a divine mandate straight out of the Bible. In its most far-reaching formulation, that of Boniface VIII (1294–1303), other parts of the New Testament were read in the light of Luke's two-swords theory of papal power.

In *Unam Sanctam* (1302), Boniface says the church's power to rule the world was prophesied in the Ark of Noah—one boat, with one pilot, and outside it "everything on earth was obliterated" (*omnia . . . deleta,* par. 1). In the same way, there is one church with one pope, and "every human creature as a condition of being saved (*de necessitate salutis*) must be subject to the Roman Pontiff" (par. 7). Another scriptural warrant for papal rule was the "seamless garment" of Christ for which soldiers gambled at Golgotha. This could not be cut into pieces; it had to be taken whole—and the pope is the one who dons this seamless garment (par. 2). This parallel is tricky—the pope is figured in the soldier who is killing Jesus as he gambles for the cloak as booty.[2]

But Boniface's main argument from scripture comes from Luke's two swords. One of these belongs to Peter, since Jesus tells him to put it back in its "place" (presumably on Peter's body). The other sword is not put in Peter's scabbard—in fact, the Gospel tells us nothing more about it. Boniface says the other sword must be outside Peter's scabbard—but not for just anyone to use any way. It must belong to someone else, but not for use against Peter—for use, rather, by someone other than Peter on Peter's behalf, directed by Peter, reinforcing Peter's own (scabbarded) spiritual sword. Here he repeats, almost verbatim, Bernard's distinction:

> [Peter's sword in the scabbard] belongs to the church, a spiritual sword like the material one—but the latter is to be used *for* the church, while the former *by* the church, this one held by the priest, the other by kings and their troops, but used only by the direction and permission of the priest (par. 4).

Those who deplore "caesaropapism" as Constantine taking over the church miss the real union that was proclaimed by the popes of the high Middle Ages, who took over the state, claiming to direct its "sword" on crusades, inquisitions, interdictions, in the christening and excommunicating of kings. It would not be long till the church absorbed this indirect control of nations into its own "papal states," with all the physical swords now deployed by the pope's armies, and prisons, and spies, and torturers.

Everyone who used the two-swords theory of power ignored what Jesus went on to say while he was being arrested: "All who take to the sword are killed at (*en*) the sword" (Mt 26.52). Boniface was all too ready to take up the sword. In fact, a favorite scripture text of his, especially when calling people to join a crusade, was Jeremiah 48.10: "A curse on him who withholds his sword from bloodshed."

The sword that Boniface praises for its power is a debilitating thing. As if to fulfill this teaching, King Philip IV of France, at whom *Unam Sanctam* was aimed, sent his forces to capture Boniface at his family estate in Anagni and imprisoned him in Rome, where he was "a broken man, roaming round his apartments crying out in rage and humiliation."[3] He died a month later, powerless, hated, and reviled. Dante plunges him upside down in the "hell-pockets" (Malebolge) of *Inferno* 19.22ff., where his protruding legs semaphore his fate: "Above, I stuffed my pockets; here, I am stuffed."[4]

One has to wonder how the church could have spent centuries wielding the sword of state yet pretending to follow the Jesus of the Gospels, who expressly said that his reign was not to be served with troops. Pilate put the question directly:

> Pilate came back into his headquarters and called in Jesus, and asked him, "Are you the king of the Jews?"
> Jesus answered, "Do you ask this on your own, or did others tell you this about me?"

Pilate answered, "Can you think me a Jew? It is your own people and their archpriests who have given you over to me. What did you do to them?"

Jesus answered: "My reign is not of this temporal order. If my reign were of this temporal order, my supporters (*hyperetai*) would be fighting for me not to be handed over to the Jews. But my reign is not here."

Pilate asked him, "Does that mean (*oukoun*) you are a king?"

Jesus answered, "You use the word king of me; but I was born for one thing, and for it came into this order, to be a witness for truth. All who side with truth listen to my voice."

Pilate says to him, "Truth, what is that?" (Jn 18.33–38).

The Gospels could not have made it clearer that Jesus desired no earthly kingdom. He abjured the sword. He did not ask his followers to fight for him (though many would proclaim they were doing that in later ages). He said that people should turn the other cheek, that all who take up the sword rightly fall by the sword. When Pilate put "King of the Jews" on the cross, it was a derisive term. He was doing what the soldiers did when they crowned Jesus and clothed him in a royal garment. Scourging him was a regular part of the punishment of those to be crucified; but they improvised the mock coronation to show how ludicrous was any kingdom of his. Those who later created Christian kingdoms, papal or otherwise, were joining the Roman soldiers in their grotesquery. They were saying, inadvertently, that Jesus needed armed supporters. They were crying, with the Crusaders, "God wills it," when Jesus had expressly said that was not what he wanted or needed. To worship Jesus in this temporal order is to mock him, along with the soldiers who killed him.

NOTES

1. Bernard of Clairvaux, *De Consideratione* 4.7. Cf. Elizabeth T. Kennan, editor, *The Works of Bernard of Clairvaux* (Cistercian Publications, 1976), vol. 1, 118. Bernard reassured Eugenius III, after the defeat of the Second Crusade, that he still owned the swords (Letter 256, in Kennan, 202).
2. Another unfortunate use of scripture to endorse papal authority is Bernard's claim, in *De Consideratione* (2.16), that Peter's role is prefigured when he walks

on water to get to Jesus, leaving other disciples (in the comparison, other bishops and rulers) behind. Bernard does note that Peter is foolishly trusting his own power, which fails him. He sinks (Mt 14.30)—hardly an endorsement of Peter's power.

3. Eamon Duffy, *Saints and Sinners: A History of the Popes,* third edition (Yale University Press, 2006), 162.

4. Dante, *Inferno* 19.72: *"Che su l'avere e qui mi misi in borsa,"* glossed by Charles Singleton: "the 'hole' in which the sinner is thrust is his 'purse.'"

TEN

Churches and States

WHO OWNS THE POPE?

I n the eighteenth century, republican revolutions in France and the
United States began the slow dismantling of inherited monarchies. No
monarch felt more threatened by this eruption than the papal one. Popes
would still be fighting the French Revolution into the twentieth century,
and they had little better to say for the American system, despite the fact
that Catholics in America were fairly prosperous (and sent heavy donations to "Peter's pence" in Rome). Leo XIII (1878–1903), who is still praised
for his "liberal" encyclical on the working class, *Rerum Novarum* (1891),
issued a number of warnings against any government that did not recognize Catholicism as its one official church.

In a series of encyclicals Leo denounced the derivation of authority
from the people (*Diuturnum Illud*, 1881), governments that tolerated Free-
masonry (*Humanum Genus*, 1884), religious pluralism (*Immortale Dei*,
1885), and freedom of the press (*Libertas Praestantissimum*, 1888). All these
documents were at least obliquely critical of American democracy, with
its separation of church from state; but to resolve any doubts about the
pope's attitude, he used two letters to make a direct attack on "Americanism," which he defined as extremism in the cause of liberty (*Longin-
qua Oceani*, 1895, and *Testem Benevolentiae*, 1899). These were signs that, in
J. N. D. Kelly's words, "towards the close of [Leo's] reign, his attitudes
hardened perceptibly," with stricter censorship, a new Index, and a condemnation of Christian Democracy in Italy (*Graves de Communi Re*, 1901).[1]

This barrage of encyclicals, an outright war against religious pluralism, was hard to ignore, since encyclicals had become the papacy's
weapon of choice after it was deprived of its temporal realm. In earlier
times, serious papal edicts took the form of bulls (named for the *bulla*, the

government seal attached to them). Boniface VIII's *Unam Sanctam* was a bull. So was Pius V's *Regnans in Excelsis* (1570), excommunicating Elizabeth I and freeing her subjects of any duty to her. (Protestant iconography showed the queen treading down a bull—the animal.) But legislative bulls looked ridiculous after the pope's external powers to command were attenuated. Pius IX, following the pattern of papal overreach when the Vatican is vulnerable, had got the Vatican Council to declare him infallible. But John Henry Newman saw this as a sign of weakness, not strength, invoking powers too sweeping to be usable: "There are gifts too large and too fearful to be handled freely."[2] And, sure enough, the technical power (*ex cathedra*) to define infallibly has been used only once, on a noncontroversial subject—Pius XII's *Munificentissimus Deus* (1950) on the Virgin's bodily assumption into heaven.

The encyclical seemed the most powerful form of statement after the bull and the *ex cathedra* statement began to look ludicrous. The encyclical was the main vehicle for getting world attention. As John O'Malley puts it, "Today pontificates are largely defined by the encyclicals the popes produce, and their publication is eagerly awaited." Issuing encyclicals, he says, is now "the papal job description":[3]

> The pope's increasing use of the genre is indicative of its growing importance. In twenty-four years Pius VI issued two, in twenty-three years Pius VII issued one, but Pius IX issued thirty-eight and his successor, Leo XIII, issued seventy-five.[4]

As usual, when a thing becomes part of the church arsenal, people are instructed that it was always there. A 1961 *New York Times* article on the subject was headlined, "Encyclicals Issued 20 Centuries."[5] In fact, the first modern papal encyclical (*Ubi Primum,* 1740) was issued by Benedict XIV, a church historian who remembered that the term "circulating letter" was used by fourth-century bishops as they traded information and formed alliances.[6] The idea that it could be a one-way pronouncement from the pope was Benedict's invention, and not much used until Pius IX grabbed for weapons in his desperate condition. Pius used an encyclical, *Quanta Cura* (1864), to introduce his Syllabus of Errors condemning free speech, the free press, and democratic governments. As Shakespeare's queen says of Richard II:

> The lion, dying, thrusteth forth his paw
> And wounds the earth, if nothing else, with rage
> To be o'erpowered.
>
> (*Richard the Second* 5.1.29–31)

There was a largely successful effort by Catholics—led by Acton and Newman in England and Félix Dupanloup in France—to belittle the Syllabus of Errors.[7] Owen Chadwick rightly said, "By the time Dupanloup had finished with the *Syllabus*, it was almost as if it had never been."[8] But Leo XIII's artillery discharge of encyclicals was not so easily dismissed. For one thing, many people in the labor movement took his *Rerum Novarum* as the founding document of "the church's social teaching." For another, successors like Pius XII found it easier to defend Leo's more moderate tone than Pius IX's vituperative outbursts.

Encyclical Wars

During the twentieth century, Catholic conservatives and liberals picked their favorite parts of encyclicals to use against each other. It was repeatedly said that an encyclical ended all further discussion of any matter. Monsignor Joseph Fenton—the most powerful voice of theology in midcentury America, through his professorship at Catholic University, his journal the *American Ecclesiastical Review,* and his highest contacts in Rome—stated often that no Catholic could in conscience criticize a papal encyclical. And Father John Courtney Murray, S.J., who published a rival journal, *Theological Studies,* when he wrote that different interpreters of an encyclical should "get a say" in his journal, was warned by his Jesuit superior in Rome that "after the supreme authority has spoken, there can only be one 'say.'"⁹ Quoting pope against pope was the readiest way to defend one's own orthodoxy. Who was a real Catholic became a matter of who owned the pope.

Thus, when William F. Buckley Jr. dismissed John XXIII's encyclical *Mater et Magistra*, Catholic liberals were hysterical in denunciation. The Jesuit journal *America* said it would not accept ads for the magazine Buckley edited. A Jesuit newspaper columnist, William Smith, wrote that Buckley, compared with the pope, was "a hypercritical pigmy," issuing "the stuff from which seedling schisms sprout."¹⁰ Many of the liberals demanding such reverence for one encyclical would soon find they could not put enough distance between themselves and another encyclical, Paul VI's *Humanae Vitae* (1968), repeating the condemnation of birth control in Pius XI's encyclical *Casti Connubii* (1930).

American Catholics were asked to accept their country's religious pluralism as being a second-best system tolerated by Rome because of unfortunate circumstance. In the theology manuals, Catholicism as the state's established church was an ideal held as "the thesis." Where the thesis had to be compromised by untoward conditions, at least for a while, this adjustment was branded a "hypothesis" (something sub-ideal). This thesis-hypothesis was what Father Murray called the "reigning view" in Rome (*opinio recepta*), buttressed by Leo XIII's attacks on American-style pluralism. This meant that regimes which, by concordat with the Vatican, recognized Catholicism as the one official church were the ideal, from which American pluralism was a second best, tolerated till a single church could prevail. Franco's Spain was, in this reading, the thesis, America only the hypothesis. Father Murray, and his ally, the leading American church historian John Tracy Ellis, chafed under this absurd evaluation.

As commonly happens where there is an official prescription, avoiding departure from it becomes a matter of self-censorship, making it unnecessary for authority to exercise itself. This made Americans hoping to keep on the good side of Rome shy away from most ecumenical action. Some remembered that Cardinal Gibbons of Baltimore caused "a scandal" when he attended the World's Parliament of Religions at Chicago in 1893—which led Leo XIII to ban attendance at the 1900 Paris Congress of Religions.[11] Catholics did not join ecumenical groups like the WCC (World Council of Churches), since this would suggest an "indifferentism" about the one true church. It would be tolerating error, and a favorite maxim of the Roman Curia was that "error has no rights." One should not recognize the right of other "religions" to exist when there is only one true religion.

Thus Catholics were told they could not enter Protestant churches or synagogues, even to attend weddings or funerals. That would be "countenancing error." When Father Murray contributed an essay to a patriotic volume on Americans of different faiths serving in the armed services, his Jesuit superior in Rome objected to any reprint of it, writing him, "Why should you take space to pay tribute to the spiritual influence of Jew and Protestant religion?"[12] Earlier, when Father Murray was asked to go to Europe as part of a world youth meeting, the Jesuit provincial of Maryland ordered him not to, since this would involve mingling with other religious spokespersons on an equal footing.[13]

Rome so opposed recognition of other religions that Pope Pius XII was "almost wroth" (according to Father Murray's superior in Rome) at the appointment of Clare Boothe Luce as U.S. ambassador to the Vatican, since she had delivered a presidential Thanksgiving message in a Protestant church in Texas. Murray feared he would be caught up in this matter because he had helped prepare Ms. Luce for her Senate confirmation by coaching her on church-state relations.[14] Murray, as the editor of *Theological Studies,* had to answer for things he published as well as those he wrote himself. He was often accused of departing from the Roman line. When *Theological Studies* criticized Franco, alarms went off, and again Murray's superior warned, "Leave Spain out of it."[15]

Murray had less maneuvering room than the ordinary Catholic scholar, or even than any American bishop. Those bishops, carrying out their public duties, often had to cooperate with Protestants and Jews. They professed adherence to the Roman line, but lived comfortably within the conventions of American civility between the faiths. Murray was not allowed such hypocrisy. He normally had to clear his writings with a whole range of people overseeing his career. His Jesuit superiors were, most of them, friends; but that just made them more worried about Vatican reaction to him. As a result, he had to keep looking over his shoulder at a large flock of people watching his every word. In his own order he cleared things with the rector of the seminary where he was a professor (Joseph Murphy), the superior of his American province (John McMahon), the American assistant to the Jesuits in Rome (Vincent McCormick), and the general of the entire Society of Jesus (Jean-Baptiste Janssens).

These were just the friends he kept reporting to. He also had a range of enemies trying to outmaneuver the friends. They were led by Monsignor Fenton, along with other writers he favored at his journal (the *American Ecclesiastical Review*), theologians like Monsignor Francis Connell and George Shea. Fenton had many close allies in Rome, beginning with the head of the Holy Office, Alfredo Ottaviani, and the apostolic delegates to America (first Amleto Cicognani, then Egidio Vagnozzi). Whenever Murray was pressured to shut up, which happened often in the 1950s, it was either by Ottaviani, at Fenton's request, or by people trying to appease Ottaviani by preemptive silencings. This would reach its climax in 1955. The assistant in Rome (McCormick), having asked for opinions on a Murray article about church and state, relayed and endorsed the judgment of the general (Janssens) that it should not appear:

> These men have your interests at heart, and they know the scene over here . . . It seems to me a mistake to wish to carry on with that controverted question under present circumstances . . . provoking those who will not be appeased. Fr. General [Janssens] agrees with the final verdict . . . *Fiat.*[16]

Father Murray, an obedient Jesuit, threw in the towel, answering McCormick:

> All the books on church and state and on allied topics have been cleared from my room, in symbol of retirement, which I expect to be permanent. When Frank Sheed [the Catholic book publisher] returns [from abroad], I shall cancel the agreement I had with him to edit and revise the articles on church and state for a book. Fortunately, my gloomy prescience impelled me to refuse an invitation to give the Walgreen Lectures at the U. of Chicago. And all other practical measures will be taken to close the door on the past ten years, leaving all their mistakennesses to God.[17]

Murray, defeated by foes and deserted by friends at home and abroad, made what seemed a final retreat from the field of his chosen studies— only to be rescued, improbably, by John F. Kennedy. American Catholics were excited in the late 1950s by the prospect of a Catholic president. He had to face charges that his religion did not recognize the American separation of church and state. Theodore Sorensen, his speechwriter, was also his liaison to religious groups; he knew Catholic liberals like John Cogley and non-Catholic friends of Murray like Arthur Schlesinger Jr. So Kennedy took to quoting Murray and (minimally) consulting him. In fact, Kennedy proclaimed his freedom from papal direction in ways that went beyond what Murray had taught.[18] But Rome could not criticize Kennedy, the center of so many Catholic hopes and ambitions. Then how could it keep drawing attention to the far more moderate "Americanism" of Father Murray?

American bishops who had been afraid to support Murray now took heart from the Kennedy campaign and election. They needed Murray's help in defending the separation of church and state on which Kennedy's career was now based. Murray went from being silenced to being celebrated. The book he had canceled with Sheed & Ward, *We Hold These Truths,* appeared in 1960 to such acclaim that Murray was put on the cover of *Time,* which was still at that time a kind of secular canonization.

When Monsignor Fenton and Cardinal Ottaviani got Murray banned from the first session of the Second Vatican Council, in 1962, the conservative Cardinal Spellman brought him as his own personal expert (*peritus*) to the second session. In Rome, Murray addressed gatherings of the bishops, drafted criticisms of earlier drafts of the Declaration on Religious Freedom, and was a principal author of the fourth and final one. The remnants of the "integral" church-state monarchy, which had been constructed over centuries, were discredited with amazing rapidity. Americanism had gone from silenced heresy to orthodox belief. To the amazement of Ottaviani and the horror of Fenton—who thought they owned the pope—change could indeed occur, and had.

NOTES

1. J. N. D. Kelly, *The Oxford Dictionary of Popes* (Oxford University Press, 1986), 312.
2. John Henry Newman, "Letter to His Grace the Duke of Norfolk," in *Newman and Gladstone: The Vatican Decrees,* edited by Alvan S. Ryan (University of Notre Dame Press, 1962), 199.
3. John O'Malley, S.J., *A History of the Popes: From Peter to the Present* (Sheed & Ward, 2009), 245.
4. Ibid.
5. *New York Times,* July 15, 1961, 7. Some Catholic sources even called the letter written by the Roman community to the Corinthians at the end of the first century "the first papal encyclical." It was probably written by Clement, who had no title even as bishop, much less as pope, and he did not sign or authorize the letter. Its authority was that of the community.
6. O'Malley, op. cit., 244.
7. Newman, op. cit., passim. Acton, Letter to the *Times* of London, November 8, 1874, in Acton, *Essays,* edited by J. Rufus Fears (Liberty Classics, 1988), vol. 3, 366.
8. Owen Chadwick, *A History of the Popes, 1830–1914* (Oxford University Press, 1998), 178.
9. Donald E. Pelotte, *John Courtney Murray: Theologian in Conflict* (Paulist Press, 1975), 35.
10. Garry Wills, *Politics and Catholic Freedom* (Henry Regnery Company, 1964), 5–13.
11. E. E. Y. Hales, *The Catholic Church in the Modern World* (Eyre & Spottiswoode, 1958), 180–81, 187–88.
12. Pelotte, op. cit., 51–53.
13. Ibid., 9–10.

14. Ibid., 40–41, 66. Clare Luce's biographer described Father Murray as "the Luces' Richelieu": Wilfrid Sheed, *Clare Boothe Luce* (E. P. Dutton, 1982), 160. Henry Luce's biographer says Murray was "a fixture in the Luces' many houses": Alan Brinkley, *Henry Luce and His American Century* (Alfred A. Knopf, 2010), 412. Sheed (125), says that Murray took part in Clare Luce's experiments with LSD, which Brinkley (433–36) says were extensive.

15. Pelotte, op. cit., 52.

16. Ibid.

17. Ibid., 53.

18. Murray's friend and disciple Richard Regan, S.J., detaches him from Kennedy's excesses in *American Pluralism and the Catholic Conscience* (Macmillan, 1963), 4–5.

ELEVEN

Churches and States

A PLURALIST WORLD

I t is a little embarrassing to read John Courtney Murray's early works on church and state, which seemed so heretical to Catholic conservatives at the time, and so trailblazing to Catholic liberals. He had to "interpret" papal statements without outright rejecting them. He was maneuvering through the Argonauts' *Symplegades*—the "Clashing Rocks" of (on the one side) Vatican denouncers and (on the other side) Jesuit protectors. This involved him in continual trimming and tacking to slip past his friends as well as his foes. He had to criticize the *opinio recepta* without being branded a heretic. The quibbling over encyclicals and other papal statements was bound to look "jesuitical," despite the good intent of this learned Jesuit. The Second Vatican Council made it possible for him to speak more coherently as it vindicated him retrospectively. But the only way he could stay in the game when he first began writing on the subject was to play by the rules set for him in Rome.

"Two There Are"

The only resort for disagreeing with the pope, back in the 1940s, was to invoke another pope. Murray did not have many popes to enlist in his cause, and the one he chose was only convincing if no one looked very carefully at the history of the fifth century. This card on which he relied was, *faute de mieux,* the fifth-century pope Gelasius I (492–96). Though Gelasius was subject to the Arian ruler of Italy (Theodoric) in the West, he wrote to the Eastern emperor, Anastasius, that the pope had a spiritual domain independent of temporal power. The letter has his famous words, "There are of course two (*duo quippe sunt*) who preside over the world."

Murray shortened this to "Two there are" (*duo sunt*), and made the phrase a kind of mantra, frequently intoned. He said that the true Catholic doctrine for all later time was "the Gelasian thesis." He quotes a few sentences from Gelasius's letter, as if they were the whole of it, and the standard of all later thought on the matter of church and state: "We are here in the presence of a Great Idea, whose entrance into history marked the beginning of a new civilizational era . . . It was the charter of a new freedom, such as the world had never known."[1]

Murray says, for instance, that Boniface VIII got the Gelasian thesis backward in *Unam Sanctam*. The earlier pope had said that the priest has *auctoritas* and the prince has only *potestas*. Boniface reversed the attributes, giving *potestas* to the priest and *auctoritas* to the prince. This is a meaningless quibble. For one thing, the terms were used interchangeably, as practical synonyms, in late antiquity and the Middle Ages.[2] *Auctoritas* without *potestas* is impotent, and *potestas* without *auctoritas* is tyranny.

Besides, Boniface could not have cared about the phrasing of a distinction he did not recognize—he claimed that both swords, spiritual and temporal, belonged to him (though in fact he could not use either of them). Moreover, Gelasius was not claiming a really separate power from that of Anastasius—he said he would assist at the emperor's consignment to hell if he did not suppress the Monophysite heresy. This was an argument for the establishment of religion, and Ottaviani could more justly quote Gelasius in defense of Francisco Franco than Murray could in defense of the First Amendment.

Murray's Vatican critics said he was trying to make the American separation of church and state the *thesis* (ideal), and Spain (along with other nations establishing the Catholic religion by concordat with the pope) the *hypothesis*. Murray answered that, on the contrary, he rejected this "disjunctive" approach, replacing it with a "unitary approach." According to him, the only valid tradition is that "the freedom of the church" must temper secular power—and this can happen under different forms of government, for the Spanish as well as for Americans.

Murray's claims for the basic importance of "the freedom of the Church" are very sweeping. He says it was the first important challenge in history to the "omnicompetent" state. Before the church challenged it, all states were totalist, claiming the entirety of a citizen's allegiance:

> The question has always been that of identifying the limiting norm that will check the encroachments of secular power and preserve these sacred immunities. Western civilization *first* found this norm in the pregnant principle, the freedom of the Church [emphasis added].[3]

This was Murray's tool for preserving a basic core to Leo XIII's rebarbative encyclicals. In Leo's documents, he noted, "the phrase, the 'freedom of the Church,' appears some eighty-one times."[4] If Leo condemned democracy, it was because the only form of it he knew was the anticlericalism of the French Revolution. That denied the freedom of the church—as have all state totalisms, that of ancient Rome, of eighteenth-century "royal absolutisms," and, more recently, of Nazi and communist governments. These all asserted, in their own way, "One there is," not allowing the church to say, "Two there are."[5]

Murray, placating his foes, says that Leo was right to warn Americans that even their democratic government can become monist if it goes to the extreme that Madison did in his *Memorial and Remonstrance.* Murray exerts great ingenuity in distinguishing the First Amendment from Madison's own writings, to which he attributes the religious "indifferentism" his critics charged Murray himself with. He even anticipated modern right-wing arguments that disestablishing religion is a theological position, and is therefore proscribed by the First Amendment:

> This is the essence of Madison's concept of separation of church and state. Its ultimate ground is a religious absolute, a sectarian idea of religion. The separation therefore is itself absolute. And no other grounds may be assigned for its absoluteness but its theological premise.[6]

Thus does disestablishment become, jesuitically, an establishment:

> In the effort to prove that "no establishment of religion" means "no aid to religion," the Supreme Court proceeds to establish a religion—James Madison's.[7]

Murray distorts Madison's teaching to validate Leo XIII's attacks on "Americanism." The pope was right because he was attacking Madison, not the First Amendment. Murray labored so hard to get on the right side of the popes that he agreed with the "Gelasian" aspects not only of Leo XIII but of Pius IX's Syllabus of Errors:

> As the Syllabus and its explicatory documents—as well as the multitudinous writings of Leo XIII—make entirely clear, it was this thesis of the juridical omnipotence and omnicompetence of the state which was the central object of the Church's condemnation of the Jacobin development. It was because freedom of religion and separation of church and state were predicated on this thesis that the Church refused to accept them as a thesis.[8]

The idea that the church introduced freedom of religion into Western history reverses the order of fact. Ancient governments were tolerant of belief so long as patriotic rituals were observed. Creedal tests were introduced by Christianity, in its energetic suppression of heresy. This gave special impetus to the idea that a polity must be truth-based (a tradition Murray honors in his book title, *We Hold These Truths*). The idea that power must be based on a creed was the very essence of papal monarchism. In order to say, "Two there are," one must be able to define exactly what the two are saying, what different truths they embodied. It took a greater fifth-century thinker than Gelasius to deny that truth is the basis of human societies. Augustine of Hippo came by a long route to make that denial.

Three There Are

It might seem surprising, at first, that Murray, with his two-powers theory, does not cite Augustine's famous two "cities" from the *De Civitate Dei*—the City of God and the Earthly City. In the Middle Ages, Augustine was sometimes taken to be describing church and state in his two cities. But Murray at least avoided that trap. Augustine made it clear that the City of God was a lasting society (that is, heaven), and no one knows which persons now on earth will inhabit it lastingly. Being a member of the church on earth at any point does not mean one will end up in heaven, since people enter and leave the church. Augustine had been out of it before he was in it, and he could be out again. No one has any assurance of what the Last Judgment will reveal. Augustine constantly opposed the idea that there was a manifest providence. God's judgments are secret judgments (CD 4.33, 20.2).

It was essential to Augustine's thinking that the church on earth *not* be the City of God. Many in his time—Donatists next door to him in Africa, Novationists to the north in Italy, Melitians in Alexandria—claimed that only the pure, the perfect could be Christians. Augustine drew on a maverick Donatist, Tyconius, to emphasize that the church we see on earth is a very mixed bag. It is the net of Christ's parable, full of good fish and bad, to be sorted out at the end of time (Mt 13.47–50).[9] It is a field of wheat growing entangled with weeds, to be separated only after harvest (Mt 13.24–30, 36–43).[10] It is wheat mixed with chaff, to be winnowed (Lk 3.17).

One becomes clearly a member of the City of God only when love of God is confirmed forever in heaven. Here on earth one may, as a pilgrim, be traveling toward the City of God. But membership in the visible church does not mean the journey will be completed. There are Christians whose love of self rather than God will make them end up in the Earthly City—just as there are those in earthly government who may be headed toward the City of God.

The Earthly City is the opposite of the City of God—which means it is eternal, but with an eternity of unhappiness:

> I speak by analogy (*mystice*) of two "cities"—that is, two human groups, of which one is destined to reign eternally with God, the other to undergo eternal punishment with the Devil (CD 20.1).

These two eternal cities do not provide a template to be imposed on the historical church and state. If the visible church is a mixed bag, the visible state is bound to be the same. After the fall of man by original sin, justice is no longer to be expected in any temporal order. The temporal church is partly made up of sinners. The temporal state is partly made up of thieves:

> Take away justice, and what is government but a magnified gang of thieves (*magna latrocinia*)? For that matter, what is a gang of thieves but a small-time government (*parva regna*)? It is a human group, following a leader, observing its own rules, splitting the booty by an agreed procedure. If this nuisance grows large by recruiting enough scoundrels, it establishes its own territory, sets up headquarters (*sedes*), occupies cities, subdues inhabitants, more openly calls itself a government, until its claims are confirmed—not by less of greed, but by more of effrontery. As a captured pirate cheekily explained to Alexander the Great, when asked by what right he terrorized at sea, "By the same right that you terrorize the world. I have only my little ship, so I am called a thief. You have a great fleet, so you are an emperor" (CD 4.4).[11]

Is Augustine describing all states, or just the ones that lack justice (*remota justitia*)? In this fallen world, after original sin, all states, in greater or less degree, lack justice. Augustine was a constant critic of unjust court decisions (CD 19.6).[12] States are based on violence and deception. Does that mean they cease to be states? Then there could be no state at all. Cicero, in his dialogue *Government* (*De Re Publica*), had Scipio, who voiced his own views, define government this way:

> Government (*res publica*) pertains to a nation (*populus*), and a nation is a gathering of many individuals held together by an agreement on the just (*juris consensus*) and a mutuality of advantage (*utilitatis communio*).[13]

Scipio makes it clear that the first of those two conditions is the key one. He says that the state must not only be just, it must be the signally just thing in people's lives.[14] Indeed, the nation where justice does not prevail is not only ill governed—it is not governed at all. It is not even a state.[15]

Augustine did not agree with the Scipio of Cicero's dialogue. Governments do not go out of existence because they lack justice. The effort after justice is required of all humans. People want and need that, however they fail to attain it. He had said the state is a gang of thieves. But he read that equation backward as well. A gang of thieves has to have some elements of government. Even thieves demand their rights. Remember, from the passage I quoted above, that the gang may be lawless in how it gets loot, but it will insist on some "agreed procedure" (*placiti lege*) in divvying the take (CD 4.4). Elsewhere Augustine writes, "Thieves themselves, if only to terrorize others more fiercely and safely, want good relations with other members of the gang" (CD 19.12). Even a lone criminal has to think of continuing social relations, of at least seeming to be just, not a criminal:

> If, however, one man relies so much on his own power, and distrusts so much his fellows, as to commit his own crimes, scheming and succeeding to get booty from those he quells or kills, he keeps up a simulacrum of good relations with those he has not been able to kill or from whom he can hide his acts (CD 19.12).

Augustine, then, did not think all social relations impossible where justice was lacking. That is what made him recast Cicero's definition of government:

A nation is a gathering of many rational individuals held together by a heartfelt mutuality (*concordi communione*) on things it holds dear (*rerum quas diligit*) (CD 19.24).

The last three words are most often translated, in English, as "the things one loves." But *diligere* is not *amare*. The *Oxford Latin Dictionary* defines *diligo* this way: "To love, hold dear . . . a milder emotion than *amo*." But it is an *emotion*. It is not the *reason* that makes one recognize justice. The emotional tie is seen in the adjective given to mutuality, *concordis* (from *cor,* heart). Peter Brown says that Augustine's *dilectio* "stands for the orientation of the whole personality."[16] He develops this line of thought:

> So much of our modern study in sociology and social psychology has shown the degree to which political obedience is, in fact, secured, and political society coheres by the mediation of a third party, a whole half-hidden world of irrational, semi-conscious and conscious elements, that can include factors as diverse as childhood attitudes toward authority, crystallized around abiding inner figures, half-sensed images of security, of greatness, of the good life, and, on the conscious plane, the acceptance of certain values. These make up an orientation analogous to Augustine's *dilectio*.[17]

The Aristotelian-Thomistic politics was a matter of right reason, since it held that humans' highest gift is the intellect. Augustine thought that the will is an equal gift, with love as the supreme achievement.[18] Satan is smarter than men or women. That does him little good without love. It is easy to dismiss Augustine's politics as sentimental, or merely tribal. But it is closer to reality than the claim that people can associate only if they agree on justice. No citizen agrees with everything his or her government says or does. People are bound to differ on important matters—on wars and treaties, on the distribution of state assets, on rules concerning sex, marriage, children, and inheritance. If each point on which there is a disagreement over justice instantly erased all one's ties to the government, we would continually be dissolving countries and falling into anarchy. What prevents this? What makes people hesitate to secede from a formed social entity unless there is an ultimate and fatal break?

Usually, we do not want to sever all the many bonds that unite members of a nation. These are not a series of propositions that we must argue and agree on (as Murray said). John Henry Newman was closer to our experience of political life together. He wrote that each nation develops its own constellation of values, sentiments, memories, properties, legacies—all the things, silly as well as serious, that hold it together:

> Growing out of these varieties or idiosyncrasies, and corresponding to them, will be found in these several races, and proper to each, a certain assemblage of beliefs, convictions, rules, usages, traditions, proverbs, and principles; some political, some social, some moral; and these tending to some definite form of government and *modus vivendi* . . . It is something more than law; it is the embodiment of special ideas . . . These ideas are sometimes trivial, and at first sight, even absurd; sometimes they are superstitious, sometimes they are great or beautiful; but to those to whom they belong they are first principles, watchwords, common property, natural ties.[19]

Newman's view may be considered sentimental by those who consider themselves "realists." That kind of realism often reduces politics to power relationships abroad and at home.[20] But people often act against narrow interests to maintain emotional relations with others, nostalgic or aspirational, involving family loyalties, shared experiences, mutual understanding. People are held together by their common language—not just of words but of memories, mental associations, and hopes.

Newman's insight on what really holds society together is one others have recognized, independently of him. John Ruskin identified the importance of "social affections" as the basis for human organization.[21] Lord Shaftesbury said that a moral sense held people together by the delight they experience in doing good. Francis Hutcheson and his followers of the Scottish school said this sense was a positive appetite for "benevolence." Hume described "the social disposition of mankind."[22] The danger of their position is mere tribalism. Hutcheson recognized that danger. But for him benevolence is a universal impulse that, though strengthened by proximity, should not become exclusively focused on one part of humanity. None of these men felt that there was one ideal concept of the state that could be reached by reason.

Augustine argued that there is only one ideal community, and it does not exist on earth. The City of God beckons men who strive for it by love of God; but it is countered in fallen mankind, by a love of self that can lead to hell (the Earthly City). Since none of us, while we live, can inhabit either of the two lasting communities, we share for a while a third city, a mixed one in both the political and the religious spheres. This third city is a place of divided loyalties, not only in its social relations but in the individual soul. Nothing could be further from the Aristotelian concept of the polis as a thing that exists by *autarkeia,* "self-sufficiency."[23]

The Scholastics took this to mean that self-sufficient societies (including the church on earth) should be "complete"—*ecclesia perfecta,* fatally translated as "perfect." Saint Thomas accepted this definition of government as consisting of completed community: *Civitas est communitas perfecta.*[24] This went into theology textbooks and papal statements on the historic church as "a perfect society."[25] Nothing could be further from Augustine's view of the church in time as a mixed bag. Both church and state have citizens imperfect, striving, undecided. Here is his description of the church in time:

> In this hostile age, in these bad days, when the church strives in its present lowliness toward a lofty future, learning by the provocations of fear, the trials of sorrow, the weights of effort, the dangers of temptation—happy only in hope (when hope is justifiable)—where many recalcitrants are mingled with good people, and both are collected in a kind of Gospel dragnet, both swimming in this world, unsorted, as in a sea until they reach the shore, where the bad will be separated from the good, and God is to be everything in every way for the good, arrived as to a temple (CD 18.49).

Paula Fredriksen admitted that Augustine had, before the fall of Rome in 399, entertained Eusebius's claim that Constantine had founded a Christian state. But his long meditation on politics in *City of God* made him see through that pretense. She sums up his considered judgment this way:

> The empire, neither demonic before 312 nor holy thereafter, lacked any absolute religious significance. And events whether positive (such as the universal proclamation of the Gospel) or negative (famine, earthquake, or the fall of Rome) were eschatologically opaque. They could not be matched with scriptural prophecy to indicate anything of the divine plan. However certain in their faith, Christians could never be certain of their circumstances. For the period of time that stood outside the biblical canon, history's patterns and the ultimate significance of events, like God's standards of justice, were *occultissimi* [most secret].[26]

This does not mean that those in either the church or the state are freed from their duties to just activity. At whatever level—in the small gang of thieves acting together for efficiency and fairness, or the larger gang of thieves called the government trying to enforce justice, or the large gang of sinners called the church trying to remind one another of the love of God—we are bound to moral duty, however we fail to achieve it. Newman knew that this effort has little to do with the ideal worlds built by rational philosophers. He wrote:

> No idea or principle of political society includes in its operation all conceivable good, or excludes all evil. That is the best form of society which has the most of the good and least of the bad [available to the particular society at a particular time].[27]

To some it may seem ignoble to settle for anything less than the great shining goal of Justice. But consider the antisocial pathology of doing business only with those who judge as you do, think as you do, feel as you do, and act as you do. That kind of intellectual unanimity is what Pope Leo XIII yearned for as he looked back on the thirteenth century as an ideal "age of faith":

There was once a time when states were governed by the philosophy of the Gospel. Then it was that the power and divine virtue of Christian wisdom had diffused itself throughout the laws, institutions, and morals of the people, permeating all ranks and relations of civil society. Then, too, the religion instituted by Jesus Christ, established firmly in befitting dignity, flourished everywhere, by the favor of princes and the legitimate protection of magistrates; and Church and State were happily united in concord and friendly interchange of good offices.

The State, constituted in this wise, bore fruits important beyond all expectation, whose remembrance is still (and always will be) in renown, witnessed to as they are by countless proofs which can never be blotted out or ever obscured by any craft of any enemies. Christian Europe has subdued barbarous nations, and changed them from a savage to a civilized condition, from superstition to true worship. It victoriously rolled back the tide of Mohammedan conquest; retained the headship of civilization; stood forth in the front rank as the leader and teacher of all, in every branch of national culture; bestowed on the world the gift of true and many-sided liberty; and most wisely founded very numerous institutions for the solace of human suffering. And if we inquire how it was able to bring about so altered a condition of things, the answer is (beyond all question) in large measure—through religion, under whose auspices so many great undertakings were set on foot, through whose aid they were brought to completion.[28]

Papal authority was made to prop up, here, ludicrous history. It is also theologically ludicrous. Leo thinks that the church could abolish original sin. His thirteenth-century "great undertakings . . . brought to completion" were crusades that failed, savage slaughters of Jews, Muslims, Albigensians, and other heretics. (The Fourth Crusade's great victory was a sacking of the Christian city of Constantinople.) The harmony of church and state was achieved by interdicts, assassinations, and enslavements.

Father Murray tried to advance a better view of history, based on "truths we hold" in an America with separation of church and state. But the America of the founding, we now recognize, was terribly flawed, by slaughter of Indians, enslavement of blacks, and suppression of women, among other things. And the contemporary United States will someday be seen in retrospect as a plutocracy with impoverished citizens; as a bloated war machine with overkill stockpiles of unusable weaponry; as a place of volunteer armies ground down by constant use, of ruinously expensive political campaigning and clogged nongoverning, making ineffectual gestures toward a failing ecosystem, and with a stupor of admiration for guns. But we still love our country, and we should.

Augustine knew the consequences of original sin in both church and state. He did not mistake either of them for the City of God or the City of Man. When he described the fall of the Roman Empire, it was the Christian empire he was speaking of. When he described the bias and injustice of courts, it was under Christian emperors' rule. He knew what he spoke of, since bishops at the time had jurisdiction over local courts, and he conducted his court with exemplary fairness (without the customary torture).[29] In his little area, the church ruled better than the state. That was not an ideal to be advanced in the abstract. Nothing is ideal in this sinful world. Yet the churches and the states must both, in each era, do what Newman recommended—foster "the most of the good and least of the bad." We must cling to our flawed human society, as Augustine put it, held together by a mutuality of things we hold dear. We are, at our best, not only members but patriots of our blundering state and sinning church, muddling along in our shared third city. Three there are.

NOTES

1. John Courtney Murray, S.J., *We Hold These Truths: Catholic Reflections on the American Proposition* (Sheed & Ward, 1960), 202.

2. Milton V. Anastos, *Aspects of the Relation Between the Byzantine and the Roman Churches* (Ashgate Publications, 2001), 6–7.

3. Murray, *We Hold These Truths*, 204.

4. Ibid., 202.

5. Ibid., 206–8.

6. John Courtney Murray, "Law or Prepossessions?," in *Law and Contemporary Problems*, vol. 14 (1949), 30.

7. Ibid., 31. Murray was attacking the 1947 *Everson* decision (blocking public aid to Catholic schools) and the 1948 *McCollum* decision (banning prayer in public schools).

8. Murray, *We Hold These Truths*, 68.

9. CD 18.49.

10. CD 20.5.

11. Augustine, who was working closely from Cicero's *De Re Publica* in this section of *City of God,* took the story of Alexander and the pirate from that dialogue (3.24).

12. He especially condemned the common use of torture to get evidence: "A judge's ignorance is often an innocent man's doom . . . A judge tortures to find out if he is killing an innocent man, and then kills him because he could not find out . . . The man chooses to escape life rather than put up with more torment . . . The judge tortures to find out, then kills without finding out" (CD 10.6).

13. Cicero, *De Re Publica* 1.39.

14. Ibid., 2.70.

15. Ibid., 3.43.

16. Peter Brown, *Religion and Society in the Age of Saint Augustine* (Harper & Row, 1972), 42.

17. Ibid.

18. Albrecht Dihle rightly argues that Augustine introduced a whole new concept of the will. *The Theory of the Will in Classical Antiquity* (University of California Press, 1982), 123–44.

19. John Henry Newman, "Who's to Blame?," in *Discussions and Arguments on Various Subjects,* new edition (Longmans, Green, and Co., 1897), 315. These are eight letters sent to the *Catholic Standard* in 1855, protesting the Crimean War as opposed to the national ethos. G. K. Chesterton opposed the Boer War on similar grounds, arguing that imperialism was against the local loyalties of "little England."

20. For the narrowness of this kind of "realism," even in one of its best exponents, see Gregory Crane, *Thucydides and the Ancient Simplicity: The Limits of Political Realism* (University of California Press, 1998), especially 312–25.

21. John Ruskin, "Unto This Last," in *The Works,* edited by E. T. Cook and Alexander Wedderburn (George Allen, 1905), vol. 17, 25–114.

22. David Hume, "Of the First Principles of Government," in *Essays,* edited by Eugene F. Miller (Liberty Classics, 1985), 33.

23. Aristotle held that the polis should be large enough to supply its own needs, yet small enough to recognize and service those needs. *Politics* 1326b2–25.

24. ST I–II q 90 a3 ad 3.

25. See, for instance, Leo XIII's *Immortale Dei,* the encyclical Father Murray had to wrestle around and try to tame—pars. 10, 35 (on the church as "perfect by nature and by claim").

26. Paula Fredriksen, *Augustine and the Jews* (Doubleday, 2008), 344–45.

27. Newman, op. cit., 354.

28. Leo XIII, *Immortale Dei,* par. 21 (Vatican translation).

29. Frederick van der Meer, *Augustine the Bishop,* translated by Brian Battershaw and G. R. Lamb (Sheed & Ward, 1961), 258–70.

III

The Coming and Going of Anti-Semitism

TWELVE

Paul, "a Jew of Jews"

That the Christian church, both Western and Eastern, both Catholic and Protestant, was for so long anti-Semitic is a tragic absurdity. The church in all its branches was and is itself Semitic. Its sources and forms were and are Jewish. The church is the body of Christ, and Christ was an observant Jew. Jesus was circumcised on the eighth day after his birth, as required by religious law. Christians believe that the risen and glorified body of Jesus in heaven bears that mark of his religion. His first followers were Jewish in belief and practice, not merely by birth. His mother was purified in the Temple. Jesus himself participated in the sacrifices on High Holy Days. He preached in the Temple court. The reason he chose twelve disciples was so that they should judge the Twelve Tribes of Israel (Mt 19.28, Lk 22.30). He told the woman at the well in John 4.22, "You Samaritans worship what you do not understand; but we [Jews] worship what we do understand, since Rescue is from the Jews."

We Jews. Jesus speaks as one of his Father's chosen people. How could he not? Even Paul, who took the Jewish promise to Gentiles, spoke always as "a Jew of Jews":

> If one is to rely on lineage, my claim is better [than that of Jewish Christians opposing Gentile Christians]—circumcised on the eighth day; by nation, an Israelite; by tribe, of Benjamin, a Jew of Jews; in Law, a Pharisee; in dedication, a persecutor of the gathering; in vindication under the Law, a man faultless (Phil 3.4–6).

> As a Jew, I outstripped many contemporaries of my own lineage; extreme in my zealous preservation of the patriarchs' traditions (Gal 1.14).

I, for that matter (*kai gar*), am an Israelite, of Abraham's seed, of Benjamin's tribe. God has not rejected his people, previously singled out by him (*proegnō*) (Rom 11.1–2).

I could dare (*ēuchomēn*) to be outcast from Messiah myself for my brothers in the flesh, who are the Israelites. Ours is the sonship, and the splendor, and the covenants, and the gift of Law; and the rites, and the promises. From us are the patriarchs and from them, by fleshly descent, is the Messiah, the God above all, may he ever be praised (Rom 9.3–5).[1]

Paul preached the Jewish Messiah from the Jewish scriptures. Never in his own writings does he quote or use a pagan author.[2]

Later books that would be incorporated into the New Testament—especially the Gospel of John, Revelation, and the Letter to Hebrews—would be "supersessionist," claiming that faith in Jesus had superseded (made obsolete) God's covenant with the Jewish people. Paul, the earliest writer who would later be incorporated into the New Testament as it (slowly) took form, denied that absolutely:

I ask, has God disowned his people? How could that be? (Rom 11.1–2).

There is no distinction between Jew and Gentile, since there is the same Lord over all, profuse toward all who call on him; and all who call on the Lord's name will be rescued (Rom 10.12).

It is often thought that Paul opposed Jewish law because he lashed out at Peter for going back to kashrut after eating with Gentile Christians in Antioch (Gal 2.11–14). But Paul was not opposing the Jewish code—including circumcision—for Jewish Christians. He had his assistant Timothy circumcised because his mother was a Jew (Acts 16.3), though he resisted having Titus circumcised, since both his parents were Gentile (Gal 2.3). The promise was being extended to non-Jews—but that could not happen if the promise was erased in its first recipients. The ironic thing is that, close on to fifty years later, Luke would give Peter the lead in freeing Gentiles from the food code (Acts 10.1–48).

Paul argued that Gentile believers were, in Krister Stendahl's phrase, "honorary Jews."[3] They were the seed of Abraham justified by faith even before the time of circumcision (Gal 3.7–9). Stendahl even explains the parable of workers being paid the same wage, though some came only at the eleventh hour, as justifying the Gentiles (Mt 20.1–6). He paraphrases a friend: "Do you know who the eleventh hour folks are? They are we, the Gentiles. It was Israel who worked through the whole long heat of sacred history, and we lazy Gentiles came in at the last moment and got the same pay."[4] Soon there would be Christians arguing not merely to include Gentiles but to exclude Jews. Paul was not one of these. He described the order of salvation as "the Jew first, and then the Greek" (Rom 1.16):

> How then is the Jew favored? Does circumcision benefit him? Decidedly, in every way[5]—[as a sign that] they were made the trustees (*episteuthēsan*) for God's words of mystery (*logia*) (Rom 3.1–2).

Paul did not urge Jews to give up their precious legacy. He just said that Jesus was admitting non-Jews into the privileges of the chosen people.

True, there was a division between "Greeks" and Jews in the Christian ranks. But Paul thought that in the speeded-up events of the End Time, which had already begun, this was a temporary rift. The Jews would admit the Gentiles, would see in Jesus the completion of their own story—the *telos*, fulfillment of the law, not the "end" of it in the sense of its cancellation.[6] Stendahl said the temporary check in Jewish acceptance of the Gentiles was a part of God's "traffic plan"—some Jews were put on hold, to let Gentiles in, and the two would shortly join again.[7] Paul worked this out in the carefully nuanced image of a fig tree with old and new branches drawing on the life of a single root. He says that Jews had failed to see how Jesus was calling Gentiles into communion with them.

This was "a stumble" on their part (Rom 11.9). I break this passage into numbered parts to show how distinctly Paul had worked it out:

1. But, I ask you, have they so stumbled as to fall down? By no means. In fact, their misstep has rescued the Gentiles, which makes them envious. If their misstep has been the world's gain, and their loss was the Gentiles' gain, what greater gain will be their combined total?[8] I am addressing this to Gentiles. Inasmuch as I am an emissary to the Gentiles, I will vaunt this mission, provoking my own flesh and blood in order to rescue some of them. For if their rejecting us has led to interaction with God's plan, what will their rejoining with us mean?[9] Nothing less than life out of death.

2. Just as the blessing at the beginning of a meal blesses the whole meal,[10] a holy root [of an olive tree] makes the branches holy. If some branches have been stripped away, and you, an alien olive branch, have been grafted into their place, to share life and sap of the original root, do not crow over the replaced branches. How can you crow, when you do not feed the root that feeds you? You may say, "Those branches were stripped away so I could be grafted." Grant it so—but they were stripped away because they failed in trust, and you were grafted in because of trust. That is no cause for elation but for caution. For if God did not spare the natural growth, why should he spare you? Take heed of God's graciousness and his harshness—harsh to those who failed, gracious to you, but only if you retain his graciousness and are not yourselves stripped away.

3. And they, if they give up their mistrust, will be grafted back in. It is easy for God to graft them in again. If you, torn from a wild olive, were unnaturally grafted into the cultivated tree, just think how naturally they will be grafted back into their native olive.

4. I would not have you, wrapped in your own conceit, ignorant of God's secret—that part of Israel is hardened, to let in the full number of Gentiles, after which all of Israel will be rescued, as Scripture [Isaiah] says:

> From Zion the Rescuer will come,
> to strip iniquity from Jacob
> and this is my pact with them
> that I wipe away their sins.

In terms of the [new] revelation, they oppose you; but in terms of their privilege, they are God's beloved from their fathers. God's gifts and promise to them are not subject to second thoughts (*ametameléta*). You, after all, were once heedless of God, but now have been shown mercy because of their heedlessness. In the same way they, heedless now, will be shown the same mercy as you—when God, finding all enclosed in their own heedlessness, will have mercy on all.

5. What depth there is to God's wealth and wisdom and knowing:

> How unsearchable his decisions!
>   How untrackable his movements!
> Who has plumbed the mind of the Lord?
>   Who has advised him?
> Who first exchanged gifts with him
>   To receive gifts in return?
> For all comes from him, by way of him, to end with him,
>   His is the splendor of all ages. Amen (Rom 11.11–36).

Each stage of this carefully built argument deserves consideration:

1. Paul says he is addressing the Gentiles, but that he means by this to prod his own "flesh" to join with the Gentiles in their new relationship with the world, opened up by Christ. The Letter to the Romans is Paul's most ambitious explanation of the Gentiles' place in the Jewish world of sacred scripture. It is addressed to the Romans before his new missionary trip to Spain, sent as he was traveling to Jerusalem to deliver the collections taken up for James at the "mother church," to show his continuing loyalty to it (Rom 15.25–28). He is literally poised between two worlds, and he is obviously sending a copy of this letter to the church in Jerusalem, explaining why the Gentiles should be admitted into their fellowship. The dead relations between some of the Jewish and Gentile Christians will gain a new life if they unite now, as a condition for reunion with "all of Israel"—as Paul foresees them doing in the near future.

2. Though Paul says he is addressing the Gentiles (Christian ones), he uses a very Jewish formula for blessing the "first fruits" as a parallel

for the holy root (Israel) from which all branches must spring if they are to live. If Gentiles have replaced some of the Jewish branches, the Gentiles must be reverent to the root, not engage in coarse boasting (*katakaukhasai,* "sneer down")—the very sin Christians would commit for centuries of anti-Semitic attacks. Stendahl rightly says that this section, if heeded, would have prevented all the horrible later treatment of Jews.[11] The Jews had failed in trust (*pistis*) since they did not rely on Jesus to fulfill God's promises to Israel. But Gentiles can fall too. Paul is like Augustine, not claiming to know who is permanently in or out of the church. That is still in God's mysterious hands.

3. Paul's optimism about the fate of the Jews is expressed here. They are the natural heirs, while the new believers are adopted children. The Jews draw their own life from the root, which is Israel. The Gentiles had to learn about the sacred writings, which Jews have heard from their childhood. They know the world to which they are being reconnected. Paul speaks as sharing their own flesh and blood. That the ingrafted wild olive might not take easily to a cultivated olive was a fact that would have been familiar to Paul's contemporaries. Modern science has shown that some wild olives have a different DNA from cultivated ones.[12]

4. Again Paul warns the Gentiles about being too smug ("wrapped in your own conceit"). That can become a prison ("enclosed in their own heedlessness"). They were converts once, they can slip out of the brotherhood they did not own from their birth. God will not go back on his promises. If the Gentiles forget that those promises were given to the Jews, they have severed their life from the root that all share.

5. To stress again God's mystery, Paul does not say how the Jews and Gentiles will be united so soon. *How* it will happen is unknown. *That* it will happen is as firm as God's word. Paul here composes a Jewish poem, based on things like God's questions to Job (did God consult Job on making the winds and the world?).[13]

It is interesting to contrast this image of olive branches living off a single root with a later passage of scripture about tendrils living off a single grapevine:

I am the true vine,
  and my Father tends it.
A branch of mine that bears no grapes
  he cuts off
and any branch bearing grapes
  he prunes, to bear more.[14]
You are already pruned
  by the words I spoke to you.
Stay in me
  as I stay in you.
As a branch can bear no grapes
  if detached from the vine,
so you cannot [bear grapes]
  unless you stay in me.
I am the vine,
  you the branches.
The one who stays in me
  and I in him,
bears many grapes;
  but detached from me
he bears nothing,
  since apart from me,
you cannot do anything.
  If one does not stay in me,
he is a withered branch, broken off
  to be gathered and thrown out
into the fire and burnt there (Jn 15.1–6).

Olive groves and vineyards were omnipresent in the ancient Middle East, and olive graftings and vine prunings were familiar to the audiences of both Paul and John. Yet the differences between these two passages, roughly forty years apart, are striking.[15] Roots are as important for grapevines as for olive trees, but the root has disappeared in the Johannine passage. Jesus is the one source of life for all the vine branches. The spiritual life has been literally deracinated, detaching Christianity from its roots in God's action for and through Israel. This is what Stendahl (in a different context) calls "a holy rope trick."[16] Raymond Brown contrasts the vine image in John with Isaiah's tale of the beloved vineyard of the Lord that produces sour grapes (Is 5.1–7).[17] "The vineyard or vine [in Isaiah] stands for Israel, while John identifies the vine with Jesus and not with a people."[18] The division between Jew and Gentile is apparent in the first verse of this vine image. Jesus is made to say "I am the true (*alēthinē*) vine." Brown has to admit, grudgingly, that this true vine is contrasted with "the false vine represented by the Jewish synagogue."[19]

Stendahl argues that the separation of Jesus from his people led to the neglect or misreading of Paul for three centuries (up to the time of Augustine). The Paul who was remembered in that period was the figure described in Luke's Acts of the Apostles (written in the mid-eighties), which never cites the letters, or even seems to know that they exist. When the Gospels began to enter the canon of a New Testament, they were soon taken to be accounts of Jesus written by his disciples, who were eyewitnesses to the life of Jesus. As such, they would be listed before the letters of Paul, who never saw Jesus in his lifetime. Thus Paul, who wrote the earliest parts of what would become the New Testament, was reduced to a later and less important figure than the evangelists.

When Augustine took up Paul, he was not interested in Paul's effort to get the Gentiles admitted into the promises made to Israel. The church by that time was almost entirely made up of Gentiles. Augustine imposed his own needs on the Pauline text. Where Paul said that Abraham's faith made it possible for Gentiles outside the Law to be saved, Augustine said that faith made up for individual guilt over the Law not observed—though in fact Paul said he observed the Law faultlessly (Phil 3.6). This Paul would become dear to those who read him with "the introspective conscience of the West" (the title of Stendahl's groundshifting lecture in 1961). This Paul, Luther's Paul, would become the lodestar of Protestants.[20] Paul was also blamed for much of the church's anti-Semitism. It was not until the Second Vatican Council that Paul's philo-Semitism was vindicated in the council document *Nostra Aetate*. It was the end of a long tragic tale, which had circled back to the real Paul—and the real Jesus.

NOTES

1. The relative pronouns in this sentence are normally translated as "*Theirs* are the prophets" and so on. But the antecedent of these masculine relative pronouns is "my brothers" (*synggenon mou*), so Paul is part of the group being referred back to.

2. Luke, at Acts 17.23, makes Paul quote (once) a pagan inscription, which shows the little accord Luke had with Paul's writings, of which he shows a total ignorance.

3. Krister Stendahl, *Paul Among Jews and Gentiles* (Fortress Press, 1976), 37.

4. Ibid., 38.

5. Stendahl paraphrases this as, "Do the Jews have an advantage?—oh, plenty!" *Final Account: Paul's Letter to the Romans* (Fortress Press, 1976), 21.

6. Ronald Knox, in his tendentious translation of Jerome's Latin *finis enim legis Christi* (for Paul's *telos gar nomou Christos*), actually gives us this: "Christ has *superseded* the law"! (Rom 10.4).

7. Stendahl, *Final Account,* 7.

8. *Plērōma,* "full count," has often been treated as the "fulfillment" of revelation. But Paul is talking of divided numbers being reunited, Jews and Gentiles together—as the Pauline author of Colossians realized.

9. Rejecting (*apobolē,* throwing away) is contrasted with rejoining (*proslempsis,* taking close). "Interaction" for *katallagē,* normally translated as "reconcile," like the verb *katallassein* at 2 Corinthians 5.19, "God in Christ reconciling us to him." But there the verb has a direct and indirect object of the two things being reconciled. Here there is only a genitive *kosmou. Katallagē,* "exchange," is originally said of commercial or political exchanges—transactions or treaties. The reconciling Paul has in mind in this passage is that between Jews and Gentiles, but that has not taken place yet in this part of the sentence. Some people think the Gentiles are being reconciled with the *kosmos.* The noun does not mean cosmos as a *thing,* the universe in whole or part (heaven or earth, or heaven and earth). Paul thinks of it as God's ordering act, his plan carried out in history. The Gentiles are interacting with a history that was previously just that of the Jews. When the Jews see that this is so, the withered branches will again be grafted onto their own root, life springing from death.

10. Literally, "If the first offering is consecrated, so is the whole bread." See Joseph A. Fitzmyer, *Romans* (Doubleday, 1993), 613.

11. Stendahl, *Paul Among Jews and Gentiles,* 4–5.

12. "Genetic Structure of Wild and Cultivated Olives in the Central Mediterranean Basin," *Annals of Botany,* June 30, 2006, 935–42.

13. On Paul's own composition of this passage, see Fitzmyer, op. cit., 633–34.

14. Pruning, literally "cleaning"—tidying up by nipping off superfluous buds. The verb for cleaning, *kathairein,* is a homophone of that for cropping (*hairein*) in 15.2.

15. Raymond Brown dates Romans to the late sixties, and the various layers of John's Gospel between 80 and 110. *An Introduction to the New Testament* (Doubleday, 1997), 559, 334.

16. Stendahl, *Final Account*, 22.

17. The vineyard is called beloved since it needs constant tending (cropping and pruning). For the vineyard to resist such care was a recurrent image of God's difficult relations with his people—see Jeremiah 5.10 and 12.10.

18. Raymond E. Brown, *The Gospel According to John, XIII–XXI* (Doubleday, 1970), 670. The same attempt to cut off all connection with the first revelation to Israel is seen in John's image of the good shepherd. There, Jesus is not only the shepherd but the gate of entry into the sheepfold (Jn 10.7), where Paul would have said that the Jewish scriptures he always preached from were the gate of entry.

19. Ibid., 674.

20. Though Stendahl was a Lutheran priest and bishop, he blamed Luther for much of the modern misreading of Paul.

THIRTEEN

After the Temple

After the Jerusalem Temple was destroyed in 70 CE, things went terribly wrong for Jews and Christians. Jacob Neusner described the impact on the Jews:

> The single most important event in the history of Judaism from the destruction of the Temple by the Babylonians in 586 B.C. to the conquest of Palestine by the Arabs in ca. 640 A.D. was the destruction of the Second Temple by the Romans in 70 A.D. . . . The Temple represented the nexus between heaven and earth. God had revealed his will in the Torah—the revelation to Moses at Sinai—which contained numerous cultic laws. Those laws were kept in the Temple, where the daily sacrifices and the exact sacrificial technology represented a primary means by which Israel served their father in heaven.[1]

With the loss of priests in the Temple and Sadducees in the Sanhedrin, the role of rabbis in the synagogues became essential to preserving cohesion throughout the Diaspora. No matter how scattered, Jewish communities had felt a strong connection with the Temple, paying the Temple tax and treasuring pilgrimages to it. Though Roman troops had destroyed the center of Jewish life, the traditional Roman toleration of local religions let Jews be absent from work on the Sabbath, gather in synagogues, and maintain markets for special foods.[2] The loss of the purity code for the Temple led to a compensatory strictness of observance overseen by Pharisees. These became experts in the Oral Torah built up around memories of leading rabbis like Hillel:

> The Pharisees were Jews who believed one must keep up the purity laws outside of the Temple . . . Successive groups found it important to shape [pre-70] Hillel materials, and the conditions reflected in these materials

are often not of actual historical realities (no Pharisee, even Hillel, ran the Temple), but rather the realities of life and fantasies of the shapers of the pericopes.[3]

Destruction of the Temple also affected Christians, changing their relations with the synagogues that were filling in for the absence of the Temple. Christians were a challenging element in and around the synagogues, which had established their exempt space. The Christians were seen as competitors with or confusers of relations with the Roman authorities. They not only challenged the new Pharisaic discipline of post-Temple observances but imperiled the recognized immunities under Roman law. Even worse, they were stripping away some of the potential proselytes who attended synagogue services, the so-called God-Respecting (*Theosebeis*).[4] The Jews, maintaining their own esprit in the post-Temple period, did not want to debate scripture with Christian Jews, who emphasized a different part of the sacred writings (heavily using the Psalms and the prophets rather than the Torah's laws). Christians were expelled from the synagogues, which they took as a form of persecution by the Pharisees.[5]

This clash was retrojected by the Gospels into the Pharisees' opposition to Jesus, from a time when Pharisees were not as important as during the post-Temple clashes between synagogue and basilica.[6] The Christians, who were formulating their own accounts of Jesus at the same time as the Jews were sorting out the traditions of Hillel, saw in Pharisaic opposition to Christians the desire to kill Jesus again in his mystical body. With the sole exception of Paul's authentic letters, all of the New Testament writings come from the time after the Temple was destroyed. Paul knows nothing of that event, but the Gospels all refer to it, and make Jesus predict it.[7] They were written, therefore, when the tension between synagogue and basilica was acute.

The Jews had good reason to fear that Christians were trying not simply to share but to replace their allowed status with Roman authority. In the Acts of the Apostles, Romans are consistently made more reasonable and reliable than perfidious Jews. As Claudia Setzer writes:

> The Romans in Acts are surprisingly passive and the Jews are unable to get them even mildly excited about the Christian troublemakers . . . As depicted in the Acts, the Romans are peculiarly apathetic about Christians.[8]

There is a pattern whereby Jews denounce Christians to Roman authority, only to have the Roman ruler dismiss the charges (Gallio at Acts 18.12), or want to dismiss them (Felix at Acts 24.1–17), or would have dismissed them if Paul had not asked for a change of venue (Agrippa at Acts 26.32). When an associate of Paul, Jason, is hauled before an official, he simply pays bail and is released (Acts 17.9). One reason Paul is treated better by Romans than by Jews in Acts is that Luke presents him as a Roman citizen (Acts 22.25–29), though Paul never claims that in his own letters, even where it would have served his purpose (as in the Letter to the Romans). Of course, Paul seems to have been put to death by the Roman emperor, which somewhat embarrasses Luke's picture of his standing. That may be one of the reasons Luke never treats Paul's death.

The flattering of Rome is not restricted to Acts. The pattern of Jewish denunciation and Roman lenity is registered in the Gospels, where Pilate wants to dismiss Jesus but the Jews will not let him. Pilate tells the crowd he has not found Jesus guilty of a crime (Mk 15.14, Lk 23.14, Jn 18.38). The crowd's clamor "won out" (*katischuon*, Lk 23.23), because Pilate "feared the crowd" (*ephobēthē*, Jn 19.8), he "wanted to pacify the crowd" (Mk 15.15), which was "on the verge of rioting" (Mt 27.24). Pilate accepts no responsibility for what is happening. "I have nothing to do (*athōos eimi*) with this killing (*haima*, Mt 27.24)."

Why should Pilate accept any responsibility when Jesus himself exonerates him? "The one who handed me over to you is more guilty [than you are]" (Jn 19.11). The "one handing over" is often taken to be Judas, but Jesus seems to be thinking more of Caiaphas, or of the priests generally, as Raymond Brown argues: "John attributes to the Jewish nation and the chief priests or to 'the Jews' the handing over of Jesus to Pilate."[9] Certainly Luke thinks it was the Jews, since he has Peter say to a Jewish crowd, "this Jesus whom you crucified" (Acts 2.36). Peter then tells "you men of Israel" (Acts 3.12) that "you brought him to trial and denounced him before Pilate, who decided to release him; but you denounced the holy and just man and begged him to release a murderer" (Barabbas, Acts 3.13–14).

People have debated fine points of law in attributing Christ's death to Romans, or to Jews, or to some combination of the two, or endless calibrations of responsibility in the passion narratives. But the blame for the death is made clear throughout the Gospels, not just at the trial of Jesus. It could not have been stated more clearly than in the parable of the vineyard, given in substantially identical form in all three Synoptic Gospels, showing dependence on an early tradition conventionally called Q (for *Quelle,* "source"). I noted earlier how Isaiah made the "beloved vineyard" a type of Israel. All three Synoptic Gospels give a new and deadly use to that image, so uniformly that it shows dependence on the earlier Q source:

> "A man planted a vineyard and walled it around, and dug a wine-trough, and posted a tower, and leased it to vintners, and then left the country. And as the time came near, he sent slaves to collect from the vintners his profit. But the vintners seized the slaves and thrashed one, killed one, and stoned one. Then he sent slaves again, more of them than before; but they treated them the same way. Finally he sent his own son to them, saying, 'They will honor my son.' But the vintners, recognizing his son, told themselves, 'Here is the heir. Then up, let us kill him and claim his estate.' So they grabbed him, dragged him outside the vineyard, and killed him. Now, then, when the owner of the vineyard comes, what will he do to the vintners?" They answered, "He will slay the vile ones vilely,

and transfer the vineyard to other vintners, who will render his profit at the right times." And Jesus said, "Have you never read in the scripture, 'The stone which the builders despised has become the main cornerstone; the Lord made it happen, and it is splendid in our eyes'? Thus I tell you the reign of God will be taken away from you, and granted to a people who pay the vineyard's profits on time" (Mt 21.33–43).

Matthew has taken the basic story he shares with Mark and Luke and added detail to make its meaning almost painfully clear. The different punishments dealt to slaves trying to collect for the owner match the different ways prophets were either stoned or otherwise killed. The son of the owner is Jesus, who is predicting his own murder by telling the parable. He is dragged outside the vineyard, just as Jesus will be taken outside Jerusalem to the Crucifixion. The transfer of the lease to a whole new people is the cancellation of God's covenant with the Jews.

But theologians have spent great efforts to keep scripture clear of such obvious supersessionism. In 1961, Gregory Baum was still trying to do that. He claimed that Matthew was just repeating Isaiah's view of the vineyard, trying to call the Jews back to their covenant:

> It was not dislike of his own nation, but on the contrary his love for the people called by God, which prompted Matthew to be so severe with the Jewish people.[10]

Baum would later repudiate his own book and accept the obvious meaning of this passage in all three Synoptics.[11] That meaning was spelled out in detail by Douglas Hare, who says it means the total rejection of Israel, by contrast with Paul's claim that God could not go back on his word to his own people:

> Matthew does not suggest that Gentile members of the Church are related to Abraham by faith or that they have been grafted onto the elect remnant of Israel. The doctrine of the remnant is not employed. The

Church is in no sense a continuation of Israel but a different *ethnos*, non-Israel, which replaces Israel . . . He regarded the Church as non-Israel.[12]

For the church father John Chrysostom, Israel was so much the anti-Jesus that it adhered to a reversal of meaning in the creed's profession of the Trinity:

> Wherever the Christ-killers (*Christoktonoi*) gather, there the cross is banned, God is blasphemed, the Father is unknown, the Son is insulted, the Spirit's graces rejected.[13]

The scriptural rejection of the Jews is not indicated only in the parable of the vineyard. It is the point of the wedding banquet tale, in which those first invited to the feast refuse to attend:

> "The angry host told his slave: 'Go straight into the streets and byways and bring here poor people, crippled ones, blind ones, limping ones.'
> "And the slave said, 'Master, what you ordered has been done, and there is still room.' And the master told his slave: 'Go into the paths and bushes, and drag them in (*anangkason*) to fill up the hall. I tell you that none of those who were invited will feast with me'" (Lk 14.21–24).

That part of the Gospel is not less intransigent than Chrysostom would be:

> Because you killed Christ, because you lifted your hand against the Lord, because you poured his precious blood out, there is no correcting you, no final pardoning of you, no defending you.[14]

We have seen that the Acts of the Apostles was kinder to Romans than to Jews. Even in the Gospels, Jesus gets along better, at times, with Romans than Jews, as when he works a miracle for the centurion because of his trust:

> "I tell you solemnly, I have not found such trust in Israel. I tell you, many will come from East and West to banquet with Abraham and Isaac and Joseph in the reign of heaven, but those who were heirs to the reign will

be hurled into outer darkness, a place of howling and gnashing teeth" (Mt 8.10–12).

It is not only in the Synoptics that supersessionism is voiced. In John's parable of the good shepherd, Jesus is not only the shepherd but the entryway into the fold (*thyra tōn probatōn*, Jn 10.7). The entry into the new covenant would be through the old one unless the old was superseded. Thus Jesus says, "I am the entry. If anyone comes in by way of my entry, he will be rescued" (Jn 10.9). John is in fact far harsher on the Jews than any other Gospel. The very term "Jews," rare in the earlier Gospels, is used seventy-one times in John, and over half the references are hostile.[15] After collecting learned articles on John's treatment of the Jews, three professors at the Catholic University of Leuven (Belgium) made this judgment:

> We thus affirm three convictions: (1) the Fourth Gospel contains anti-Jewish elements; (2) the anti-Jewish elements are unacceptable from a Christian point of view; and (3) there is no convincing way simply to neutralize or to remove the anti-Jewish dimension of these passages in order to save the healthy core of the message itself.[16]

This may seem a radical position—that one of the Gospels of Christianity cannot be considered Christian. But what else is one to make of passages like this, where Jesus says that the Jews are no longer children of Abraham but children of the devil?

> If you were children of Abraham, you would follow the actions of Abraham. But instead you are seeking ways to murder me, the man who tells you truths I heard from God. Abraham did not try that [murder]. But you are following the actions of your [real] father . . . You have the devil as your father, and you are eager to follow his actions. He does not stand for truth, there is no truth in him. When he speaks falsehoods, it is his innate idiom, for he is false and the father of falsehoods (Jn 8:39–41, 44).

Raymond Brown's comment on this passage is incisive:

> It would be incredible for a twentieth-century Christian to share or to justify the Johannine contention that "the Jews" are the children of the devil, an affirmation which is placed on the lips of Jesus (8.44); but I cannot see how it helps contemporary Jewish-Christian relationships to disguise the fact that such an attitude once existed.[17]

If it were not for Brown's eminence as a scholar, and for the fact that this statement appeared in a book given the ecclesiastical *nihil obstat* and *imprimatur,* one would think it heretical to say that a decent Christian can no longer say what one of the canonical Gospels says. So far have we come in recognizing that supersessionism is not a later perversion of scripture, but one of the deepest strains in the sacred writings, and especially in John's Gospel, of which Paula Fredriksen writes:

> John's Gospel, the bane of modern interfaith dialogue, contains some of the harshest language about Jesus' Jewish contemporaries of any writing in the New Testament. Most of these statements come out of the mouth of its main character. John structures his story around high-contrast polarities: light/darkness, above/below, God/Satan, spirit/flesh, sight/blindness, knowledge/ignorance. Jesus and his followers belong to and embody the positive cluster. "The Jews" throughout John's story are their opponents. John's Jesus tells them forthrightly, "You are from below, I am from above" (John 8.23).[18]

One of the most telling symbols of supersession of the old by the new is the report that at the moment of Jesus's death, the veil that curtained off the Holy of Holies in the Temple was torn completely apart (Mt 27.51), canceling the Covenant and symbolizing the coming destruction of the Temple. Jesus himself replaces the Temple, as he predicted to the Samaritan woman (Jn 4.21–26). His flesh is now the veil through which one approaches the holy (Heb 10.19–20). It would become part of Christian tradition that the Temple was destroyed because the Jews killed Christ. Chrysostom, as usual, voiced this dramatically:

The wondrous thing, Oh Judea, is that the one you wanted to crucify was crucified; and after his crucifixion, he then destroyed your city, he then dispersed your people, he scattered them everywhere to show that he is risen, is living, and is now in heaven. Because you did not recognize his power from his blessings on you, he taught you from his harshness and punishments that his power cannot be defeated or resisted.[19]

The suffering of Jews becomes in this way a proof of God's power and Christ's divinity. Christianity was defined against this image of Jewishness. Chrysostom expressed their total exclusion from each other:

If you are so impressed by the Jews, what mode of thought can you share with us? If their rites have mystery and grandeur, ours are a trumpery. But if ours are genuine—and they are—theirs are false through and through.[20]

The rivalry of synagogue and basilica had reached such a point in Revelation that its author thinks only Christians are the "real" Jews chosen by God, and those who attend synagogue are fake or failed Jews. The angel tells the author:

"A message from the First and the Last, who was dead but returned to life: 'I know your ordeal and deprivation (yet you are wealthy), your vilification by those who say they are Jews and are nothing but Satan's synagogue'" (Rev 2.9).

Another message:

"I will give over to you from Satan's synagogue those who say that they are Jews and are not, but are lying. I will make them come and kneel at your feet and recognize that you are the one I love" (Rev 3.9).[21]

Passages like that made loathing the synagogue a Christian duty—and Chrysostom lived up to that assignment, attacking Antioch's Christians who actually went into synagogues to see the service there:

The place for whoring is a brothel; a synagogue is not only a theater and brothel but a den of thieves and nest of animals . . . not only of animals but of unclean beasts . . . When God abandons a place it becomes the residence of devils.[22]

Gregory Baum, who had denied that the Gospels were supersessionist, renounced that view after attending the Second Vatican Council as a theological expert (*peritus*). He admits that he erred because "I thought that it was my religious duty as a Christian theologian to defend the New Testament itself from the accusation of prejudice and falsification."[23] But now he recognizes that the New Testament "reflected the conflict between the Church and Synagogue in the first century," and not in "peripheral and accidental" ways, so that "the Church has produced an abiding contempt among Christians for Jews."[24] What made Baum change his reading of the Bible? The Holocaust. It changed the church. After Paul and after the fall of the Temple, we can see the coming of anti-Semitism into the church. Since the Second Vatican Council, we can see its going. It is not gone, by any means; but it is now ashamed to show its face in decent surroundings.

NOTES

1. Jacob Neusner, *From Politics to Piety: The Emergence of Pharisaic Judaism*, second edition (KTAV Publishing House, 1979), 2–3.
2. Ibid., 68.
3. Ibid., 83, 42.
4. Joseph A. Fitzmyer, *The Acts of the Apostles* (Doubleday, 1998), 449–50.
5. Douglas R. A. Hare, *The Theme of Jewish Persecution of Christians in the Gospel According to St. Matthew* (Cambridge University Press, 1967), passim. Hare argues that "a beleaguered Jewry" was threatened in "the traditional solidarity of the Jewish people" (13).
6. Neusner, op. cit., 68.
7. Of course, the Gospels draw on earlier traditions, reshaping them to fit the prayer needs of their various communities. The first Gospel, Mark's, may have been begun just before the fall of the Temple, but it was completed afterward. See Raymond Brown, *An Introduction to the New Testament* (Doubleday, 1997), 163–64; Joel Marcus, *Mark 1–8* (Doubleday, 2000), 37–39.

8. Claudia Setzer, *Jewish Responses to Early Christians* (Fortress Press, 1994), 73, 176.

9. Raymond E. Brown, *The Gospel According to John, XIII–XXI* (Doubleday, 1970), 879.

10. Gregory Baum, *The Jews and the Gospel* (Blooomsbury Publishing Co., 1961), 44.

11. Baum, in Rosemary Ruether, *Faith and Fratricide* (Wipf & Stock, 1997), 1–22.

12. Hare, op. cit., 157–58.

13. John Chrysostom, *Against the Jews* (Migne, *Patrologia Graeca*, vol. 48, Homily One, Column 852).

14. Ibid., Homily Six, Column 907.

15. Raymond Brown, *An Introduction to the Gospel of John* (Doubleday, 2003), 157. See also 168: "If the Johannine writers and many of the Johannine Christians were of Jewish birth, their generalizing use of 'the Jews' for those hostile to Jesus indicates deep alienation from their ancestral people."

16. R. Bieringer, D. Pollefeyt, and F. Vandecaster-Vanneuville, eds. *Anti-Judaism and the Fourth Gospel* (Westminster John Knox Press, 2001), 33.

17. Raymond Brown, *The Community of the Beloved Disciple* (Paulist Press, 1979), 41–42. Compare Adele Reinhartz's words: "[Nothing] defuses the anti-Jewish potential of the text. There is in fact no solution that gets the Fourth Gospel 'off the hook.' It is not possible to explain away the negative presentations of Jews or to deny that the Johannine understanding of Jesus includes the view that he has superseded the Jewish covenant and taken over its major institutions and symbols. An honest and engaged reading of the Gospel must surely acknowledge, and lament, the presence of these themes." Paula Fredriksen and Adele Reinhartz, eds., *Jesus, Judaism, and Christian Anti-Judaism* (Westminster John Knox Press, 2002), 114.

18. Paula Fredriksen, *Augustine and the Jews* (Doubleday, 2008), 304–5.

19. Chrysostom, op. cit., Homily Five, Column 884.

20. Ibid., Homily One, Column 852.

21. On these passages, see Jan Lambrecht, "'Synagogue of Satan' (Rev. 1.9 and 3.9): Anti-Judaism in the Book of Revelation," in Bieringer et al., op. cit., 279–92.

22. Chrysostom, opt. cit., Homily One, Column 847.

23. Gregory Baum, in Ruether, op. cit., 2.

24. Ibid., 3, 5.

FOURTEEN

After the Holocaust

The Holocaust was a world-altering event, and a church-altering event, for Jews, for Christians, for everyone. At first, there was a nervous effort to narrow the scope of its horror, and of responsibility for it. People who had not openly opposed it said they had secretly worked against it, as if that would be enough to let them escape blame. This was the Pius XII approach, used by many people with less than his claim on the excuse. Others argued that anti-Semitism was a new product of pagan "science," which had nothing to do with previous (Christian) forms of anti-Judaism. Hitler's men "proved" that Jews were genetically tainted and inferior. Theological anti-Judaism just said that the Jews' mandate from God had been replaced by the new covenant of Jesus. The fact that the old covenant was canceled did not, they claimed or hoped, mean that Jews were subhuman or should be killed.

But the idea that Jews were subhuman did not have to wait for Hitler's scientists to find a voice. We have seen John Chrysostom say they were "unclean beasts." We have heard the Gospel of John say they were children of the devil. We have read Revelation stating that they attend Satan's synagogue. The Holocaust was just a *reductio ad horrendum* of long years of hate and vilification. There had been a slower, less visible holocaust occurring over the centuries.

At times this quiet hate broke out in frenzy, especially around made-up Jewish atrocities used to justify real Christian atrocities. Chrysostom had called Jews "Christ-killers" (*Christoktonoi*). Thomas Aquinas too had called them Christ-killers (*Occisores Christi*).[1] For much of Europe's population this meant that Jews were still trying to kill Christ—in his church, in young baptized children, in the Eucharist. This feeling gave the hatred of Jews its peculiar quality. Though the Jews were sequestered, labeled, extruded, and denied rights of free speech and movement, they were always seen as preying on victims. The larger culture acted out of fear. Though it had tied down Jews in many ways, that larger culture itself felt persecuted. The boys supposedly murdered by Jews, for blood used in their rituals, were called (and sometimes canonized as) martyrs—like "Little Saint Hugh of Lincoln," the martyr celebrated in Chaucer's Prioress's Tale, or "Saint William of Norwich," "Little Richard of Pontoise," "Good Werner of Overwesel," or "the boy Saint Simon" of Trent. The sequestered Jews were recast as Roman emperors creating Christian martyrs.[2] How could the marginalized Jews be seen as so powerful and threatening?

We have seen that John's is the most outspoken Gospel against the Jews. David Nirenberg points out that this Gospel has a cosmic vision of a great struggle of light against the darkness.[3] The "prince of this world" may be overthrown in the long run, but he has license to fight the light coming into the world, and he seems at times to extinguish it. Jews, as the killers of Christ, were doing the devil's work, and had his power behind them, even in their confined areas of activity. The whole of medieval Christianity thus felt picked on. The Jews were given some of the devil's own license to defy God. They were devils who continually threatened the good order of God. One could not kill the devil. But one could kill a witch—or a Jew.

This explains the personal feeling of endangerment wherever Jews seemed to encroach on ordinary people's lives. The stories that originated or excused pogroms, mass burnings, harsh repression have the air of last-minute rescues of endangered Christian values. Massacres of Jews were celebrated in processions and pilgrimages as triumphs of God. Even the scholarly Jesuit Bollandists, who introduced scientific method into hagiography in the seventeenth century, validated the tales of Jewish ritual murder and host desecration as defenses of an imperiled Christianity.[4] The highly personal engagement in this struggle is expressed in the tale of a Bavarian Jewish massacre in 1337.[5] In the poetic work memorializing this event we read how:

1. The Jews got a female servant to take communion on Easter, but to bring the host to them to be tortured.
2. The Jews tried to torture the host, stabbing it, burning it, trying to eat it, but it remained unconquerable.
3. The torture continued through the night, until the Virgin Mary appeared to the Jews and asked why they were murdering her child. Her cries were heard by people outside the house.
4. The town council, alerted, came to capture the host's captors, upon which Jews outside the house poisoned the city's wells.
5. A group of Christians in a neighboring village, swearing on the cross to take vengeance (approximating themselves to Crusaders), came and set fire to the house, burning much of the village and killing Jews who opposed them.
6. The host flew intact out of the fire, was retrieved by a priest, and was installed in a shrine that became an object of pilgrimage. The inscription on the shrine read

> Anno 1337, the day following Michaelmas Day
> here were the Jews slain:
> they had set the city afire.[6]

7. The Duke of Bavaria rewarded the citizens by giving them the Jewish property.
8. The miraculous events were celebrated in an annual procession.

The only parts of this tale that are verifiable in history are numbers 5 (the burning and massacre), 6 (the existence of the shrine and its inscription), 7 (the bestowal of Jewish property), and 8 (the later commemorations). The other parts could have been made up to explain the massacre and seizure of property, but they were clearly believed, then and after, by many of the local devotees of the shrine.

I choose this tale, out of a heartbreakingly large number of tales proudly commemorating the defeat of Jews, because it contains the elements of so many of the other local traditions. Consider the story, point by point:

1. Tensions often came to a climax in the conjunction of the principal feasts of the two cultures, Easter and Passover. Easter recalled the foiling of the Jewish murder of Jesus by his resurrection. Passover was treated as an anti-Easter, according to legend, when Christian blood was used to commemorate Jewish deliverance. Another common feature in this tale of a servant girl stealing the host was the distrust of servants given access to family or religious activities—something seen in the prominence of servant girls in witch hunts.[7]

2. The torture of the host combines the most hallucinatory irrationalisms of the legend. The Jews are made to believe that Jesus is in the host, a belief that was embattled even among Christians of the Middle Ages. Then, to top that absurdity, they are made to believe they can harm or desecrate Jesus by abuse of the host. The various ways they try this are all foiled, yet they keep trying to stab, drown, or incinerate the host. Gavin Langmuir and others think this part of the legends had more to do with giving negative reinforcement to Christian belief in the Eucharist, which was still uncertain in the eleventh and twelfth centuries. The defeat of the Jews was the reverse side of the Corpus Christi processions.[8] The importance of the host desecrations as an adjunct to host devotion is indicated from the fact that some authorities exonerated Jews of the ritual murder of boys, but courts and communities continued to uphold judgments against the even crazier idea that Jews tried to murder hosts ritually. These were not just events of the Middle Ages. In 1492, twenty-seven Jews were judicially executed in Sternberg. In 1510, thirty-nine were burnt at the stake in Berlin while the Christian charged with supplying the host was torn apart with red-hot irons.[9]

3. The Virgin Mary was often brought in on the side of the victimized host or the boy martyrs.[10] In one tale, popularized by Saint Gregory of Tours, a Jewish father learns that his son has received a host, throws the boy into an oven, and Mary comes to rescue him. In the Bavarian tale treated here, Mary does not seem to know that the Jews cannot hurt her son, but wails as if she were still standing at the cross—in effect making her symbolically denounce the Jews at the actual Crucifixion.

4. Poisoning of wells was a common crime attributed both to witches and to Jews. This is an example of the way disasters had to be caused by some alien intervention. In the Middle Ages, the Jews were behind it all. In modern times, conspiracies are behind bad happenings (Pearl Harbor, the death of Kennedy, the Twin Towers, etc.). Modern "truthers" are descendants of the witch trials and inquisitorial tribunals.

5. The mob gets lionized as a set of heroes saving the village by burning it down. This was the way of sacralizing mass violence.

6. Though the Bavarian tale begins on Easter, it reaches its climax on September 29, the feast of Saint Michael the Archangel, celebrated as a Holy Day of Obligation in the Middle Ages. Since Michael led the army of angels throwing Lucifer out of heaven, he is the right patron for the defeat of hellish agents, either in crusades against the Saracens or in local victories over Jews.

7. The confiscation of Jewish property was often justified as redress for some prior assault—often for their usurious practices, imposed on them by Christian doctrine. This concept still lives in anti-Semitic hatred of "the banks."

8. Devotion to Christian feasts was often deepened by seeing them as triumphs over the Jews. Pilgrimages to the sites of massacres was a way of sweetening their memory.

Anti-Jewish hysteria was not necessarily encouraged by church authorities. In fact, bishops feared that such movements could get out of hand. (The same was true of witch hunts.) There were papal bulls and other statements against belief in Jewish ritual murder of Christian boys—notably by Calixtus II in *Sicut Judaeis* (1120) and Innocent IV in *Lachrymabilem Judaeorum* (1247). But as Joshua Trachtenberg notes, the need to repeat such defenses shows that the abuse was a continuing one.[11] And Kenneth Stow shows how persistent was belief in fictional Jewish murder, with real murderous consequences:

> Charges of ritual murder were clearly magnets to which any of the various ills afflicting the Christian body politic, or some part of it, might be attached.[12]

Even though popes denied belief in ritual murder, their statements are most notable for what they did not deny—especially that the Jews had killed Christ, that their religion was superseded, that Catholics should not "Judaize" by reverting to it.

The whole tradition of Christian protection for Jews came from Augustine, who might be called a modified supersessionist. He believed the Jewish religion was no longer valid, but it was useful to keep it as an independent verifier of the prophecies that confirm Christ's Messiahship. Augustine's view was perfectly summed up in what was then (and for a long time) a mistranslation of Psalm 59.11, which said the opposite of the Hebrew. Augustine read a Latin text like that of the King James translation of the verse: "Slay them not, lest my people forget: scatter them by thy power."[13] Augustine took that as warrant for keeping Jewish scripture alive to bolster Christian belief, and to scatter Jews in a protected Diaspora, to bear wider witness to the proof texts of Christianity.

This misunderstanding served as a slogan, "Slay them not," that was used by popes and others to protest the recurrent massacres of Jews. As such, the misreading probably saved Jewish lives down through the years. As for Augustine himself, Paula Fredriksen, in her excellent book *Augustine and the Jews*, argues that the psalm had little influence on his thought. It was just a memorable way of pressing home a line of thought he had hammered out for himself long before he thought about this convenient slogan:

> Within his own lifetime and thus within the contemporary context of his own work, Psalm 59 . . . never had this status as a major proof text in his arsenal. He had come to it too late . . . By the time he found Psalm 59, he did not need it.[14]

Fredriksen claims that the important early text for his thought on Jews was *Contra Faustum*, in which he refuted Manichean dismissal of the Jewish scriptures in general. This was a part of the widespread Gnostic attack on the "Old Testament" as too material and earthy a teaching to express

anything truly divine. Augustine defended such "earthiness" as necessary to the Incarnation of Jesus in a physical body.[15]

Even though the psalm verse served some good purposes, it did not
shake the tendency to see Jews as the Gospel of John did, as on the devil's
side in fighting Christ. As David Nirenberg points out, even the most favorable reading of Augustine reduced Jews to mere milestones by which
Christians proceeded on their way, leaving the immobile stones behind
them as they passed.[16] And as Gavin Langmuir argues, the Augustinian
valuation of Jews, as keepers of the Old Testament, was blunted by the
belated discovery (in the thirteenth century) that contemporary Jews
were living as much by the Talmud as by the ancient texts. If they were
not going to be seen solely as witnesses to the Old Testament, their Augustinian value dwindled or disappeared. That protection, as flawed as it
had been, was gone.[17]

But the debate about real Jews always weighed little against the fear
and hatred of what Nirenberg calls artificial Jews or the Jewish construct.
He says that anti-Judaism put a Jewish mask on any evil feared or despised at the time.[18] Ordinary Christians had little contact with Jews
themselves, who, when they were not expelled from a country (as in
England), were confined to ghettos or met only in straitened ways. But a
mental picture of the Jews was instilled in popular culture and devotion,
making them convenient stereotypes for people to use about anything
they hated. John Chrysostom had begun his series of anti-Semitic sermons as an attack on Arians. It was a natural to move on, in his pulpit, to
the Jews, since Arians, attacking the divine status of the Son in the
Trinity, were also trying to kill Christ.

Anything hostile to Christianity was seen as in alliance with the Jews,
or becoming as bad as Jews, or simply being Jews. Paganism was Jewish.
The Antichrist of the End Time was a Jew.[19] Saracens who took the Holy
Land were enemies of Christ, indistinguishable from Jews—so Crusaders
slaughtered them both indiscriminately. The Enlightenment began a
long tradition of seeing in Jesus "the modern man," opposed to Jewish

legalism and obscurantism.[20] Hitler attacked "degenerate" artists of any ethnicity as Jews. My grandfather hated bankers, and referred to them as uniformly Jewish. He also hated Franklin Roosevelt, so he was sure that the president was a Jew.[21] Pius X, XI, and XII thought that communism was a largely Jewish phenomenon. They could oppose the Jews on the excuse that they were just opposing communism. Even a pious Christian could find a Jew in himself if he disappointed Jesus. The great religious poet George Herbert lamented in prayer:

> He that hath made a sorry wedding
> Between his soul and gold, and hath preferr'd
> False gain before the true,
> Hath done what he condemns in reading:
> For he hath sold for money his dear Lord
> And is a Judas-Jew.[22]

Krister Stendahl said that Paul believed Christians were "honorary Jews." He meant it in a favorable sense, to all involved. But what has been beaten into the Western mind was a whole series of *dis*honorary Jews, people of all sorts sifted down into a bag of despised things as "Jewish." Christian art has helped set the fashion for making any opponents of Christ or Christians become artificial Jews. The ugly humans conducting Jesus on the way of the cross were caricatured Jews. In pictures of the betrayal of Jesus, Judas was given the red hair and yellow cloak of a Jew, no matter that he had been a follower of Jesus like Peter and John—who were given Caucasian features. The synagogue was personified in the arts as blindfolded—notably in a striking mosaic in Venice's San Marco.

Christians who may not ever have met a Jew had seen his inner nature revealed in the artworks that showed the ritual murder of Christian boys, or the desecration of the host. Many of these were in woodcuts or engravings widely distributed as prints or in books; but others are permanent parts of famous churches—the ten windows of Brussels cathedral that tell the story of the desecrated host of a 1370 "miracle," also depicted in a tapestry of the church. Or the paintings of ritual murder by Charles de Prevot that hung in the Polish cathedral of Sandomierz and in the neighboring church of Saint Paul. Or in Paolo Uccello's Urbino altarpiece of a Jew being burnt at the stake for "torturing" the host. In general, wherever a supposed miracle or rationalized massacre took place, artworks were used to memorialize it as a triumph of Christianity.

What point is there in distinguishing "racism" from theological supersessionism when all the torrent of filth down the ages had stigmatized the Jew as diabolic? The distinction between theological and racist prejudice was erased in all the Christians who sympathized with Hitler and were not criticized for that by the Vatican. A striking instance of this was the writings of Karl Adam, a theologian widely revered in Europe and America. He greeted the rise of Hitler as if it were the Second Coming: "And he came, Adolf Hitler. From the south he came, but we knew him not." Hitler's Jesus was not a Jew, Adam said, because his mother was immaculately conceived:

> Jesus' mother Mary had no physical or moral connection with those ugly dispositions and forces that we condemn in full-blooded Jews. Through the miracle of the grace of God, she is beyond these Jewish hereditary traits, a figure who transcends Judaism. And what had occurred in Mary took place too in the human nature of her son.[23]

Jesus had to be saved from being Jewish, with all the ugly dispositions we rightly condemn, because "the Jew" was made a synecdoche for everything dissenting, oppositional, subversive, or clandestine. Forced into marginality, the Jew was blamed for being shadowy. Exiled from many lands, he was condemned as alien. The Holocaust's monstrous quality shed a terrible light on all the prior history of "Christendom." It made Jews too much the victims of a threatening world for us ever to see them again as agents for threatening the world. We all feel (or should) a pang of guilt for what "our" culture produced. It shook every kind of smugness or self-satisfaction. Even those who did not actively engage in anti-Semitic talk or action did not either engage in talk or action defending the Jews. There was something intimidating about so much anti-Semitism woven into the very fabric of our lives. It was easy to think one should not, in the slang term, "go there." It resembles the way the white majority in the South did not protest against the treatment of blacks in the Jim Crow days—they were inhibited by the then-effective deterrent term "nigger lover." It is time now for all of us to become, as Stendahl put it, "honorary Jews."

NOTES

1. ST III q47 a5 ad 3.
2. Making martyrs of the Jews' boy victims was a priority analyzed at length by Kenneth Stow in *Jewish Dogs* (Stanford University Press, 2006). He deals with boy martyrs like Little Robert of Bury St. Edmunds and Richard of Pontoise, among others. See also R. Po-chia Hsia, *The Myth of Ritual Murder* (Yale University Press, 1988), 43–50.
3. David Nirenberg, *Anti-Judaism: The Western Tradition* (W. W. Norton, 2013), 80–83.
4. Stow, op. cit., 99–118.
5. The narrative is laid out in Christopher Ocker, "Ritual Murder and the Subjectivity of Christ: A Choice in Medieval Christianity," *Harvard Theological Review*, vol. 91 (1996), 171–72. See also Hsia, op. cit., 47, 128.
6. The inscription is given in Joshua Trachtenberg, *The Devil and the Jews* (Jewish Publication Society, 1983), 90.
7. See Hsia, op. cit., 45–51.
8. Gavin Langmuir, *History, Religion, and Antisemitism* (University of California Press, 1990), 259–64. See also Caroline Walker Bynum, *Wonderful Blood* (University of Pennsylvania Press, 2007), 71–72, and Hsia, op. cit., 55–56.
9. Bynum, op. cit., 68–69.
10. Stow, op. cit., 27, 57, 61, 71, 76, 79.
11. Trachtenberg, op. cit., 134.
12. Stow, op. cit., 77.
13. Translators mistook Hebrew *El*, a divine name, for the negative *al*. The meaning is, "Slay them, God!" See Mitchell Dahood, *Psalms II* (Doubleday, 1968), 71–72. Even in the translation Augustine used, the rest of the psalm repeatedly asks that enemies be crushed and obliterated. In fact, verse 14 of the same psalm describes the enemies prowling and growling like a dog—an image constantly used against Jews, as Kenneth Stow shows exhaustively in *Jewish Dogs*.
14. Paula Fredriksen, *Augustine and the Jews* (Doubleday, 2008), 349.
15. Ibid., especially 260–89.

16. Nirenberg, op. cit., 130–31.

17. Langmuir, op. cit., 295–97.

18. Nirenberg, op. cit., 10.

19. Norman Cohn, *The Pursuit of the Millennium,* revised expanded edition (Oxford University Press, 1970), 77–80.

20. E. P. Sanders, "Jesus, Ancient Judaism, and Modern Christianity," in *Jesus, Judaism, and Christian Anti-Judaism,* edited by Paula Fredriksen and Adele Reinhartz (Westminster John Knox Press, 2002), 34–35.

21. This absurdity was not restricted to the United States. An Italian newspaper charged in 1938 that Roosevelt was "the Pope of world Jewry." David Kertzer, *The Pope and Mussolini* (Random House, 2014), 352.

22. George Herbert, "Self-Condemnation."

23. Karl Adam, "Jesus, the Christ and We Germans" (1943), quoted in Robert Krieg, "Karl Adam, National Socialism, and Christian Tradition," *Theological Studies,* vol. 60 (1999), 448.

FIFTEEN

The Return to Paul

Many Jews, converts to Christianity, brought about the conversion of the church in relation to the Jewish people

—Hans Ucko, World Council of Churches[1]

G regory Baum was one of those Jewish converts to Catholicism mentioned by Hans Ucko. He knew the church must change at the Second Vatican Council. But he knew it was an almost impossible task:

> The presence of the anti-Jewish trend in the Christian tradition, confirmed by a host of historical studies, and the connection of this trend, however indirect, with the genocide of European Jewry, left Christian thinkers speechless and stunned. They recognized that the effort to liberate Christian teaching from the contempt for Jews and Jewish religion would shake the foundation of the Christian faith. And yet it had to be undertaken.[2]

The recognition that anti-Semitism was not just an excrescence on the Catholic faith, but deeply embedded there, was so unpleasant that some at the Vatican tried to ignore or downplay the issue. Some fathers said they had not even heard that Jews were Christ-killers. Had they not read their own sacred texts? John Courtney Murray said he had lived the first forty years of his life without hearing of such a thing—yet he had spent his whole professional career studying church history, which is filled with the Christ-killer charges.[3] Baum again faces the unpleasant facts:

> Many years ago I had occasion to write that I had not learned what ideology was—that is, the distortion of truth for the sake of collective

interests—from Karl Marx. I had learned it instead through the painful discovery of the church's anti-Jewish rhetoric, an ideology that has marred almost the entire Christian tradition.[4]

Almost all the bishops and *periti* at Vatican II had studied Thomas Aquinas in their seminary days. And Thomas said that killing Jesus was the worst kind of sin (*peccatum gravissimum*), and the Jews had committed it.[5] They wanted to stone him to death, but could not while they were under Roman rule—so they gave him over to the Romans to kill in their way.[6] The Romans had taken part in this sin, but they were partly forgivable because they did not realize who Jesus was. Not taught by the prophets as Jews were, they were only committing homicide. The Jews committed deicide—they were *Dei crucifixores*.[7] Thomas has to admit that Jesus said on the cross, "Father, forgive them, since they do not realize what they are doing" (Lk 23.34). But that applied only to the executioners. They and other Jews had been kept in the dark by their priests and leaders (*principes*), who had every reason to recognize their Messiah from the prophecies and his miracles:

> It must be held that their ignorance does not exculpate them, because it was an ignorance they found a way to contrive (*ignorantia quodammodo affectata*). Though they saw the miracles that proved him divine, out of hatred and resentment of Christ they twisted the miracles' significance, and they willed their disbelief in the words by which he proclaimed that he was the Son of God.[8]

They were blinded to the truth because hatred made them put on their own blindfold.

How were bishops at the council, men who had been steeped in this teaching from their youth, going to change what they had been taught? The scriptures themselves, amply cited by Thomas, condemned the Jews. Some of the bishops were not going to change. In fact, Maximos IV Sayegh, the respected patriarch of the Melkite Catholic Church, said that he would have to depart from the council if it denied a teaching so old and strong as that the Jews killed Christ. Paul VI, who had succeeded John XXIII as the council continued its work, told Cardinal Augustin Bea, the head of the commission considering the Jewish issue, that the defection of so important a member of the council might force him to disband the council.[9] This is believable, since the pope actually agreed with the patriarch. In a Passion Sunday sermon delivered in Rome while the council continued, he described "the clash between Jesus and *the Jewish people*":

> That people, predestined to receive the Messiah, who awaited Him for thousands of years and was completely absorbed in this hope and in this certainty, at the right moment—when, that is, Christ came, spoke, and presented Himself—not only did not recognize Him, but fought Him, slandered and injured Him; and, in the end, killed Him.[10]

Another issue involving Jews, supersession, was perhaps even harder to deal with since it seemed less invidious than the charge of deicide. The bishops had been taught and continued teaching that there is only one true church, that of the only-begotten son of God. What room does that leave for any other religion, including that of the Jews? The fathers gathered for the council felt they had spent their lives carrying out what is called the Great Commission, delivered by the risen Christ at Matthew 28.19: "Journeying out, then, make disciples of all nations, baptizing them into the name of the Father and the Son and the Holy Spirit." Even ordinary Catholics were urged to be "apostolic" by calling others to convert. John Connelly put the situation squarely:

> Christians could not suddenly close their eyes to teaching dating back to the second century, according to which Jews were fated to suffer until they turned to Christ. With the exception of the Anglican minister James W. Parkes, no Christian theologian of note dissented from this point of view before 1945: not Charles Journet, Jacques Maritain, Karl Barth, Martin Niemöller, or even the martyrs Dietrich Bonhoeffer and Bernard

Lichtenberg. Though horrified by Nazi antisemitism, leading Catholic theologians Romano Guardini and Erich Przywara—both inspirations to the White Rose resistance group in Munich—remained silent. The prominent French anti-fascist theologian Henri de Lubac said nothing publicly against anti-Judaism before 1945. Those few Christians who opposed antisemitism in the interwar years, such as Maritain, Karl Thieme, or Dietrich von Hildebrand, still said to Jews, in essence, "The Jew Jesus of Nazareth has become my savior, redeemer and King; and because of that, I would like that he finally be recognized by his own people as their redeemer, because then they will be saved."[11]

How, then, at Vatican II was the church to give up its whole missionary obligation to go out to the world and convert everyone to Christ? Yet Rabbi Abraham Heschel, one of the Jewish observers invited to the council, said that day was over for him and his fellow believers. He would "go to Auschwitz anytime, if faced with the alternative of conversion or death."[12] Heschel, of course, remembered the times of forcible conversions, in Spain and elsewhere, that degraded both religions by coercion, subtle when not minatory. Gregory Baum understood the logic of Heschel's position: after the Holocaust, he wrote, "asking the Jews to become Christians is a spiritual way of blotting them out of existence and thus only reinforces the effects of the Holocaust."[13]

Most of those called to the council did not want to deal with such an embarrassing question. They were asked, while the council was in preparation, to write in suggestions for what it should deal with. None thought that relations with Jews should be on the agenda.[14] But John XXIII, who had called the council, was determined that redress must be undertaken. Pope John was an admirer of the great French Jewish historian Jules Isaac, who had labored to expose the tragic Christian past but also to build new ties with the Christians—and especially with the Jewish converts to Catholicism, who would play such a vital role as the council developed.[15] So Pope John commissioned the German Jesuit Cardinal Bea to shepherd the Jewish question through the council's deliberations.

When John XXIII died in 1963, after the first session of the council, the new pope, Paul VI, said that the council must go forward. He was nonetheless frightened by the energies of change that Pope John had unleashed, and he tried to rein them in. He listened to voices in the Curia that tried to control what was becoming a majority of bishops, now heeding progressive theologians they had enlisted as their own non-Roman experts. Paul tended to agree with those—Cardinals Pericle Felici, Amleto Cicognani, and Ottaviani—who thought the Gospel teaching on deicide could not be abandoned without defying the clear message of the Gospels. Paul at first tried to work with Bea to change the text of the declaration on Jews:

> It soon became clear that the pope and Bea did not see eye-to-eye on the [draft] text, particularly on what was to be said about the crucial issue of deicide, and the document was reworded several times in attempts to reach a compromise. Bea was intent on absolving of the crime not only contemporary Jews but also the Jewish people of Christ's time, as distinct from certain of their leaders. On that issue the pope prevailed in the text Bea presented to the council, which contained only one sentence on the subject: "Let everyone take care not to impute to the Jews of our times what happened during the Passion of Christ."[16]

But this victory for Paul did not satisfy the Curial types, who called for more changes, or even for withdrawing the draft text. When these attempts failed, Cardinal Felici dropped what Father O'Malley calls "the bomb" of October 9, 1964. He moved that the matter be transferred from the Secretariat for Promoting Christian Unity (Cardinal Bea's responsibility) and placed in a new subcommission whose members would be chosen by Cardinal Ottaviani, the most ardent opponent of Bea.[17] This caused a sensation in the penumbra that had gathered around the council—the religious press, the secular press, *periti* serving the bishops, Protestant observers, and Jewish observers. A storm had already hit this community and reverberated in the bishops' ears, caused by Rolf Hochhuth, whose play *Der Stellvertreter* (*The Deputy,* more accurately *The Vicar*) had been translated and performed in Berlin, New York, and London during the council's sessions of 1963 and 1964, creating a worldwide controversy. Its thesis, that Pius XII had ignored the plight of the Jews in the Holocaust, was resented or resisted by many bishops—who nonetheless did not want to incur the same suspicions about their own acts at the council. A backlash returned the matter to Bea's care.

Bea was working with and drawing on the opinions of Jewish priests and theologians who had become Christian priests and theologians (some Protestant, most Catholic). They were called "converts," though some did not accept that term. They were as Jewish as they had ever been. There was a large group of them, acutely aware of each other's views—John Oesterreicher, Karl Thieme, Paul Demann, Leo Rudloff, Jean-Roger Héné, Irene Marinoff, Bruno Hussar, Sophie van Leer, and Gregory Baum. Most of these people were at a 1960 meeting that passed on its recommendations for improved Jewish-Christian relations to Pope John XXIII. Three of them, Oesterreicher, Baum, and Hussar, would join in the drafting of what became the council's document on the Jews, *Nostra Aetate.*[18] They could play such a prominent role, well recorded in John Connelly's book, because they shared the experience of Paul, as *both* Jews *and* Christians.

It is ironic that Cardinal Giovanni Montini took the papal name of Paul and yet opposed Paul's view of the faith. Bad as the Gospels are on Jewish Christ-killers, Paul said that God did not go back on his promises to the Jews, which are *ametamelēta,* not subject to second thought (Rom 11.29). David Nirenberg, quick to spot any anti-Judaism, found none in Paul: "Paul the Pharisee, writing before the destruction of Jerusalem and before the predominance of gentiles in the church, had never aligned the Jews with Satan, nor opposed their world of Temple and covenant to God's."[19] With the Letter to the Romans on their side, the drafters of the council document could boldly assert, "The apostle Paul maintains that the Jew remains very dear to God, for the sake of the patriarchs, since God does not take back the gifts he bestowed or the choice he made."[20]

There could be no better instance of a long course of error followed by the church, corrected at last from the original springs of faith. The church can live because it can learn, correct, and change under God's direction. We are never more Christian than when going back to Paul, "a Jew of Jews." The council did not "forgive the Jews" for killing Christ. It asked them for forgiveness so that, once having fought, we can at last be friends.

NOTES

1. Hans Ucko, "Towards an Ethical Code of Conduct on Conversion," *Current Dialogue,* no. 50 (February 2008), 18.
2. Gregory Baum, ed., *The Twentieth Century: A Theological Overview* (Orbis Books, 1999), 244.
3. John Connelly, *From Enemy to Brother: The Revolution in Catholic Teaching on the Jews, 1933–1965* (Harvard University Press, 2012), 266.
4. Baum, op. cit., 244.
5. ST III q47 a6 resp.
6. ST III q47 a4 ad 3.
7. ST III q47 a5 ad 3.
8. ST III q47 a5 resp.
9. John O'Malley, S.J., *What Happened at Vatican II* (Harvard University Press, 2008), 250.
10. Paul VI, 1965 sermon reported in *New York Times,* April 8, 1965, cited in Jeremy Cohen, *Christ Killers* (Oxford University Press, 2007), 179.
11. Connelly, op. cit., 175.
12. Heschel quoted in ibid., 257.
13. Gregory Baum, quoted in Ucko, op. cit., 7.
14. O'Malley, op. cit., 219.
15. Ibid.
16. Ibid., 222.
17. Ibid., 224.
18. Connelly, op. cit., 7, 179.
19. David Nirenberg, *Anti-Judaism: The Western Tradition* (W. W. Norton, 2013), 85.
20. *Nostra Aetate* 4, in *Vatican Council II,* edited by Austin Flannery, sixth printing (Costello Publishing Company, 2007), 573.

IV

The Coming and Going of "Natural Law"

SIXTEEN

The Pope as Sex Monitor

M any of the most prominent and contested stands taken by Catholic authorities (most of them dealing with sex) have nothing to do with the Gospel, with anything revealed, with the so-called deposit of faith—things like contraception, oral sex, anal sex, stem cell research, artificial insemination, masturbation, tubal ligation, vasectomy, transgender surgery. All these are condemned, the Vatican says, not on any scriptural grounds, but according to "natural law." Natural law is native to human beings, as perceived by natural reason. By that measure, men and women should be able, with basic intelligence and information, to discover what it means. No special revelation is required to tell people what is native to them. Yet on the moral acceptability of all of the issues I just listed, there is widespread disagreement. Then how can a church teaching be so confident, firm, and unrelenting?

The solution has been to shift the grounds for condemnation—relying not on natural law alone, but on a religious pronouncement about the natural law. Yet Newman said the pope has no special vocation to what all people are supposed to be perceiving and obeying: "The Pope, who comes of Revelation, has no jurisdiction over Nature."[1] When, in a televised debate, I quoted that maxim, the Jesuit priest Joseph Fessio answered that the pope has a special charism for declaring what natural law is, even when many disagree with him. Natural law is what the pope says is natural. In this way, agreement with him becomes a religious test. And those who disagree with his reading of natural law are infringing on the "religious freedom" of his followers.

There was a shock to this view of natural law on the subject of contraceptives when the Anglican bishops at their decennial Lambeth

Conference of 1930 came out in favor of birth control. Here were educated men, adherents both of scripture and of natural law, saying they saw no reason to oppose responsible ways of family planning. Pope Pius XI, responding to the panic of the eminent Jesuit theologian Arthur Vermeersch, issued the encyclical *Casti Connubii* (largely drafted by Vermeersch), saying that the pope had the right to declare what is natural law:[2]

> The Catholic Church, *to whom God has entrusted the defense of the integrity and purity of morals,* standing erect in the midst of the moral ruin which surrounds her, in order that she may preserve the chastity of the nuptial union from being defiled by this foul stain, raises her voice in token of her divine ambassadorship and *through Our mouth proclaims* anew: any use whatsoever of matrimony exercised in such a way that the act is deliberately frustrated in its natural power to generate life is an offense against the law of God and of nature, and those who indulge in such are branded with the guilt of a grave sin [emphasis added].[3]

Those who might reach a different conclusion on the matter were condemned for pride of intellect, pitting mere human reason against the pope as God's voice:

> Let the faithful also be on their guard against the overrated independence of private judgment and that false autonomy of human reason. For it is quite foreign to everyone bearing the name of a Christian [including the Lambeth bishops] to trust his own mental powers with such pride as to agree only with those things which he can examine from their inner nature, and to imagine that the Church, *sent by God to teach and guide all nations,* is not conversant with present affairs and circumstances; or even that they must obey only in those matters which she has decreed by solemn definition as though her other decisions might be presumed to be false or putting forward insufficient motives for truth and honesty. Quite to the contrary, a characteristic of true followers of Christ, lettered or unlettered, is to suffer themselves to be *guided and led in all things* that touch upon faith or morals by the Holy Church of God *through its Supreme Pastor the Roman Pontiff,* who is himself guided by Jesus Christ Our Lord [emphasis added].[4]

Teleology

Of course, a pope who proclaims what natural law dictates must indicate what form of natural law he is proclaiming. There have been many versions of natural law invoked in various cultures—from Antigone's "unwritten laws," to Paul's "laws written on the heart," to Jefferson's "laws of nature and of nature's God."[5] But each of these (and many others) have had different and disputed contents. The papal appeal has been to a very specific biological school of natural law, that of Aristotle, mediated by Aquinas. Aristotle was a Greek, and the Greeks were great taxonomists, ranking things within carefully defined categories, to decide what is best (*ariston*) in each field. This has been called their agonistic (competitive) culture—sorting out the best seven sages, the best ten orators, and so on. Not only in sports but in singing contests, in tragedy and comedy presentations, an award was given to the best. There was a rhetorical format (German scholars called it a *Priamel*) that declared what was the best of all things.[6] Aristotle decided what was best by teleology—what best met the goal (*telos*) of any act or thing. In this way he decided what was the goal of tragedy—a *katharsis* (cleansing) of fear and pity, by a reversal of fortune (*peripeteia*) and a realization of what has happened (*anagnōrisis*)—and said that Sophocles' *Oidipous Tyrannos* best met these criteria.[7]

Aristotle held that his scientific studies were based on universal principles, of which the first is: "Nature makes nothing purposeless, but for the best (*ariston*) of all things any type of animal is essentially capable of."[8] He breaks things into their specific functions. In animals (and humans) the stronger right hand/foot means that is the origin of heat and motion, and it should therefore prevail. "Since all animal movements come from the right, and it moves the rest of the body, all must be right-handed."[9] Left-handed people should remedy their defect by using only the right hand until it becomes habitual. In the same way, the upper part of the body is superior to the lower, the front to the back.[10] Everything is sorted into its proper function by its particular *telos*.

The hierarchy that "by nature" puts the right over the left is reflected in the language of "dexterity" over things "sinister." The right-hand side is the favored one—where Jesus sits by the Father in heaven, or Mary stands at Last Judgment paintings, or the Gospel is read from the altar. The right is the spear hand in phalanx formations or in jousts. Signs on the right are of good omen, on the left are bad. By the same logic, Aristotle says that the stronger thing is superior to the weaker—the man to the woman, the master to the slave. The strong child should be kept, the weakly one abandoned in the wilderness: "The law should prevent the raising of any defective child."[11] That is how nature works, and we have to follow nature. Much of this "natural law" went straight into Aquinas, who passed it on to Catholic teachers and rulers. As Saint Thomas said, "All things are ordered to their proper exercise and end."[12] The *telos* of Aristotle became the *finis* of Aquinas.

Each thing or act has its own *telos/finis*. Nature has provided men and women with the equipment for producing offspring.[13] Any use of sex other than for this purpose is unnatural for Thomas, and therefore a sin. It is not a sin against others, but it is one against God himself—for breaking his law, which is declared in the order of nature.[14] Once accept this limit on the use of sex—i.e., only for procreation—and all kinds of things are forbidden as unnatural: homosexual sex, abortion, masturbation, oral sex, anal sex, *coitus interruptus,* tubal ligation, vasectomy, the use of male condoms, female diaphragms, postcoital douches, or any medication that inhibits or prevents conception. In early Scholasticism, there was only one legitimate position for intercourse—man above, woman below— which Aquinas called the natural way of having intercourse (*naturalis modus concumbendi*).[15] This not only observed the proper symbolism of male superiority; it was thought to ease procreation. Thomas's own mentor, Albertus Magnus, explained that semen would not travel up into a woman on top of the man, and even side-by-side intercourse could make insemination difficult, acting as a possible abortifacient.[16]

It was hotly debated whether intercourse during pregnancy or with a woman after menopause, where no conception could occur, had to be banned also. Aquinas said no, because the integrity of the act was preserved, though failure of procreation was outside the partners' control.[17] (This idea of the integrity of the act would come back to haunt the discussion when artificial insemination was forbidden by the Vatican.) Even to have sex with one's spouse is sinful unless, each time, one is intending to have a child—though Augustine admitted, "Never, when talking openly with a man who is or was married, did I hear him say that he did not ever have sex with his wife except in the hope of conceiving."[18]

Though I said above that there is nothing about the current controversies over contraception in scripture, Pius XI thought he had found a scriptural condemnation of it. In Europe, as opposed to America, birth control was known as onanism, since a passage in Genesis was taken to condemn it—so severely that God punished a man with death for sinning in that way:

> Then Judah told Onan to sleep with his brother's wife, to do his duty as the husband's brother and *raise up issue for his brother.* But Onan knew that the issue would not be his; so whenever he slept with his brother's wife, he spilled his seed on the ground so as not to *raise up issue for his brother.* What he did was wicked in the Lord's sight, and the Lord took his life (Gen 38.8–10, emphasis added).

This passage was first used to condemn masturbaters. They were "onanists," spillers of seed on the ground instead of into women. But Vermeersch and others held that "onanism" could be used of any ejaculation that frustrates conception (e.g., use of a condom in penetrating the vagina), with the horrible punishment given Onan. That is the extended meaning Pius gave it in his 1930 encyclical *Casti Connubii,* which said (paragraph 55) that Genesis condemns all sex used for nonprocreative purposes. But modern scholars agree the passage does not condemn "spilling one's seed" in general. Onan has avoided the duty assigned him by his father, Judah, of a levirate marriage—making sure that his dead brother's line will continue through his widow. Onan's sin is against his dead brother, who had the right to demand this of him. Onan is trying to blot out a rival for his inheritance.

As scripture scholars agreed that the pope had misrepresented the Bible, references to Onan were quietly retired from papal pronouncements on contraception. That would have been a powerful argument if Pius had been right about it, but Paul VI would not use scripture in his own encyclical on the subject, *Humanae Vitae* (1968). If a pope can err in his interpretation of scripture, which might be called his bailiwick, what confidence can we have in his interpretation of natural law, which is everyone's area?

The flaw in the Aristotle-Aquinas version of law is what might be called biologism. If nature works in a purposeful way, no one should interfere with nature's design. If you are left-handed, make yourself right-handed. Biology dictates morality. If nature "wants" sex to be procreative, we cannot frustrate it. Hume called this the is/ought fallacy. What *is* determines what *should* be:

> The author proceeds for some time in the ordinary way of reasoning and establishes the being of a God, or makes an observation concerning human affairs when, of a sudden, I am surprised to find that, instead of the usual copulations of propositions, *is* and *is not,* I meet with no proposition that is not connected with an *ought* or an *ought not.* This change is imperceptible but is, however, of the last consequence. For, as this *ought* or *ought not* expresses some new relation or affirmation, it is necessary that it should be observed and, at the same time, that a reason should be given for what seems altogether inconceivable, how this new relation can be a deduction from others which are entirely different from it.[19]

The papal view of natural law lets biology define morality. It assumes that one way nature works must *always and only* be the way humans engage with it. This would manifestly be absurd if we applied it outside the area of sex. Eating, for instance, has the obvious natural purpose of nourishment. Does that mean that anything beyond the *telos* of nourishment is "against nature"? Can there be no banquet to honor a person, no champagne toast at (of all things) a wedding, no extra treat cooked for a special person? As Sir Toby Belch says, "Because thou art virtuous, there shall be no more cakes and ale?" (*Twelfth Night* 2.3.116). Granted, great excess can mean gluttony or drunkenness, but not every calorie consumed beyond the body's need is a sinful departure from nature. Ascetics who starved themselves in penance would be sinning by defect of food's purpose.

Or consider exercise. The natural goal of that is to keep the body functioning well. Can one not strain the body, even risking its normal functions, to do acrobatic feats, or climb mountains, or get a "running high" out of sheer delight in achievement? Are all these things, going beyond natural need, against nature and therefore sinful? Of course, "nature" is gone against in all kinds of medical procedures. Each of these raised serious doubts among Catholic theologians who bought the idea that nature is destiny. If sterilization was condemned as mutilation of the body, what about other "mutilations," like cosmetic surgery, trying to "improve" nature?[20] At first, organ implants were condemned by Catholic theologians.[21] Even blood transfusions were questioned. What about removal of blemishes that do not threaten life? The ban on sterilization as mutilation of the body led to casuist discussions of medical amputations. In these areas, Catholic thought veered toward Christian Science. The papacy was expected to weigh in on each medical practice as it arose—for instance, on growth hormones for abnormally short people. When was a hysterectomy medically justifiable? If only one life could be saved in a medical emergency—the mother's or the child's—which should it be? A famous controversy in the 1950s arose around Henry Morton Robinson's novel *The Cardinal* for suggesting that the baby gets a religious preference.

"Rhythm"

In the nineteenth century, the growth of urban populations over rural ones, along with the scientific and industrial revolutions, made large families less desirable and in some cases debilitating. Improvements in medicine cut down the "natural" control on family sizes from miscarriages and early deaths. The need for longer education meant that extra children, far from helping the family subsist in farm conditions, damaged the chances of some siblings for advancement. In response to this concatenation of forces, the spacing of births became desirable when not imperative. Reduction of childbirths became a goal, if not a duty. Contraception was advocated as a social improvement of the economy and culture. A lower birth rate correlated with national prosperity.

All these trends were intensified in the twentieth century, and Pius XII sought a loophole from the maximal childbirths imposed on Catholics by *Casti Connubii*. He offered believers the dubious gift of "the rhythm method." You could now plan to have sex only on a woman's infertile days. This was not to avoid altogether the "natural" duty to have sex only for procreation. It simply counseled continence (a monkish recommendation anyway) on the fertile days, if one was planning to have a smaller number of children.

This, Pius said, was a response to the science the church was accused of opposing. It endorsed the biological discovery (in 1924) of a Japanese doctor, Kyusaku Ogino, that ovulation takes place (approximately) at the midpoint between menstrual periods (twelve to sixteen days before the next menstruation). Ogino used this to promote conception for parents who could track this fertile period. But when a European doctor, Hermann Knaus, independently made the same discovery about ovulation in 1929, some Catholic doctors began to recommend the Ogino-Knaus method for those who wanted to *avoid* the fertile time.

Pius XII, in what he conceived as a timely response to the science that had been around for twenty years, gave his blessing to Ogino-Knaus in a

1951 address to a Catholic midwives' convention in Rome. He claimed that the use of such rhythmically spaced intercourse did not go against nature, since the infertile period is itself natural, and the intercourse had during that period does not depart from "the integrity of the act." A minor cottage industry grew up to show a Catholic woman how to find her infertile period—which was far more difficult than it might seem from a slight acquaintance with the Ogino-Knaus teaching. John Noonan gives a summary of the problem:

> Menstrual cycles varied by the age of the woman and from woman to woman; even in a given year one woman might have considerable variation in her cycle. Cycles as short as 17 days had been found, and as long as 40 days. If statistics were to establish the norm, the average cycle would be 30.1 days for women aged 19 to 23, and 27.4 days for women aged 34 to 38.[22]

How was a woman to know during each cycle when her fertile period was about to occur and when it would end, so she and her husband could refrain from intercourse then? There were only indirect indicators, which a woman would have to measure constantly and accurately:

> We cannot know precisely and directly when ovulation is occurring. We have knowledge only by signs—changes in the cervical mucus so that it becomes wet, stretchy, and lubricative, and increasing basal body temperature. These signs indicate that intercourse may be fertile because ovulation is about to occur, is occurring, or has just occurred. A couple cannot determine more precisely when ovulation occurs.[23]

These two signs—basal temperature and mucus viscosity—had to be checked every day by special means. The basal temperature, the lowest bodily temperature in any one day, is best recorded before a woman rises in the morning—and it helps to wake at nearly the same time every day. A special (basal) thermometer is needed with minor calibrations, since hormone changes will make the temperature go up (slightly) two or three days after ovulation. By that time, of course, it is too late to avoid this fertile time, so one must chart one's cycle over several months, to find where you can anticipate ovulation's inception. A problem, of course, is that temperature can fluctuate unpredictably for various reasons—sickness, anxiety, stress, indigestion, and so on.

So another indicator should be coordinated with the basal thermometer results:

> Over the course of your menstrual cycle, the amount, color, and texture of your cervical mucus will change, thanks to fluctuating hormone levels. Checking your cervical mucus and keeping track of these changes can help you figure out when you're ovulating.[24]

But how can one check one's mucus?

> When your period is over, you'll most likely be dry for several days. After that, you'll start to have cloudy-colored mucus that's roughly the consistency of sticky rice. You're not very likely to conceive on any of these days. As you approach ovulation (typically a few days beforehand), the mucus will become clear and slippery, very much like raw egg white, and you'll have more of it. (You can remember that this is baby-making time if you think of how its clear, slippery quality makes it easier for the sperm to travel to the egg.) . . . Some women have enough cervical mucus discharge that they can check it by looking at the toilet paper after they wipe. Others need to collect some mucus with their finger. While sitting on the toilet, simply insert a clean index or middle finger into your vagina and reach toward your cervix. Get some of the liquid on your finger, if you can, so you can examine it.[25]

Pope John Paul II would praise the rhythm method as making a couple's life more spiritual, with denial of intercourse letting them earn their time of indulgence by ascetic preparation. Indeed, the husband will make a more perfect gift of himself to the wife if he has undergone the exercise of self-mastery: "Man is precisely a person because he is master of himself, and has self-control. Indeed, insofar as he is master of himself he can give himself to the other."[26] But Catholic couples would find that the constant fixation on a woman's bodily functions—anxiety that one had missed a day of record keeping, or misread the complicated accounting system, or let other cares intervene (health or family crises of distracting kinds)—led to a materialism that little resembled love.

When Patrick and Patricia Crowley, a pious Catholic couple who had given their lives to the Christian Family Movement, surveyed couples they dealt with, the results were disheartening. Sixty-three percent of those responding said that "rhythm" had harmed their marriage rather than elevated its spirituality. These couples were observant of the condemnation of contraceptives, but they found the unrelenting attention to the mechanics of sex far from natural—deadening, rather, and separating husband's and wife's needs and desires in subservience to charts and thermometers.[27] Then, by a cruel irony, after all that effort, couples failed—over and over—to prevent conception. Sixty-five percent of the two thousand polled by the Crowleys said that "rhythm" was not only deadly in its demands, but that it does not work. Pope John Paul would take such failure to mean the couple was "open to life," that they had not blocked their self-giving by an "artificial" means like a condom.[28] One advantage of the method was, in his eyes, its failure to be effective.

A staple of Catholic conversation in the 1950s was the fact that the harder a couple tried to limit childbirths by the rhythm method, the larger their family became. David Lodge, in his early novel *The British Museum Is Falling Down,* imagined future visitors to a ruined earth:

Martian archaeologists have learned to identify the domiciles of Roman Catholics by the presence of large numbers of complicated graphs, calendars, small booklets full of figures, and quantities of broken thermometers, evidence of the great importance attached to this code. Some scholars have argued that it was merely a method of limiting the number of offspring; but as it has been conclusively proved that the Roman Catholics produced more children on average than any other section of the community, this seems untenable.[29]

The Going of Contraception

By the end of the twentieth century, Catholics had solved the problem of the rhythm method. They had overwhelmingly adopted easier and more certain ways of doing what the rhythm method had intended in self-thwarting ways—the prevention of unwanted pregnancies. Poll after poll showed a majority of Catholics calling the use of contraceptives acceptable. In fact, the most thorough poll of Catholics under thirty found, in the 1990s, so few people agreeing with this papal teaching that they were falling within the margin of error, making them statistically nonexistent.[30] Even general polls of Catholic women as a whole showed that 97 percent of sexually active Catholic women used some form of contraception—about the same as the average for the population as a whole.[31] How did this happen?

It happened because the argument for a "natural law" on this subject was at last given a fresh look, out from under the shadow of Vatican pronouncements, precedents, and protection of continuity. The Lambeth Conference had indicated that good Christians could find no basis in the natural law argument. But Catholics could still suspect that those Protestants were biased by an anti-Roman attitude or history. What if a fair sample of loyal Catholics, both lay and clerical, both male and female, reached the same conclusion? Pope Paul VI, against what he was intending, supplied just that kind of test. John XXIII had set up a commission to study the problem of contraception, with a view to presenting its findings to the council. But Paul inherited that commission, and was determined to keep it away from the council. To give it strength as a free and final report for him alone to consider, he expanded the membership, swore it to secrecy, and thought it would surely endorse what the church had been saying ever since *Casti Connubii* had been promulgated.

When the expanded commission was finding no valid argument from natural law, Paul let Cardinal Ottaviani stack it with more (presumably more conservative) members. But every move they tried to make things better just made them worse. At last Ottaviani limited the final vote to the six-teen bishops he had shoehorned into the commission. But even with the exclusion of all laypeople and priests and theologians under the rank of bishop, the *bishops* voted nine-to-three (with three abstentions) for abandon-ing *Casti Connubii*. Ottaviani, at the end of his rope, decided he must rescue the church by confecting—with his favorite American Jesuit, John C. Ford—a rival document supporting "the church." He then presented this to Pope Paul as a "minority report" *of the commission,* saying that the pope could make the decision by himself since the commission had been divided.[32]

To the dismay of the authorities, the report of the majority of the commission was leaked to the *National Catholic Reporter.* Ottaviani said the commission was trying to force Paul's hand. If the church could change on this, what authority would it have in moral matters? The whole natural law would be discredited. John C. Ford had told the commis-sion that masturbation would now run wild. Souls had been sent to hell for committing the mortal sin of contraception. Would they now be given passes to leave? Paul agreed with Ottaviani that if he gave way on this, the entire structure of Catholic teaching would crumble. Paul confided his real concern to his friend, the philosopher Jean Guitton, telling him:

> Any attenuation of the law would have the effect of calling morality into question and showing the fallibility of the church . . . The whole moral edifice would collapse, and with it the edifice of the faith.[33]

The authorities had painted themselves into a narrow corner, thinking the church's teaching on sex was a revealed truth (though contraception is not in scripture). Actually, much of the moral authority of the Vatican was lost because Paul issued his encyclical *Humanae Vitae.* Many bishops around the world agreed with their brethren who had voted against this teaching. They made pro forma gestures of respect for the document while telling their people that this was a matter of individual conscience.

The German Jesuit Josef Fuchs, who had taught at the Gregorian

University in Rome, said he would have to withdraw his moral textbook, since he now realized it had wrongly condemned contraceptives.[34] After the role of John C. Ford in thwarting the commission was reported to his students at the Jesuit seminary, Weston in Massachusetts, they stopped attending his classes.[35] The Catholic version of "natural law" was in the dustbin of history. But John Paul II would not recognize this. He doubled down on *Humanae Vitae* with his own lengthy apostolic exhortation, *Familiaris Consortio* (1981). He argued that married partners cannot truly share their life unless they share the risks involved in abjuring contraceptives. He carried the biologism of "natural law" teaching to a kind of reductio ad absurdum when he called rhythm's temperature-taking and mucus-testing and chart-making the means of entering into a "dialogue" with the woman's body:

> The choice of the natural rhythms involves accepting the cycle of the person, that is the woman, and thereby accepting dialogue, reciprocal respect, shared responsibility and self control.[36]

The pope himself had to be sole monitor of the sex life of all the faithful. And all bishops, in order to qualify as bishops, had not only to adhere to that preposterous claim, but to call it "natural law." During his long (almost twenty-seven-year) papacy, John Paul had a strict litmus test for appointing new bishops. As Peter Hebblethwaite, the great Vatican reporter for London's *The Tablet,* observed:

> Opposition to contraceptives, to the ordination of married men and even the discussion of the ordination of women has been made the criterion for becoming a bishop. No one who so much as finesses on such questions has the slightest chance of being chosen.
>
> The result is that John Paul has created an intellectual desert and called it peace. Bishops and theologians have been cowed into silence. Synods have been reduced to papal rallies. Heads that pop up above the parapet are lopped off.

Laypeople have greater freedom than clergy, which is partly why Brazilian Fr. Leonardo Boff left the Franciscans earlier this year [1992]. St. Francis had not wanted to be a priest, he pointed out. He can be a better Franciscan as a layman.[37]

The pope created a huge army of ecclesiastical yes-men. People willing to meet his requirements would naturally tend to be mediocre in intellect or character, willing to use what abilities they had to repress the superior insight or initiative of outsiders. They were, after all, the pope's hatchet men, the sole ones he felt should act, since they were chosen for not acting outside his direction. As Hebblethwaite wrote, "The favorite theme, deployed by both John Paul and Cardinal Joseph Ratzinger, was that bishops, and not theologians, were the 'true teachers' of the church."[38] God forbid that any others—even *women*—should have a say in what affects their lives, health, minds, and marriage. The bishops, this dreary group of unmarried men, were the pope's only immediate arbiters on marriage.

It is often asked how church authorities could have ignored or covered up the abuse of children by priests all over the world. The answer lies in the men who had to face this challenge of accountability—the bishops. How could men trained in submission as apparatchiks of Rome muster the wisdom, empathy, and resolution to face such an issue? Every instinct of their situation told them to stay ignorant, or feign ignorance, or evade, or hide— anything but face or prevent or do penance for the multiplying scandals. They had to do this, by their lights, "for the good of the church." Acting otherwise would have required courage, and openness, and humility, from which they had been systematically disabled. It would have made the church embrace what Paul called the real scandal of the faith, "Christ on the cross, a *skandalon* [impasse] to Jews, and insanity to Gentiles, but to those responding to the call, whether Jew or Gentile, the throughway [*dynamis*] of God and the sanity of God" (1 Cor 1.23–24).[39]

NOTES

1. John Henry Newman, "Letter to His Grace the Duke of Norfolk," in *Newman and Gladstone: The Vatican Decrees,* edited by Alvan S. Ryan (University of Notre Dame Press, 1962).
2. On Vermeersch's important role in the matter, see John Noonan, *Contraception: A History of Its Treatment by the Catholic Theologians and Canonists,* enlarged edition (Harvard University Press, 1986), 424–25.
3. Pius XI, *Casti Connubii,* par. 56.
4. Ibid., par. 104.
5. Sophocles, *Antigone* 454–55; Paul, Letter to the Romans 2.15; Jefferson, Declaration of Independence.
6. A famous example is Sappho's fragment 16: "Some say the most beautiful thing on the black soil is a formation of cavalry, others say of infantry, but I say it is whatever you are in love with." She trumps male and military culture with her female value. See Garry Wills, "The Sapphic 'Umwertung Aller Werte,'" *American Journal of Philology,* vol. 88 (1967), 434–42.
7. Aristotle, *The Poetic Art (Peri Poietikēs)* 1452a24–26.
8. Aristotle, *Animal Locomotion (Peri Poreias Zōōn)* 704b16–18.
9. Ibid., 706a16–18.
10. Ibid., 705b7–11, *Animal Breeding (Peri Zōōn Geneseōs).*
11. Aristotle, *Polis Affairs (Peri Politikōn)* 1335b19–21.
12. ST I–II q91 a2 resp.
13. Aristotle, *Animal Breeding (Peri Zōōn Geneseōs)* 732a2–4.
14. ST II–II q154 a12 ad 1.
15. ST II–II q154 a11 resp.
16. Albertus Magnus, *Animals (De Animalibus)* 10.2.
17. Thomas Aquinas, *Evil (De Malo)* 15.2 objection 14.
18. Augustine, *On the Good of Marriage* 13.15.
19. David Hume, *A Treatise of Human Nature,* edited by L. A. Selby-Bigge (Oxford University Press, 1888), 469–70. See A. C. MacIntyre, "Hume on 'Is' and 'Ought,'" in V. S. Chappell, *Hume* (Doubleday, 1966), 240–64.
20. Noonan, op. cit., 452–53, 464. Pius XII said cosmetic surgery was allowable so long as it did not go beyond "attributes which already conformed to the canons of normal aesthetics" (453).
21. Ibid., 453–54.
22. Ibid., 464.
23. Ibid., 549.
24. "Basal Body Temperature and Cervical Mucus" (reviewed by the BabyCenter Medical Advisory Board), 1.
25. Ibid.
26. John Paul II, *A Theology of the Body* (Pauline Books, 1997), 398.

27. Crowley survey reported in Robert Blair Kaiser, *The Politics of Sex and Religion* (Leaven Press, 1985), 95.

28. John Paul II, *Familiaris Consortio,* sections 30–32.

29. David Lodge, *The British Museum Is Falling Down* (Holt, Rinehart and Winston, 1965), 16.

30. The Lilly Endowment survey was published as *Young Adult Catholics,* edited by Dean R. Hoge et al. (University of Notre Dame Press, 2001), 200.

31. See the mutually confirming polls of the Guttmacher Institute in 2011 and the National Survey of Family Growth in 2008, reported in Reuters article of April 17, 2011, "Most Catholic Women in U.S. Use Birth Control."

32. The story of the birth control commission is told in Robert McClory, *Turning Point: The Inside Story of the Papal Birth Control Commission* (Crossroad, 1995), and Kaiser, op. cit.

33. Peter Hebblethwaite, *Paul VI: The First Modern Pope* (Paulist Press, 1993), 472.

34. McClory, op. cit., 122.

35. Kaiser, op. cit., 214–15.

36. John Paul II, *Familiaris Consortio,* section 32 (Vatican translation).

37. Peter Hebblethwaite, *Pope John Paul II and the Church* (Sheed & Ward, 1995), 222.

38. Ibid., 199.

39. The contrasting pairs define each other: impasse and power to clear the way, the insanity (*mania*) and the sanity (*sophia*).

SEVENTEEN

Male God

The female is a defective male (*arren pepērōmenon*).

—Aristotle[1]

The female is an accidental male (*mas occasionatus*).

—Aquinas[2]

Natural law, that slippery concept, gave no more evil gift from Aristotle to Aquinas than the doctrine that women are incurably, indeed structurally, inferior to men. We have to go back to that oracle of natural law—to Aristotle—to discover that males are "naturally" superior to females, in human beings just as in the animal kingdom. If the male is bigger, he was framed to rule and must therefore be obeyed, in order to observe the good order, the economy (*oikonomia*, "good housekeeping") of the universe. In his words, "The male is by nature stronger, the female weaker, so one should rule and the other be ruled."[3]

Aristotle taught us in the last chapter that the right hand is superior to the left hand, as the source of heat and energy. In exactly the same way, male semen is superior to female as the hotter and more active initiator of life. The male needs the female to beget its own like, as form needs matter.[4] But the male semen is not only more energetic—more pure—than the female seed (which Aristotle took to be a part of menstrual blood).[5] When the male seed prevails over the female, the right outcome occurs— a male embryo. When the female, the lesser seed, prevails, a female embryo results.[6] This less happy event can happen for any one of several reasons—the male seed may be less vigorous because of the man's youth or old age; a cold wind could be blowing; there could be a freakishly strong female seed; the moon could be waning.[7] The result is a *necessary* swerve from the ideal, since the male will always need the female in order to extend his lineage; but the female will have a less degree of the divine spark of reason that was given to the embryo by the male semen:

> That is why, in each and every case the male should be set apart from the female, since the former is better and more godly (*theioteran*), in the way it imparts activity to what is generated. The female supplies the matter [for male form].[8]

Thomas follows Aristotle almost slavishly in his discussion of female inferiority:

> In natural function, the female is an accidental male, since the active male seed means to produce a perfect image of itself; but if a female results, it is because there was lessened effect in the active seed, or because there was some inadequacy in the matter, or because of some interference by an external cause, like the humidity of the south winds.[9]

Like Aristotle, Thomas says that the inferiority of the woman is necessary for the propagation of the race. If the "mistake" of women did not occur, there would be no human race bred from them. But Thomas deepens Aristotle's account by drawing on the creation account in Genesis. The Bible says that it was not good for man to be alone, so woman was created to be his helper (*adjutorium*). In most ways, other men could help Adam more than a woman could. But only she can beget his heirs.[10]

If it is asked why Eve was not created directly, as Adam was, but taken from his rib, Thomas says this is to keep the primacy of the male clear: "In this way, the first man's eminence would be preserved: Since he was made in the image of God, he should be the head of the whole human race, as God is the head of the whole universe."[11] Though some males governed as tyrants after the fall, Adam was the governor of Eve even in Paradise:

Some subordination would have occurred even before the fall. For the benefit of order in human affairs would have been lacking if some were not governed by wiser others. Thus, by that natural subordination, the female is subject to the male, since the control of reason is greater in the man.[12]

It is clear from this teaching how the church would conceive of gender differences. Once again, biology would dictate morality—the *is* would become an *ought*. The church read backward the Genesis claim that man was made in the image of God. God would be made in the image of man. If man has reason, and women do not, then it would be an insult to say that God was a female. He had to be male, and had to be the sole head of the universe. Which means the church could have only one parent, and that divine parent would be reflected in the structure of his church on earth, which had one sole Papa (Daddy), the pope (another single parent). All priests too would have to be single and male. The entire structure from heaven to earth would exclude the female. When the American Catholic commission let women slide partway into the Bible by giving "inclusive" translation of the generic "man" and "mankind" as "man and woman" and "humankind," Cardinal Joseph Ratzinger of the Congregation for the Doctrine of the Faith blocked the effort, since the singular "man" in Old Testament passages can sometimes be interpreted (more often misinterpreted) as referring prophetically to Christ.[13]

When this claim of female inferiority began to wear thin as a reason to exclude women from church ministry, Paul VI added pseudo-biblical justifications for their subordination. As the Anglican Lambeth Conference had prompted Pius XI's *Casti Connubii* by allowing contraception, the Anglican decision to ordain women priests in 1976 made Paul VI quickly order up a document from the Congregation for the Doctrine of the Faith, *Inter Insigniores,* which he issued with his blessing later that year. This said that women could not be priests since Jesus had never ordained a woman.[14] True enough. But neither did he ordain any men. There are no priests (other than the Jewish ones) in the four Gospels.[15]

Peter and Paul and their fellows neither call themselves priests nor are called priests by others. Jesus himself is called a priest only in the late and anonymous Letter to Hebrews—*and it says his priesthood is unique, it cannot be shared or passed on.*

The document added two more "biblical" reasons why only men can be priests. First, if Jesus had meant women to be priests, surely he would have ordained his mother as one, since no one could better represent him.[16] In fact, since he ordained no one, it would have been more than odd to appoint the Virgin Mary to an office that did not exist in his lifetime. The twelve were appointed, it is true—but not to exercise a priestly office on earth. They were to judge the Twelve Tribes at the end of time (Mt 19.28)—which explains their number, and the reason they had to restore the number after Judas's defection (Acts 1.12–26).

The second argument from scripture is even flimsier. Women cannot be priests *because they do not look like Jesus:*

> The priest is a sign, the supernatural effectiveness of which comes from the ordination received [*sic*]. But a sign must be perceptible, one which the faithful must be able to *recognize* with ease . . . The same natural *resemblance* is required for persons as for things; when Christ's *role* in the Eucharist is to be expressed sacramentally, there would not be this "natural *resemblance*" which must exist between Christ and his minister if the *role* of Christ were not taken by a man: in such a case it would be difficult to *see* in the minister the *image* of Christ. For Christ himself was and remains a man . . . The incarnation of the Word took place according to the *male sex* [emphasis added].[17]

One has to wonder whether porky young priests or shriveled ancient ones remind one of the appearance (or what we take to be the appearance) of Jesus. And if this resemblance is the basis for ordination, do we get holier sacraments given out by a handsome priest than by an ugly one? One might as well argue, in modern America, that no woman can be president because she does not look like George Washington. These "biblical" arguments are as absurd as was Pius XI's use of the Onan story to condemn contraception.

But John Paul II repeated most of the arguments of *Inter Insigniores* in his 1994 apostolic letter *Ordinatio Sacerdotalis*. He too thought that if the Virgin Mary had not been ordained, no woman could be.[18] Women had their own sublime roles, as "martyrs, virgins, and mothers."[19] He concluded, "I declare that the Church has no authority whatsoever to confer priestly ordination on women, and that this judgment is to be *definitively* held by all the Church's faithful" [emphasis added].[20]

Paul

As the bad history and evil teaching on the Jews had to be corrected by a return to Paul on the part of his fellow Jewish Christians at Vatican II, so we should correct the church's exclusion of women by looking at what Paul experienced and taught. He, after all, reflects the earliest church situations, since he wrote before the destruction of the Temple in 70 CE, and the other New Testament authors wrote after it (some of them well after). For a long time it was thought that Paul favored the suppression of women because the First Letter to Timothy was assigned to him, though almost all scholars now date it to the end of the first century, thirty years after Paul's death:[21]

> Let a woman quietly learn with all submission. I do not permit a woman to teach, nor to lord it over a man. Adam, after all, was fashioned first, then Eve. And Adam was not deceived, while Eve, because she was deceived, strayed first. But she will be rescued by childbearing if she retains fidelity, love, and the sacredness of good judgment (1 Tim 2.11–15).

The tone of Paul is very different from this—as is shown in his many dealings with women and his indebtedness to them. He is dependent on them, a coworker with them, a fellow prisoner with them, and gives them the highest functions he knows of in the church. So, far from saying they must stay quiet in the gathering, he tells them to rebuke the brothers and sisters—the function of prophets (1 Cor 11.5). It is true that he says a woman must wear a modest veil while prophesying; but that does not reduce the importance of women prophets:

> The speaker in strange tongues does not address men but God. No one [else] understands, since he is inspired to speak mysteriously. The prophet by contrast tells men something constructive, protective, and heartening. The speaker in tongues says something constructive of himself, while the prophet says something constructive for the gathering. I will gladly let anyone speak in tongues, but I would prefer you to prophesy. The prophet is better than the speaker in tongues, unless he later explains his meanings, to give the gathering some constructive message. So, brothers, if I speak in tongues when I visit you, what good does that do you, unless I reveal something to you or deepen your knowledge or teach you by prophecy? (1 Cor 14.2–6).

Paul asks for a certain decorum for all prophets, while not doubting that God speaks through them to the community:

> When you gather, one sings a psalm, another instructs, another reveals, one speaks in tongues, another explains. But all must be constructive. If there are speakers in tongues, there should be only two or three doing so, one after the other. If one does not have an interpretation, he should not speak in the gathering, but only to himself and God. But let two or three prophets speak while others digest their meaning. If someone sitting there receives an inspiration, let the preceding one pause. You should all have the chance to speak, one by one, so that all may learn and all be heartened. The order of prophecy should be observed by prophets, since theirs is not a God of chaos but of calm (1 Cor 14.26–33).

Paul says that all (men and women) have the right to prophesy, and he considers this important to the community's learning and fervor. This openness to women prophets seems to have lasted in churches other than the Pauline ones. In Acts 2.17, it is said that the Christians are fulfilling

Joel's prophecy, "I will pour out from my spirit on *all* humans (*pasan sarka*), and your sons *and daughters* will prophesy" (emphasis added). Later, the four daughters of one of the original seven "deacons" (*diakonoi*) are identified as prophets (Acts 21.9).

But if Paul says that women may prophesy in the gathering, how can he go on immediately to say that they are not even allowed to speak there?

> In all the gatherings of the holy, let women be silent in the gatherings. It is not permitted for them to speak. But let them be submissive, as the Law requires. If they want to learn something, let them inquire of their husbands at home. It is matter for shame if a woman speaks in the gathering (1 Cor 14.33–35).

If it is asked how Paul could say that, the brief answer is that he didn't. He never speaks of the Law that way, especially about women. When it was still thought that he wrote the First Letter to Timothy, with its later church discipline, there was an obvious attempt to make him consistent with himself by interpolating the silencing of women in 1 Corinthians to exactly what was written in 1 Timothy. As the Dominican scholar Jerome Murphy-O'Connor wrote:

> Not only is the appeal to the law (possibly Genesis 3:16) un-Pauline, but the verses contradict 1 Corinthians 11:5. The injunctions reflect the misogyism of 1 Timothy 2:11–14 and probably stem from the same circle. Some mss. place these verses after 40 [suggesting uncertainty where to put the interpolation].[22]

We know how later church practice corrupted the Pauline manuscript from the change that made female Junia become male Junias in the Letter to the Romans. There Paul praises Junia and her husband, Andronicus, as "eminent emissaries" of the Lord (Rom 16.7). Emissary, the proudest title he gives himself, is *apostolos*. It was unthinkable to some later Christians that a woman could be an "apostle," so with a simple change of an accent mark they turned her name in the objective case to a male form for Junias. One of the many problems with this is that there are no men known with the name Junias, though there are many women with Junia (naturally, since it is derived from the female Juno). Here is another case where what Paul said does not dictate the treatment of women, but the treatment of women seems to dictate what Paul said.[23]

Junia and Andronicus were a preaching couple who were very close to Paul. They were "related to me" (*syngeneis*) and "my prison mates" (*synaikhmalōtoi mou*). Such preaching couples were common in the early church, as Paul had said when he called himself the exception (1 Cor 9.5). Another couple he mentions in Romans is Prisca and Aquila, his co-workers (*synergoi*) who risked their lives for him (16.3–4). Another prominent woman he knew and worked with was Phoebe, a "deacon" (*diakonos*) and protectress (*prostatēs*) of the church (Rom 16.1–2). He obviously depended on his fellow workers, preachers, and church organizers (Lydia of Thyatira, Acts 16.14–15). The deeper reason for this collaboration is given in what Krister Stendahl calls "the Galatian breakthrough."

Galatians 3.26–28

Stendahl changed the whole course of Pauline scholarship on the Jews when he treated Paul's defense of the permanent covenant. He does something similar in his work on Paul's attitude toward women. This comes out in the baptismal hymn for the churches of Galatia. These communities had been changed since the time Paul was with them. Judaizing Christians had convinced the communities that they needed to observe Jewish practices like circumcision.[24] Paul recalls his own teaching at their baptisms, using the very formulas used then. "Paul quotes and interprets for the Galatian setting an early Christian liturgical tradition formulated for use in baptism."[25] This is one of the places where Paul quotes a community hymn, proving that it is not just his own particular teaching:[26]

> All you baptized into Messiah,
>   have been clothed in Messiah,
> no longer Jew or Gentile,
>   no longer slave or free
> no longer "male and female,"
>   since you are all one in Messiah-Jesus (Gal 3.26–28).

The disjunctive clauses "not . . . nor" (*ouk . . . oude*) are varied by "not . . . and" (*ouk . . . kai*) for just one pairing, "male *and* female." Why is that? Stendahl explains:

> In the Greek text, *arsen kai thēlu* ("male and female") is more of an inter-ruption than English translations would indicate. These words are the technical terms from Genesis 1.27 ("male and female created he them"). And their technical character is clear as they are not the ordinary words for "man" and" woman" but actually mean "male and female." The con-nection "and" also interrupts the "neither/nor" series. We therefore have good reason to put "male and female" in quotation marks. Paul shows that the Law of Moses—for that is the Law of which Galatians 3 speaks—has been transcended in Christ at the following points: (1) The boundary line between Jews and Greeks has been abolished, the wall of partition which God himself had raised through the Law, the foundation of Israel's glory and faith. (2) The boundary line between slave and free, which also is well attested in the Law and belonged to the order of life in the Gentile world, is overcome. (3) And, finally, the most primary division of God's creation is overcome, that between male and female—the terminology points directly back to Genesis 1.27 and in the direction of man as the image of God, beyond the division into male and female.[27]

Louis Martyn makes the same point:

> The variation of the wording of the last clause suggests that the author of the formula drew on Gen 1.27, thereby saying that in baptism the struc-ture of the original creation had been set aside. One senses in the formula itself, then, an implied reference to new creation, a motif Paul will use in crafting a dramatic conclusion to the entire letter . . . Religious, social,

and sexual pairs of opposites are not replaced by equality, but rather by a newly created unity. In Christ (in what Paul will later call "the body of Christ"), persons who were Jews and persons who were Gentiles have been made into a new unity that is so fundamentally and irreducibly identified with Christ himself as to cause Paul to use the masculine for the word "one." Members of the church are not one *thing;* they are one *person,* having been taken into the corpus of the One New Man.[28]

Stendahl wrote his book on women in the Bible as part of the 1958 debate over ordaining women in the Church of Sweden. The argument of some was that emancipation of women in the secular sphere should be imitated by the church, while others said that it should be defied. Stendahl thought that got things backward:

> If there is to be change in the relation between male and female, it is to take place—according to the New Testament—in Christ, in the church, and not in the world. What the New Testament has to say about the new equality between man and woman as well as between Jew and Greek, slave and free, it says concerning those who are in Christ and for those who belong to him. It is not speaking outside the church, it is not enunciating new principles for society. It would then be peculiar if the church, which wants to belong to Christ and to witness to him, saw it as its duty to turn this biblical picture upside down by saying to its faithful: "In worldly affairs you may accept emancipation—that before God there is neither man nor woman—but in the church's life and its worship it is not so."[29]

It was always against the Gospel for men to treat women as inferior, just because the surrounding culture was patriarchal. If we are all Christ, then how can one "pull rank" on a woman? She is Christ.

Pope Francis seems to sense this. Though he said a woman priesthood is settled, that probably just means he will let others bring it about. But that doesn't mean he cannot nudge an outcome along. John XXIII had to let the council listen to Jewish Catholics before reversing the rejection of the Covenant—but he encouraged them to think about it when he turned the matter over to Cardinal Bea. In the same way, Francis is indicating his views on Catholic women by his dealings with them, as well as by what he says. He easily uses inclusive language, as when he calls the hierarchy— not the church, but the hierarchy—"Mother Church." He said, "I dream of a church that is a mother and shepherdess."[30] If he says that, how can he exclude women from any offices in the church?

This pope shows by doing. He not only treats women as equals, and consults them. He befriends to this day a woman priest. She is the widow of the radical bishop Jerónimo José Podestá, who was hunted out of Argentina by the government and disowned by the Vatican. He asked to see Bergoglio, as archbishop of Buenos Aires, and be reconciled with the church on his deathbed. But in his radical days he *concelebrated Mass* with his wife, Clelia. The pope became her friend and confidant, and he still calls her from Rome. That would have been scandalous in Rome not so very long ago. We can take it, rather, as a sign of hope for the future. The official church has been one of history's sturdiest bastions of patriarchy. But it seems to be listening again to Paul, and to Jesus. "Clothed in Messiah, [you are] no longer 'male and female.'"

NOTES

1. Aristotle, *Animal Breeding* (*Peri Zōōn Geneseōs*) 737a28.
2. ST I q92 a1 ad 1.
3. Aristotle, *Politics* (*Peri Politikōn*) 1254b13–14.
4. Aristotle, *Animal Breeding* (*Peri Zōōn Geneseōs*) 729a10–12.
5. Ibid., 728b23–24. The element of soul, or reason, is in the male sperm, not the female. So when the female sperm prevails, the woman that results is deficient in reason (737a28–30).
6. Ibid., 766a14–776b8.
7. Ibid., 766b28–713.
8. Ibid., 732a7–9. "The sperm emitted by the male has the beginnings of soul, which is either inseparable from the body, or separable in those creatures that have the godly (*theion*) quality we call reason" (737a8–11).
9. ST I q92 a1 ad 1.
10. ST I q92 a1 resp.
11. ST I q92 a2 resp.
12. ST I q92 a1 ad 2.
13. Ratzinger overturned an earlier ruling by the Vatican Congregation on Di-

vine Worship and Sacraments, which had given permission for the new language. See Jonathan Kwitny, *Man of the Century: The Life and Times of Pope John Paul II* (Henry Holt, 1997), 666.

14. Sacred Congregation for the Doctrine of the Faith, *Inter Insigniores* (1976), section 2.

15. Krister Stendahl, who was himself a Lutheran priest (and bishop), rightly wrote, "The word 'priest,' which is preserved in the Swedish tradition, does not belong to the New Testament vocabulary, or to the period of church history to which the New Testament witnesses; it took some time before the priestly office of the Old Testament or of the Hellenistic-Roman times exercised an influence on the concept of the ministry." *The Bible and the Role of Women: A Case Study in Hermeneutics,* translated by Emilie T. Sander (Fortress Press, 1966), 42.

16. *Inter Insigniores*, section 2.

17. Ibid., section 5.

18. John Paul II, *Ordinatio Sacerdotalis* (May 22, 1994), section 3.

19. Ibid.

20. Ibid., section 4.

21. Raymond Brown, *An Introduction to the New Testament* (Doubleday, 1997), 653–70.

22. Jerome Murphy-O'Connor, "I Corinthians," *The New Jerome Biblical Commentary* (Prentice Hall, 1990), 809–10.

23. Most church fathers, and all of the Eastern church, honored "Saint Junia" as a female apostle. But manuscripts from the ninth century gave the masculine accent, and Giles of Rome in the thirteenth century argued that Junia could not be right. Joseph A. Fitzmyer, *Romans* (Doubleday, 1993), 737–38.

24. J. Louis Martyn, *Galatians* (Doubleday, 1997), 13–19, 236–40.

25. Ibid., 374.

26. Brown, op. cit., 489–93.

27. Stendahl, op. cit., 32.

28. Martyn, op. cit., 376–77.

29. Stendahl, op. cit., 40.

30. Interview with Pope Francis, *America,* September 30, 2013.

EIGHTEEN

"Right to Life"

> I have not discovered anything certain about the soul's origin
> in the recognized works of Scripture . . . When a thing ob-
> scure by nature exceeds our competence, and holy Scripture
> offers no clear help, it is wildly presumptuous to pronounce
> with certitude.
>
> —Augustine, Letter 190[1]

S ome Catholics and evangelicals have made opposition to abortion
the center of their spiritual life. No dogma is treated with more insistence. This is odd since the matter is nowhere mentioned in the Old
Testament or New Testament, or in the early creeds. But some people are
convinced that God must hate such an immense evil and must have expressed that hatred somewhere in his Bible. In order to disprove Augustine, they rely on a single verse, Psalm 139.13: "Thou hast covered me in
my mother's womb." That is the King James version, taking "cover" as
"protect." The psalm goes on to say, "My substance was not hid from thee
when I was made in secret" (verse 15)—so God is watching over the fetus
in the womb. But then, unfortunately for the thesis, the verse continues,
"and curiously wrought in *the lowest part of earth*." Is God protecting pri-
mal creation so that *it* may not be aborted? Modern scholars think both
"made in secret" and "lowest part" refer to Sheol, the abyss from which all
of creation was summoned.[2] If so, the psalm could more properly be used
by environmentalists, guarding all of creation, than by anti-abortionists.[3]

Since abortion cannot be forbidden on scriptural grounds, we must
again have resort to "natural law," as discoverable by natural reason. That
law was not perspicuous in condemning contraception and endorsing
male supremacy. Will it do better on the subject of abortion? Well, one

cannot take Aquinas's normal starting point for natural law argument—
namely, Aristotle. The Greek philosopher said that no one should be allowed, by law, to raise a defective child. Since direct killing pollutes one,
the child should be condemned to die by exposure (*apothesis,* "placing
away").⁴ Since parents too young or too old had the highest chance of
producing weak offspring, their offspring should be aborted (though only
before "quickening").⁵ Of course, if children are born weak or deformed,
they can be disposed of after birth. Anyone so cavalier about dismissing
children after they are born cannot be expected to care much about them
before birth.

Of course, Thomas does not follow Aristotle on these points, but he
saves what he can of Aristotle's thought on the conception process. Since
Aristotle defined *psyche* (Thomas's *anima*) as any form of life, he divided
psychai into three categories—vegetable (nutritive) "soul" for plants, sensible for animals, and rational for human animals. Not only did the human
surpass other forms of life by an injection of something rational "from
above" (*anōthen*) or "from outside" (*thyrathen*).⁶ Aristotle also made the process of conceiving a human recapitulate the process of life up the scale of
things. The fetus begins with vegetable life, able to grow and be nour-
ished; then advances to sensible life able to react to sense stimuli; and at
last to human life, able to reason.⁷ Since there is not much to exercise
reason on in the womb, Aristotle seems to suggest that the rational soul,
the last in the process, was completed at birth, its proper *telos.* "Last
comes the goal, the particular completion for which it [the fetus] was
reaching."⁸

Thomas too thinks of the fetus in terms of three stages, but he fears
that Aristotle either gives the fetus three different souls, or sees the higher
stages developing from the lower.⁹ "The physical body comes from bodily
processes, but the rational soul comes from God alone."¹⁰ Aristotle's soul
was fitted only for life here on earth, but Thomas's had to be an everlasting soul, going from life to heaven (or hell) with the sensations of the
risen body. So the rational soul comes simultaneously with a higher

sensation than that of other animals.[11] The nutritive soul will have no part to play in the afterlife, where there is no eating or starving, no growing or declining. So the nutritive must be shed as corruptible. How this applies to the fetus is uncertain; but Thomas agrees that the soul's infusion must come at the end of the process, as its *telos* is reached. "The rational soul is created by God at the end of human begetting" (*in fine generationis humanae*).[12]

The natural law against abortion has not been readily perceived by many people very well endowed with "natural reason," and that remains the situation in our time. Whatever one thinks of the *Roe v. Wade* decision, seven of the nine justices, men of some education and experience in weighing arguments, could say in 1973 that abortion is legal before viability (last three months). They were not isolated outliers in this position. Three years before the decision, John Noonan wrote:

> The deans of all the medical schools in California, the American Civil Liberties Union of Southern California, and some fourscore professors of law, teachers of gynecology and practitioners of obstetrics drawn from all parts of the nation have asked the Supreme Court of California to assert the constitutional right of a woman to have an abortion when she seeks it and the constitutional right of a physician to perform an abortion if he finds it medically appropriate.[13]

Nature does not clearly enunciate its "natural law" to these people. Only a plurality of Americans, not a majority, think abortion should be illegal. That is true even for Catholics, among whom the plurality is 42 percent.[14] In 1984, ninety-seven prominent Catholics, including fifty-five theologians, signed a full-page ad in the *New York Times* opposing the bishops' ban on all abortions.[15] They were supporting Geraldine Ferraro for vice president at a time when she was criticized as a pro-choice Catholic. She lost. But many Catholic politicians taking the same position have been elected and reelected, so citizens must have approved of them even when the bishops did not.

This is what infuriates some bishops and their supporters. Catholics are supposed to obey the commands from above. If they do not, they are supposed to admit they are excommunicated and depart. Their refusal to do that looked like a new phenomenon. The sociologist priest Andrew Greeley described the situation:

> Certainly never in the history of Catholicism have so many Catholics in such apparent good faith decided that they can reject the official teaching of the church as to what is sexually sinful and what is not, and to do so while continuing the regular practice of Catholicism and even continuing the description of themselves as good, strong, solid Catholics.[16]

"Pro-Life"

For lack of better arguments from natural law, opponents of abortion have declared a general "pro-life" premise. Life is to be protected wherever and whenever possible. This is a brilliant slogan. It implies that anyone not agreeing with it is "pro-death." Pope John Paul II gave this position support when he said that abortion manifested a "culture of death," to be opposed by "a culture of life."[17] Being for life in general is roughly the position of environmentalists, who want to preserve plant and animal life threatened by many things. But we make distinctions between support for plant life and the destruction of weeds, or for some animals and against those who devour vulnerable lives. The foes of abortion make a distinction here. They are not, we are assured, "tree huggers." They mean to preserve *human* life. Well, yes. But my hair has human life—it is not a plant, it is not canine or ursine hair; it is human hair, alive and growing. It grows so well I must frequently get it cut. I trim my growing fingernails, though they too have human life.

The answer I have heard for this is that my hair does not have the capacity to become another human being. That is true. But male semen and women's ova have that capacity, and we do not try to preserve them separately. Thomas, arguing against Aristotle's contention that male semen, as opposed to the female secretion, has a source of rationality, said that if that were true, then any ejaculation outside intercourse would give us a profusion of souls.[18] Well then, the pro-lifers say, they are for human life only after conception—that is, when the zygote is formed of the fertilized ovum. But from half to two-thirds of the zygotes fail to attain nidation—"nesting" in the inner wall of the uterus.

> Experiments with animals have shown that the prenatal loss from the time of fertilization averages about 40 to 50 percent. In view of the higher organization of man, the losses may be even greater. At least one-fifth or even one-fourth of the fertilized eggs may perish before implantation in the uterus or during this process.[19]

Is nature (i.e., God) committing a holocaust of conceived human beings by this massive destruction of zygotes? At the moment of conception, the zygote has not begun to split its cells to form twins or multiple births, so the death toll of human souls is even higher than we will ever be able to discover. In that case, the pro-lifers say we have to protect life wherever we can discern that it is happening, obviously later than conception.

But does having human life make the fetus a person? For that is what we must preserve. For the first two-thirds of the fetus's life, it looks like a human and reacts to natural electrical pulses, but it does not have the necessary equipment to feel pain or anything else. It lacks a cerebral cortex that can coordinate the signals coming at it from its nerves and limbs. Without that "signal center" to read itself as an entirety, it is not a functioning human being with a physical sense of itself as a single totum. To quote a pair of Catholic professors of philosophy:

> A pile of wires and switches is not an electrical circuit, and a collection of nerve cells is not a functioning brain. The wires and switches need to be connected in order to make a circuit or a computer, and the nerve cells in the cortex need to be connected for there to be a functioning brain. In

effect, before synapses are sufficiently formed the brain does not function because it is just a collection of nerve (and other) cells. The burst of
synapses formation, and hence the start of the cerebral cortex as a functioning entity, occurs between twenty-five and thirty-two weeks, and in
most cases toward the end of this range. It is this period that can legiti-
mately be seen as the one that gives rise to what is distinctively human
from a biological point of view.[20]

Even at this stage, is the biological entity a person? For that is what we
should be asking—not when life begins (it is there in my hair, in the semen, in the ovum, in the zygote), but when personhood is achieved. Aristotle and Aquinas thought it was at or near the end of the process, the *telos*
of the completed baby. For most of the post-Scholastic period, church authorities did not hold that life began at conception, but at "ensoulment"
(when God infused the soul), and there was no *theological* way to define
the precise moment when that happened. All Thomas said was, "The rational soul is created by God at the end of human begetting." There was
no practice of baptizing miscarried fetuses, as if they had been "ensouled."
Augustine said he could not tell from scripture when that occurred.[21]

But Augustine also thought that the key to identity is memory. If we
cannot remember ourselves as persons, we do not exist. That is the
trauma of amnesia. Augustine also thought that personality was *inter*personality. Unless we have exchanges with others, we do not form an identity of our own. Even God needs interpersonality, an engagement with
himself as having different persons, with his Logos to express himself,
and with his Spirit to love his perfect goodness. The fetus in the womb
has no memory of its own actions there, though it is equipped by evolu-
tion to begin instantly forming them in its all-important interchanges
with its mother and others, its rapid ability to imitate and understand
sounds, the language that is essential to its dealings with itself and with
the world.

One can argue when the person begins to be formed and needs to be protected. Few defend late abortions except for the protection of a person already complete (the mother). Yet even as observant a Christian as Jimmy Carter approves of abortion that results from rape or incest.[22] So do most Americans. But this makes no sense if the fetus has its own human rights, of the sort to be observed in the various "personhood" laws being proposed or passed by state legislatures. No *person* with its own *rights* should have its life taken because its father abused its mother.

There has always been a lack of certitude about the status of the fetus, even among those with good minds and goodwill. How, then, can a pope or a priest, a judge or a legislator be so certain, where others as well equipped have left room for debate? And who can weigh these considerations closer to the action than the woman most involved? Those who invoke the murky "rights" of a fetus over the undoubted rights of a prospective mother seem to be backing a cloudy prospect over an assured fact. The woman certainly does have memories and interpersonal actions that assure her identity.

The common sense of the community has never supported the view that abortion is murder. If it had, women would have been given the punishment for murder—the death penalty where that is still the law (killing a woman to "protect life"), or at least long prison sentences. She is the most responsible for the action she simply authorizes a doctor to perform. The anti-abortionists do not wish to follow their own logic to its obvious conclusion. At the most, they want to fine or deprive of their livelihood the ones performing an abortion, who are not forcing the decision on the woman. One pope tried to impose the view that abortion is murder. In his papal bull *Effraenatam* (1588), Sixtus V declared that abortion is homicide, to be punished with death. But even in an autocratic age he could not make this stick, even with his fellow clerics and political subjects. As John Noonan wrote:

> This Franciscan pope set about the reform of Rome and the Church in a draconian way . . . Like most of the efforts at righteous reform of

Sixtus V, however, *Effraenatam* overshot the mark. Within a year of Sixtus V's death in 1590, his successor, Gregory XIV, noted with suave understatement that "the hoped-for fruit" had not resulted from the bull, but that instead its rigor had led to sacrilege: those affected by it ignored their excommunicated status. Accordingly, the new pope repealed all its penalties except those applying to abortion of an ensouled, forty-day-old fetus. The other penalties were retroactively annulled, and the decree of Sixtus V was "to be in this part as if it had never been issued" (*Sedes Apostolica,* May 31, 1591).[23]

Jimmy Carter and other sincere Christians have noted a certain hypocrisy in people who claim to abhor abortion yet vastly increase its occurrence by denying the means of contraception both in America and abroad.[24] The popes denied condoms in Africa to fight not only unwanted pregnancies but the deadly spread of AIDS. American aid to African countries was refused to efforts that included abortion and contraception. It was a joke during the Vietnam War that hostilities would have been ended much earlier if bishops had thought condoms were being airdropped on the country and not napalm. We have seen how flimsy are the "natural law" arguments against contraception—yet those are used to reinforce the prohibition of all abortions. In fact, all three of the "natural law" arguments treated here—on contraception, on male superiority, and on abortion—are combined in the war on abortion. Women are not supposed to be competent to make their own choices on what will be done about their bodies. That has been left, in the past, to popes or priests, judges or lawmakers. There is a long legal tradition behind male guardianship of "legitimate" offspring, to assure proper heredity. This dates back to the levirate marriage law as it affected Onan—the woman was just the vehicle for Onan to assure the continuance of his brother's line. These "natural law" arguments come in a cluster of assumptions about a woman's subordination in all things, including the disposal of her body and her offspring. The combination of the three arguments considered in this section brings to mind three tipsy men staggering home arm in arm. They must keep leaning on each other, since each would fall if left to stand alone.

NOTES

1. Augustine, *Letters* 190.5.16–17.
2. Mitchell Dahood, *Psalms III: 101–150* (Doubleday, 1970), 283–95. That God foreknows everything is the point of Jeremiah 1.5: *"Before* I formed thee in the belly, I knew thee."
3. Some even more desperate attempts to find abortion condemned in the Bible misread Jewish Law, making the same mistake as Pius XI when he thought Onan's sin was to spill seed, not to defy his levirate duty. Exodus 21.22 fines a man for hurting a woman so as to cause a miscarriage. But the offense is not against God, punishable by death. It is against her husband, who has been deprived of an heir, and the fine is exacted by and paid to the husband. Similarly, in Genesis 38.24–26 the life of the pregnant Tamar is spared, but not to save the life in her but because she proves the fetus is the ruler's.
4. Aristotle, *Politics* 1335b19–21. Since he uses the same word (*pepērōmenon*) for "defective" that he used of women as defective men, the grounds for disposing of babies would be very broad—and especially for *female* babies.
5. Ibid., 1335b21–24.
6. Aristotle, *Animal Breeding (Peri Zōōn Geneseōs)* 731b24, 736b20.
27. He says that this rational element is potentially in the male semen and then it is actualized in the fetus, more of it to form males and less of it to form females (736b 18–73771 29).
7. Ibid., 736a35–736b29.
8. Ibid., 736b3–5.
9. ST I q118 a2 ad 2.
10. ST I q118 a3 ad 3.
11. ST I q76 a4 ad 3.
12. ST I q118 ad 3.
13. John T. Noonan, *The Morality of Abortion* (Harvard University Press, 1970), ix–x.
14. Quinnipiac Poll, October 4, 2013.
15. Patricia Miller, *Good Catholics: The Battle over Abortion in the Catholic Church* (University of California Press, 2014), 110–12.
16. Andrew Greeley, *American Catholics Since the Council* (Thomas More Press, 1985), 81.
17. John Paul II, *Evangelium Vitae* (1995), section 28.
18. ST I q118 a3.
19. Bernard Haring, "A Theological Evaluation," in Noonan, op. cit., 130.

20. Daniel A. Dombrowski and Robert Deltete, *A Brief, Liberal, Catholic Defense of Abortion* (University of Illinois Press, 2000), 13.
21. Augustine was opposed to abortion, but not to protect the life of the fetus. He was against any use of sex but for procreation. So the sin was in the parents who had intercourse but did not want to accept the procreation consequences.
22. Jimmy Carter, *A Call to Action: Women, Religion, Violence, and Power* (Simon & Schuster, 2014), 183.
23. John Noonan, *Contraception: A History of Its Treatment by the Catholic Theologians and Canonists,* enlarged edition (Harvard University Press, 1986), 362–63.
24. Carter, op. cit., 108, 112, 183.

V

The Coming and Going
of Confession

NINETEEN

The Duty to Forgive

C onservative Catholics lament a falling off in church observances after the Second Vatican Council—not only fewer people at Mass, but
the neglect of identifying practices like fish on Friday, Benediction, nove-
nas, First Fridays, public recitation of the rosary, fasting before communion, and ten-children families. None of these things meant the
abandonment of one of the seven sacraments. But that did occur with the
sacrament of penance. There used to be long lines at the confessionals
on a Saturday before the penitents could go to communion on Sunday.
Priests spent many hours in the box hearing mainly minor sins, which
people were encouraged to find, in frequent confessions, to get the extra
grace of a sacrament. Yet now the confessional boxes are being removed,
or used by church janitors to store their equipment. There is a frequently
cited maxim of Prosper of Aquitaine (fifth century): *Lex orandi lex cre-
dendi,* the way we pray is the way we believe. Here church practice sug-
gests that Catholics, by not using the sacrament of penance, have stopped
believing in it.

That is surprising. Confession was not only a normal part of Catholic
life, but a vividly experienced one, sometimes in searing ways. There was
a mystique to the thing, its "seal," making it part of a shared experience
with the priest, who could never reveal what he heard, even from a criminal. A priest was more bound than a mother or father not to speak of
what their child said; more bound than a policeman could be to shelter a
criminal after a crime he has committed; more bound than a questioner
of terrorists to keep the threat of a plot from any revelation of it. Here
was the stuff of drama, as Alfred Hitchcock knew.

There was also the stuff of trauma. The solemnity of the matter was enhanced by the dark box, the low voices, the Latin formula that magically wiped the soul clean. After Pius X, in 1910, moved back the time for receiving communion to the "age of discretion" (which he put at roughly seven), the link between confession and communion meant that children had to undergo the black box ordeal before making their first communion. They had to learn how to sift their sins before they had committed them. What was a mortal, what a venial sin? What kind of contrition (perfect or imperfect) would be required for each? It was easy for children to suspect themselves of bad sins—otherwise, why learn so much about them? It was a weight of knowledge hard for a child to carry.

Given such instruction at her "age of discretion," Mary McCarthy was sure she had committed a horrible sin of blasphemy:

> One of the great moral crises of my life occurred on the morning of my first Communion. I took a drink of water. Unthinkingly, of course, for had it not been drilled into me that the Host must be received fasting, on the penalty of mortal sin? . . . I *could not* take Communion. And yet I had to. My Communion dress and veil and prayer book were laid out for me, and I was supposed to lead the girls' procession . . . It seemed to me that I would be failing the school and my class if, after all the rehearsals, I had to confess what I had done and drop out. The sisters would be angry, my guardians would be angry, having paid for the dress and veil. I thought of the procession without me in it, and I could not bear it. To make my first Communion later, in ordinary clothes, would not be the same. On the other hand, if I took my first Communion in a state of mortal sin, God would never forgive, it would be a fatal beginning. I went through a ferocious struggle with my conscience, and all the while, I think, I knew the devil was going to prevail: I was going to take Communion, and only God and I would know the real facts. So it came about: I received my first Communion in a state of outward holiness and inward horror, believing I was damned.[1]

This fear of going to communion with an unconfessed sin on one's conscience was not only a matter for children. Graham Greene's Scobie, to spare his wife the knowledge of an adulterous affair, goes to communion with a mortal sin on his soul—damning himself out of love.

> Father Rank came down the steps from the altar bearing the Host. The saliva had dried in Scobie's mouth: it was as though his veins had dried. He couldn't look up. But with open mouth (the time had come) he made one last attempt at prayer, "O God, I offer up my damnation to you. Take it. Use it for them," and was aware of the pale papery taste of an eternal sentence on his tongue.[2]

In Catholic communities, not going to communion was practically an announcement that one had a mortal sin on one's soul. Adolescents had to hurry off to confession each time they committed the mortal sin of masturbation, or they would be conspicuous by not joining other kids in going to the communion rail.[3] In a legal case treated by Stephen Haliczer, the expert on the Spanish Inquisition, a nun drew attention to herself by not going to communion for weeks. Her prioress found, on inquiry, that she had not confessed being sexually solicited by a priest, and the superior made her denounce the priest to the Inquisition.[4] Not going to communion had branded her with being in "a state of sin."

To this generally intimidating experience, imagine the impact when a child found that he or she was being sexually inveigled by the priest prying into one's sins. The confessional box was invented, in the Counter-Reformation, to prevent the close contact of priests and women in the older form of confession, where the priest was seated on a chair, in church or convent or sickroom, while the woman was kneeling in front of him—a suggestive configuration in itself.[5] But the box made for even more secret quarters, where the priest and penitent could flirt with each other, talk sex, engage in mutual masturbation, or arrange for a tryst (with intercourse) outside the confessional.[6] The records of the Inquisition show a special concern with the problem of priests listening to women talk of their sexual sins in the confessional. Haliczer describes how clerical moralists debated the problem:

[One of them] depicts the confessional as a place where the priest could expect to experience erection and ejaculation while hearing the confessions of female penitents. Under these circumstances, ejaculation was seen as involuntary and, therefore, not sinful, but simply one of the moral risks that came with the job of the confessor . . . [But others condemned] the priest, who either induced or forced his penitent to manipulate him or, more commonly, did so himself while hearing her confession.[7]

Directions for confessors hearing about sexual sin had to walk a fine line between allowing evasion and eliciting salacious detail. Mark Twain put the Protestant suspicion about such exchanges with typical zest: "The official list of questions which the priest is required to ask [in the confessional] will overmasteringly excite any woman who is not a paralytic."[8]

There were particular problems with the confessions of nuns, at a time when families consigned the less marriageable sisters to convents, since they did not have enough money for more than one or a few dowries. It has been estimated that as many as 50 percent of the nuns in Renaissance Venice had been sent there by their families in this way, and an abbess justified lenience toward them on the basis that "the girls are placed here more for safekeeping than as nuns."[9] Not feeling that they had a vocation, they sometimes sought contact with the one man allowed into their convent. Others went mad from confinement, had visions, or were seen as possessed. Priests were called in to handle such women, sometimes intimately in the physical process of exorcising them.[10]

"The Crisis of Confession"

This earlier change—from open quarters to the enclosed box—was reversed in the wake of Vatican II, when there was an attempt to humanize the sacrament by calling it reconciliation. The idea was that sin and other problems could be discussed with a priest-counselor outside the box. This, however, gave pederast priests new venues for confession as a way to seduce boys—and to seal them to silence in a reversal of the sacrament's logic (by which priests were bound, but not penitents). The confessional was also useful to clerical pedophiles, who bound their fellow priests to silence by confessing their predations "under the seal."[11]

Uneasiness about the practices of confession both in and out of the box made the post–Vatican II church experiment with ways of maintaining the sacrament of penance. In Germany and America, there was an effort to spare children the ordeal of confession at age seven. Long-term objections at last led to some action. The objections included:

1. The effort at defining types of sin and degrees of contrition for young minds made the teaching on confession overshadow in importance that of communion.
2. The effort to impress on young minds the seriousness of sin led to anxiety and bizarre notions. A German author remembered the nun who told him that his sin made his guardian angel cry.[12]
3. The parents' right to decide what was fitting to a child's development was ignored.
4. At a time when adults were no longer going to confession in large numbers, it was strange to say that children must nonetheless do what adults no longer do.
5. The early sense of an ordeal was making children abandon the practice as soon as they could.

In response to these concerns, certain dioceses in Germany, the Netherlands, and America began giving first communion at age seven, but delaying first confession to a later time, according to the different levels of maturity in the young, and making that decision in consultation with parents and teachers. But in 1973 the Congregation for the Liturgy and the Clergy turned down a request from the United States to continue with this experiment, bringing practice back to the rigid order of Pius X in *Quam Singulari* (1910).[13] This is just one of many ways the papal Curia cut back on new approaches opened up by the Second Vatican Council.

Another example of postconciliar conflict had to do with the idea of communal confession. Paul VI, in his decree *Ordo Paenitentiae* of 1973, said there were three ways to receive absolution from one's sins—the conventional way in the confessional, one by one; or as a community, with individual confession afterward if one felt a need for it; or as a general absolution of sins in cases of need. Determining what constitutes need was left to bishops. In the Roman Synod of Bishops called by Pope John Paul II in 1983, examples were given of missionary churches in Africa and Latin America, where some people traveled for long distances to hear Mass, and could not be heard individually by one or two overworked priests.[14] Other bishops found that the crush of people desiring absolution before their Easter duty called for a general absolution. There was a precedent of sorts for this: in the case of accidents with multiple victims, not all of them conscious, conditional absolution had been given by priests arriving on the scene. The same had applied to absolution of troops on the eve of battle, where there was no time for all penitents to be heard individually. But a general absolution, without some catastrophe as its condition, was severely criticized by conservatives. They saw in it a laxness caused by Vatican II and asked for a return to Tridentine notions of penance—not paying attention to the great decline in traffic at the confessionals.

This falling off of penitents, the experiments in confession outside the box, the change from general back to individual absolution, the scandal of pederast crimes connected with confession—all these things added up to what was called, by the 1980s, a crisis of confession. The 1983 synod met for a month in Rome to consider this situation, hoping for "a pastoral rather than dogmatic orientation."[15] The first two weeks were a general discussion, with 176 "interventions" limited to eight minutes each, and then the discussion was carried out in twelve smaller groups before a vote was taken on sixty-three *propositiones* submitted to the pope and kept secret.

Such synods had been recommended by Vatican II, and the first ones held (in 1967, 1969, and 1971) had drawn up their own reports and published them. But beginning in 1974, as episcopal collegiality faded from view, the synod met but submitted its recommendations secretly for the pope to make his own decision on what to report. This inertial tug back toward authoritarianism was made evident in the use the pope made of the 1983 synod. John Paul II opened the synod with a homily, and closed it with an address, but did not make a report supposedly drawn from what was learned there for a full year, with the result that "the apostolic exhortation which was published more than a year after the closing of the Synod seems as removed in tone as it was in time" from what went on.[16] The pope said that the Council of Trent had to be the guide in these matters (ignoring the Second Vatican Council). Though the usual gestures of continuity were made to Paul VI's *Ordo Paenitentiae,* general confession seemed de facto excluded in all situations short (perhaps) of a nuclear catastrophe.

The Origins of Confession

It is clear, then, that recent history shows the sacrament of penance undergoing changes, even rapid changes—was it to be in the confessional box or outside it, given individually or socially, with the stress on reconciliation as absolution or as counseling? It should come as no surprise, therefore, that the whole idea of a sacrament of penance was the fruit of repeated innovations and drastic alterations in the preceding history of the church. The original church knew only one form of absolution from sin—baptism. Since this was thought to make one enter a sinless life, for centuries the moment of baptism was put off until late in life. Sinning after it would be a desertion from one's baptismal vows and give no chance of further cleansing. That is why Ambrose had not been baptized until he was elected the bishop of Milan. It is why the emperor Constantine was not baptized until he was on his deathbed.

The thought that one could not be forgiven for sinning again after one's baptism was accepted into the canon of scripture when the Letter to Hebrews was adopted as part of the New Testament. There we read, of those who sin against the faith after baptism:

> If we sin again on purpose, after seeing the truth, no sacrifice remains for our sins, only a terrifying judgment to come, and a wild fire voracious of recalcitrants. Anyone rejecting the Law of Moses dies without pity if two or three testify. What worse punishment will he earn who has trampled on the Son of God, disregarding the blood of the Pact in which he was cleansed, and mocking the favors of the Spirit? We know, of course, who says, "Punishment is mine, I shall exact it," and "The Lord will judge his people." Fearful it is to fall into the hands of the living God (Heb 10.26–31).

This was a harsh provision, and, as with other developments in the church, a certain "laxness" led to different practices. (See, for instance, the invention of Purgatory to make it possible for sinners to get into heaven after a waiting period.)

The early punishment for postbaptismal sin (after a publicly known scandal) was exclusion of the sinner from the community of "saints" (as they were called). Since the eschatology of the early church looked forward to an imminent end of time, it was a dire punishment not to belong to the people chosen for salvation. Yet the purity of the saints had to be maintained. That is why Jesus gave the community ("you," plural) the ability to purge itself of sinners: "Whatever (*ho ean*) you may ban on earth it will have been banned in heaven, and whatever you let in on earth will have been let into heaven" (Mt 18.18).[17] Thus Paul urges the Corinthians to expel a notorious criminal—"do not have him at table with you" (1 Cor 5.11). Paul admits that he has no power as an outsider, but the community itself should act: "Are you not the judges of your own company?" (5.12). Later, however, he requests that a person expelled from the community be readmitted in love—though again he leaves the decision up to the community (2 Cor 2.5–11).[18]

As the church outlasted the promised eschatological time, it had to deal with people living for many years beyond their baptism, and with the fact that those who could not put off baptism till their deathbed were committing sins after receiving that great absolution. The issue was not private sin, but public offenses—like Theodosius's massacre of Thessalonian rioters in 390, for which Ambrose made him do public penance and be readmitted to the community. But even then the forgiveness could not be repeated. One was given a second chance after baptism, but not a third. Ambrose said, "As there is only one baptism, there is only one penance."[19] But knowing that one had only one chance to clear one's sins away after baptism had the same effect as the first resort of baptism—a person put off the public humiliation and penance to get back into the community until the end of one's life. With only one "second chance," people did not want to "waste" it and have to live the rest of their lives excommunicated.

It was in the wilds of Ireland that a new approach to penance began to arise in the eighth century. In the sparsely inhabited country, few if any public figures could perform humiliating penances for scandalous behavior. Monks had no one to absolve but each other.[20] In this setting, confessions were treated as remedial ways of strengthening resolution. Constant spiritual counseling between a monk and his guide called for confidentiality—the first harbinger of what became the "seal" of confession.[21] The spread of Irish missions led some people to prefer this private and individual act of confession and forgiveness, and bishops tried to co-opt this new discipline, just as they had adopted the ascetic principles of the Egyptian monks in earlier times.[22]

As always, popular new trends led to new suspicions of abuse. The idea of the confessor as a private guide made people fear that clerics were the real "power behind the throne." Kings and queens, aristocratic ladies and lords, were thought of as manipulable by professional confessors. This fear was aggravated by the fact that specialists in confession were from the mendicant religious orders. Other priests could hear confession only in the diocese where they were authorized by a bishop—or, in static monasteries, by the abbot. But mendicants—Franciscans, Dominicans, and Jesuits—were mobile, traveling across dioceses, and they were given a license to hear confession anywhere.[23]

The Jesuits were especially prominent in this ministry, and their reputation as casuists made Jansenists and others fear that they were giving permission to rulers and the powerful to act with relaxed moral codes. There is a vast literature on the way Jesuits were said to manipulate or connive with their famous penitents. In a brilliant play by Shakespeare's collaborator Thomas Middleton, a Spanish Jesuit coaxes an English princess to give over her secrets so he can use them for his order's purposes. The seal of the confession was considered a weapon of diplomacy on a level with the NSA's secret prying in our time:

> Resolve you thus far, lady,
> The privat'st thought that runs to hide itself
> In the most secret corner of your heart now
> Must be of my acquaintance—so familiarly,
> Never she-friend of your night counsel nearer.
>
> *A Game at Chess* 1.1.132–36

A Forgiving God

Given this long history of widely varying changes, what made us Catholics think that frequent recurrence to the confessional was a normal part of the average believer's life? The modern discipline came only late and in two stages. The first was the order of the Fourth Lateran Council (1215) that a believer must go to confession at least once a year. This made the connection between confession and communion, as a kind of one-two punch, the norm. Then a second discipline was added by Pius X, in the decree *Quam Singulari*, which enjoined frequent communion, from the age of seven onward. The sixth requirement (of eight) was this:

Those who have charge of the children should zealously see to it that after their First Communion these children frequently approach the Holy Table, even daily if possible, as Jesus Christ and Mother Church desire.

In schools where everyone was required to go to communion, any failure to do so would brand the child as having some unconfessed sin on his/her conscience. This has departed very far from what we know of earlier beliefs and practices about the forgiving of sin.

The whole discussion of penance in recent times has been about the *authority* to forgive—who has the right to hear confession, what duty does one have to go to confession, what makes the sacrament valid, what is the sufficient degree of contrition to make absolution "take"? Since authority is at issue, the scriptural warrant for the dogma centers on possession of the keys mentioned at Matthew 16.19: "I will give you the keys to the reign in heaven. And whatever you may ban on earth it will have been banned in heaven, and whatever you let in on earth will have been let into heaven."[24] But this was a power of the church to protect itself by inclusion and exclusion of members. It was not about forgiveness of sins. There is no reason to read that passage as if it said, "Whose sins you forgive on earth, they are forgiven in heaven." There are much more important passages on "forgiving" (*aphienai*). It is a regular theme of the Old Testament, where God is often called "a forgiving God."[25]

Forgiveness is such a divine prerogative that twice—when Jesus forgives sins (of the crippled man, and of the woman taken in adultery), he is accused of blasphemy (Mt 9.2)—people grumble, "What kind of person is this, who forgives sins?" (Lk 7.49). Jesus is prodigal of forgiveness, just like Jahweh of the Old Testament. Nowhere is this more evident than when, on the cross, he forgives his executioners. "Father, forgive (*aphes*) them, since they do not realize (*oidasin*) what they are doing" (Lk 23.34). He wants his followers to be just as forgiving. "Peter came to him and said, 'Lord, how many times will a man wrong me, yet I forgive him (*aphēso*)—up to seven times?' Jesus tells him, 'Not up to seven, but up to seventy times seven'" (Mt 18.21–22).

The Lord's Prayer has the request, "Forgive (*aphes*) our defections, as we have forgiven (*aphēkamen*) our defectors" (Mt. 6.12, Lk 11.4). Matthew, in a gloss on the prayer, makes it clear that our forgiveness depends on our forgiving: "If you forgive others' misdeeds (*paraptōmata*), your heavenly Father will forgive you. But if you do not forgive others, neither will your heavenly Father forgive your misdeeds" (Mt 6.14–15). Forgiving is not something reserved to an order of priests who did not yet exist. It is a part of every Christian life.

An emphasis on this mark of faith is what the risen Jesus is inculcating when he says, "Receive the Holy Spirit. If you forgive anyone's sins, they have been forgiven. If you condemn them (*kratēte*), they have been condemned" (Jn 20.22–23).[26] Some church authorities have taken this as a parallel to the "banning/permitting" language of Matthew 16.19, as giving select members of the community the power to forgive sin; but Raymond Brown, an expert on John's Gospel, does not endorse that view: "We doubt that there is sufficient evidence to confine the power of forgiving and holding of sin, granted in John 20.23, to a specific exercise of power in the Christian community, whether that be admission to Baptism or forgiveness in Penance."[27]

In breathing on them his own spirit of forgiveness, Jesus is making the community as forgiving as the Father is. This does not make the community the legalistic judge of who sins and who does not, since Jesus had said, "Be no judge, or you will be judged" (Mt 7.1, Lk 6.37). As Raymond Brown writes:

> Johannine realized eschatology and dualism offer background for understanding the forgiveness and holding of sin in 20.23. The disciples both by deed and word cause men to judge themselves: some come to the light and receive forgiveness; some turn away and are hardened in their sins.[28]

We should hear less about the authority to forgive, which the Gospels barely mention (if at all), and more about the duty to forgive, which is often inculcated.

Jesus was always ready to forgive. Like the father of the prodigal son, he goes out to receive the sinner even before he returns: "When his father saw him coming at a distance, he melted with emotion (*esplangkhnisthē*). Running out to him, he threw his arms around his neck and kissed him" (Lk 15.20). This is a favorite text of Pope Francis:

> And the father? Had he forgotten the son? No, never. He is there, he sees the son from afar; he was waiting for him every hour of every day. The son was always in his father's heart, even though he had left him, even though he had squandered his whole inheritance, his freedom. The father, with patience, love, hope, and mercy had never for a second stopped thinking about him, and as soon as he sees him still far off, he runs out to meet him and embraces him with tenderness, the tenderness of God, without a word of reproach: his son has returned![29]

There are many places where Jesus forgives, before telling his followers to forgive each other. He is not on the side of judges—which is why he thinks the legalists have no right to stone the woman taken in adultery:

> Straightening up [from his crouch], he asked the woman, "Where are they? Has no one condemned you?" And she said, "No one, Lord." And Jesus replied, "Then neither do I. Leave, and from now on do not sin" (Jn 8.10–11).

The history of the church has sometimes been populated by stone throwers. Christians became deadly in their skill at killing people they thought of as Christ-killers, though Christ prayed that these very people be forgiven. Jesus forgives the crippled man's sins because of his trust (*pistis*, Mt 9.2). Most tellingly, he forgives the woman who had sinned greatly because she had loved greatly (*polu*, Lk 7.47). That is the great reason to forgive. He forgives Peter for deserting him three times when he asks him to profess, three times, that he loves him (Jn 21.15–17). Love is always the point. And Peter, far from being a demanding ruler, is great in love— a forgiven sinner, like all of us.

Pope Francis calls him "Peter, purified in the crucible of forgiveness."[30] Francis's personal motto, taken from the Venerable Bede, is *Miserando atque eligendo,* where he takes *Miserando* to mean "Mercying."[31] God acts by pitying and accepting. One cannot expect a pope to endorse the abandonment of a sacrament, like that of penance. But the dark past of the confessional will just fade away if we ponder his statement, noticed in my introduction: "The confessional is not a torture chamber." Sometimes church authorities do not explicitly renounce a former position—on, say, slavery, usury, interdicts, or contraception. They just accept the fact that the People of God have moved on. With regard to confession, they have voted with their feet. On the side of mercy. The pope's side.

NOTES

1. Mary McCarthy, *Memories of a Catholic Girlhood* (Harcourt, Brace, 1957), 19–20.
2. Graham Greene, *The Heart of the Matter* (William Heinemann, 1948), 225.
3. John Cornwell, *The Dark Box: A Secret History* (Basic Books, 2014), 146–56.
4. Stephen Haliczer, *Sexuality in the Confessional: A Sacrament Profaned* (Oxford University Press, 1996), 119–20.
5. Ibid., 100–112, 166.
6. Ibid., 102–4, 109, 164–65.
7. Ibid., 165. Haliczer goes on to describe women reporting their shock when they realized the priest was masturbating while he heard their confession.
8. Mark Twain, *Letters from the Earth,* edited by Bernard DeVoto (Harper & Row, 1962), 53.
9. Mary Laven, *Virgins of Venice: Broken Vows and Cloistered Lives in the Renaissance Convent* (Viking, 2003), 34–38.
10. Haliczer, op. cit., 91, 112, 177. Haliczer cites the case of a priest exorcising a nun with touches of the consecrated host, even slipping it into her vulva (171).
11. Cornwell, op. cit., 190–96. Michael D'Antonio, *Mortal Sins: Sex, Crime, and the Era of Catholic Scandal* (St. Martin's Press, 2013), 89. In 2012, Irish priests said they would defy a new law that would require them to report priests who admitted in the confessional to abusing the young. Michael Brennan, "Priests: We Won't Break the Seal," *Irish Independent,* December 2, 2012.

12. Norbert Mette, "Children's Confession—a Plea for a Child-Centered Practice of Penance and Reconciliation," translated by Graham Harrison, in *Concilium* 190, *The Fate of Confession*, edited by Mary Collins and David Power (T. & T. Clark, 1987), 64.

13. Ibid., 66.

14. Cornwell, op. cit., 210–11.

15. Catherine Dooley, "The 1983 Synod of Bishops and the 'Crisis of Confession,'" in Collins and Power, op. cit., 14.

16. Ibid., 17.

17. The verb *deomai* was used of imprisonment, and *luo* of release. The latter sense here is that the community gives a "free pass" to those they approve of. The two verbs were used of exclusion and inclusion in Jewish communities. The power of banning/permitting is given to Peter at Matthew 16.19 and to the community of disciples at Matthew 18.18, proving that the former is a symbol of the latter.

18. Victor Paul Furnish, *II Corinthians* (Doubleday, 1984), 159–68.

19. Ambrose, *De Paenitentia* II.10.

20. Joseph Martos, *Doors to the Sacred: A Historical Introduction to Sacraments in the Catholic Church*, revised edition (Liguori, 2001), 291–93.

21. John T. McNeill and Helena M. Gamer, *Medieval Handbooks of Penance* (Columbia University Press, 1938), 28.

22. Ibid., 21–27.

23. Haliczer, op. cit., 86–87.

24. For this passage as the warrant for absolution in confession, see *Catechism of the Catholic Church*, Imprimatur Joseph Cardinal Ratzinger (Liguori, 1994), entry 981.

25. See, for instance, Psalms 32.5, 86.5, 99.8. The Lord is often called on to forgive his people's lapses from the Covenant, and the *whole people* are forgiven.

26. *Kratēte* is normally translated as "maintain," but *kratein* means to exercise some kind of force (*kratos*).

27. Raymond Brown, *The Gospel According to John* (Doubleday, 1970), vol. 2, 1044.

28. Ibid., 1043.

29. Pope Francis, *The Church of Mercy* (Loyola Press, 2014), 4. See also 73: "He went every day to see if his son was coming home; this is our merciful Father. It indicates that he was waiting for him with longing on the terrace of his house."

30. Interview with Pope Francis, *America*, September 30, 2013.

31. Ibid.

Epilogue: The Future
A CHURCH OF SURPRISES

I await the surprise of each day.

—Pope Francis, 2010[1]

Dear brothers and sisters, we are afraid of God's surprises. He always surprises us! The Lord is like that.

—Pope Francis, March 30, 2013[2]

I would like to speak of three simple attitudes: hopefulness, openness to being surprised by God, and living in joy.

—Pope Francis, July 24, 2013[3]

God is always a surprise, so you never know where and how you will find him. You are not setting the time and place of the encounter with him.

—Pope Francis, September 30, 2013[4]

Pope Francis, like Chesterton, does not see the church as changeless, as permanent, as predictable, but as a thing of surprises. And he has, in his pontificate so far, surprised many by things he has said or done. Some were surprised, even shocked, when he answered a question about a "gay lobby" in the Vatican: "When I meet a gay person, I have to distinguish between their being gay and being part of a lobby. If they accept the Lord and have good will, who am I to judge them?"[5] Some people think that judging others is the pope's job description. His immediate predecessor often gave the impression that it was his most significant activity.

But the most astonishing thing Francis said early in his days as pope was how bad a Jesuit provincial he had been. How often have we heard any pope tell us how wrong he was? His fellow Jesuits asked him, in their long interview with him, whether as pope he would consult others, as is the practice recommended for Jesuit superiors. He answered:

> In my experience as superior in the Society, to be honest, I have not al-
> ways behaved in that way—that is, I did not always do the necessary con-
> sultation. And this was not a good thing. My style of government as a
> Jesuit at the beginning had many faults. That was a difficult time for the
> Society: an entire generation of Jesuits had disappeared. Because of this I
> found myself provincial when I was still very young . . . That was crazy.[6]

It should be noted here that when he talks of a whole generation of Jesuits disappearing, he was not talking about the politically "disappeared" in Argentina during the Dirty War there. He talks of that elsewhere, but here he is referring to the generation gap that pushed him into office be-fore he was ready.

Jesuit seminaries and institutions had been built on the expectation of new vocations arriving every generation, to allow a seasoning process and steady advance into positions of authority. The departure of so many from the priesthood in the 1970s, and the sharply dwindling recruitment of new members, meant that there was a smaller pool of talent for appointing su-periors. Young men of promise were called on to fill spots they would nor-mally have advanced to only after a range of previous experience. This was a problem in many Catholic religious orders and institutions (I per-sonally know several cases of such premature promotion). The untried had to be called on because there were no obvious successors. As the pope says, "That was crazy."

Father Bergoglio succeeded a Jesuit provincial, Riccardo O'Farrell, who took to heart Vatican II's encouragement of social ministry. This was an approach that had been approved by the Jesuit general, Pedro Ar-rupe, and the Society's 32nd General Congregation of 1974. But Bergoglio disagreed. He wanted to maintain old ways. As he later said, he was trained in the decadent Thomism of the manuals.[7] While Jesuits in other Latin American countries followed the lead of Arrupe's sympathy with liberation theology, he opposed it. This did not mean he was unconcerned about the poor but, as the best historian of this period in the pope's life, Paul Vallely, puts it, "Bergoglio wanted to alleviate the symptoms of poverty; Arrupe wanted to challenge them."[8]

Bergoglio felt social activism was especially dangerous in Argentina, where the military government branded as Marxist any priestly activity in the slums. Two of Bergoglio's priests who had been his own teachers in the seminary—Orlando Yorio and Franz Jalics—were deeply involved in this work. He ordered them to come out of the slums. When they refused, with the support of other Jesuits in Argentina, to leave their ministry there, he dismissed them from the order.[9] When Bergoglio told the archbishop of Buenos Aires that they were no longer Jesuits, the archbishop removed their faculties (ability to say Mass or administer other sacraments).[10] Yorio and Jalics felt this action by both of their superiors—by their provincial and by their archbishop—exposed them to the government as fair game for arrest and torture, which they promptly suffered. Though Jalics later reconciled with Bergoglio and the Society, Yorio died still feeling betrayed—he refused the offer of reinstatement as a Jesuit.

Bergoglio was out of step with the Jesuits in other Latin American countries—enough so for the new Jesuit general (John Paul II's interim appointee, Peter-Hans Kolvenbach) to bring him more into line with the other provincials.[11] When Bergoglio was sent away to Germany to work on his doctoral dissertation—he had not had time even to do that before becoming provincial—many of his Jesuit subjects felt relieved. Even when he returned to teach part-time at the Jesuit school in Buenos Aires, he still had authoritarian ways. "Bergoglio seemed to have forgotten he was no longer provincial or rector."[12] He was made to feel uncomfortable in the Jesuit residence where the new Argentine provincial assigned him.

Though Jesuits now proudly claim him as their pope, some lingering resentment of him made Bergoglio avoid staying at the Jesuits' home in Rome during his visits after he became archbishop. Before being elected pope, he had planned to die in a priests' retirement home, not in a Jesuit residence.[13] Bergoglio's later admission that he was a failure as a Jesuit superior came from no false humility, but from the real article. He not only recognized that he had been wrong—something rare enough. He did a far rarer thing. He set about atoning for it in the most thorough way. As archbishop of Buenos Aires, he not only lived like the poor but lived with them, becoming a fixture in the very slum where Yorio and Jalics had worked. He lived then the direction he gives to all priests and bishops now—devoting himself to the poor, going out to the social periphery and living with the people there.

There must have been some pungent odors in those neighborhoods. But he counsels bishops, as shepherds, to get the "smell" of their sheep—"never to lose the scent of the People of God in order to find new roads."[14] On another occasion, he said, "Be shepherds with the 'odor of the sheep,' make it real, as shepherds among your flock."[15] This is not a sense of smell developed by priests in their rectories or bishops in their palaces. The pope even praised a priest in Buenos Aires who knew the name of every dog in the slum neighborhood.[16] Francis went to the poor to learn, not to teach. He went to find God there. He admired the people's own feel for real religion, their perception of the phony and the sincere, calling it *their* own smell of the flock. "The people have a 'nose.' The people scent out, discover, new ways to walk; they have the *sensus fidei,* as theologians call it."[17] Straight Newman talk.

The pope in Rome can no longer ride the buses and subway, as he regularly did as archbishop of Buenos Aires; but he has kept reaching out to others. His kindness to his predecessor/neighbor, Benedict, has the air of one who has himself been lofty and above the people. In loving Benedict, he is forgiving his former self. Like John XXIII, he does not aspire to change the church all by himself, but to encourage others to respond with him to the Gospel call toward the poor. He resembles Pope John in other ways. Neither was a handsome athlete like John Paul II when he was elected. Nor did they have the visible austerity of Pius XII or Paul VI.

They are more ordinary in appearance, not homely but more everyday or down-to-earth. Each retained a fondnesss for the traditional practices some call "folk religion" (others call them superstitious)—the many local cults of Mary, devotion to the saints, the personification of evil as the devil. Francis praises in others a certain "naïveté," and professes it himself: "It is also true that I am a bit naïve."[18] Francis, like John, recognizes that folk religion is the language of the heart for many people. Loving the people means loving what they love. That is part of the smell of the sheep. In *Evangelii Gaudium* he wrote:

> Popular piety enables us to see how the faith, once received, becomes embodied in a culture and is constantly passed on. Once looked down upon, popular piety came to be appreciated once more in the decades following the Council . . . On that beloved continent [his own Latin America], where many Christians express their faith through popular piety, the bishops also refer to it as "popular spirituality" or "the people's mysticism."[19]

If some find Francis slow in addressing some of their anxieties—the treatment of priest pedophiles for instance—they should recognize that he has a justified caution about changing things "from the top." He has renounced his authoritarian ways and likes to use a favored New Testament word, *hypomonē*, "steadiness under pressure."[20] He told his Jesuit interviewers:

> I am always wary of the first decision, that is, the first thing that comes to my mind if I have to make a decision. This is usually the wrong thing. I have to wait and assess, looking deep into myself, taking the necessary time. The wisdom of discernment redeems the necessary ambiguity of life.[21]

He has appointed a committee to investigate the handling of the pedophile scandal. Justice must be done, but fairly and openly. The Vatican revealed to a UN hearing that hundreds of priests had been dismissed without publicity—which goes against the kind of transparency Francis aspires to. Meanwhile, I think we might trust the instincts of a man who, when told, "Many people say they believe in God, but not in priests," answered, "And that's just fine. Many priests are not worthy of their belief."[22] We should remember that his namesake, Saint Francis, was not a priest.

Welcoming change does not mean dismissing the past, as if it does not exist. It means reinhabiting it with love, a *sensus fidei,* a reliance on the People of God. There is no better recommendation of a pope than his realization of how wrong he has been and how much he still must make amends, how he must rely on others, since they too are responding to God's call. When Francis answered the standard question in the Sistine Chapel, "Do you accept the papacy?" he made the nonstandard answer, "I am a sinner, but I trust in the infinite mercy and patience of our Lord Jesus Christ, and I accept in a spirit of penance." For Francis, being heir to Peter does not mean sitting on a throne of power but following the penitence of Peter, the sinner. His favorite music of Bach is the "Erbarme dich" from the *St. Matthew Passion,* asking God for mercy toward Peter's repentant tears.[23] That kind of pope bodes well for the future of the Catholic Church.

NOTES

1. Francesca Ambrogetti and Sergio Rubin, *Pope Francis: Conversations with Jorge Bergoglio,* translated by Dail Literary Agency (G. P. Putnam's Sons, 2013), 169.
2. Pope Francis, *The Church of Mercy* (Loyola Press, 2014), 10.
3. Ibid., 62.
4. Interview with Pope Francis, *America,* September 30, 2013.
5. John Allen, "Pope on Homosexuals," *National Catholic Reporter,* July 29, 2013.
6. Pope Francis, *America* interview, September 30, 2013.
7. Ibid.: "Unfortunately, I studied philosophy from texts that came from decadent or largely bankrupt Thomism. In thinking of the human being, therefore, the church must strive for genius and not for decadence."
8. Paul Vallely, *Pope Francis: Untying the Knots* (Bloomsbury, 2013), 55.
9. Ibid., 74. Technically, they resigned, but at his insistence. In earlier interviews, Bergoglio said that General Arrupe dismissed them—but of course Arrupe was acting on information Bergoglio had given him. See Ambrogetti and Rubin, op. cit., 203.

10. Vallely, op. cit., 93.
11. Ibid., 58.
12. Ibid., 59.
13. Ibid., 61, 125.
14. Pope Francis, *The Church of Mercy,* 57.
15. Ibid., 95.
16. Ibid., 75.
17. Pope Francis, *America* interview.
18. Ibid.
19. Pope Francis, *Evangelii Gaudium* (United States Conference of Catholic Bishops, 2013), 60–61 (pars. 123, 124).
20. Ambrogetti and Rubin, op. cit., 72.
21. Pope Francis, *America* interview.
22. Ambrogetti and Rubin, op. cit., 123.
23. Pope Francis, *America* interview.

Index